Gravity,
the Glue of the Universe

Gravity, the Glue of the Universe

History and Activities

Harry Gilbert

Diana Gilbert Smith

1997
Teacher Ideas Press
A Division of
Libraries Unlimited, Inc.
Englewood, Colorado

To my children
Karen Louise, Natalie Jan, H. Paul, Sally Jo, and Diana Dee

●

TEACHER IDEAS PRESS
A Division of
Libraries Unlimited, Inc.
P.O. Box 6633
Englewood, CO 80155-6633
1-800-237-6124
www.lu.com/tip

Production Editor: Kevin W. Perizzolo
Copy Editor: Jason Cook
Proofreader: Lori D. Kranz
Indexer: Nancy Fulton
Typesetter: Kay Minnis

Library of Congress Cataloging-in-Publication Data

Gilbert, Harry, 1918-
    Gravity, the glue of the universe : history and activities / Harry Gilbert and Diana Gilbert Smith.
        xv, 207 p. 22x28 cm.
    Includes bibliographical references and index.
    ISBN 1-56308-442-2
    1. Gravitation--Study and teaching. 2. Gravitation--History.
I. Smith, Diana Gilbert, 1962-   . II. Title.
QC178.G55   1997
531'.14--dc21
                                                    97-381
                                                      CIP

Contents

Preface and Acknowledgments ix

Introduction xi

    Cast of Principal Characters xiv
    Prologue xv

1—THE ANTECEDENTS 1

Narrative 1
Lesson Plan # 1—Aristotle's Ideas About Gravity 5
Lesson Plan # 1—Student Handout—Aristotle's Ideas About Gravity—Narrative 8
Lesson Plan # 1—Student Handout—Aristotle's Ideas About Gravity—Review 10
Lesson Plan # 2—Galileo Asks Nature a Question 11
Lesson Plan # 2—Student Handout—Galileo's Ideas About Gravity 18
Lesson Plan # 2—Student Handout—Experimental Data 20
Lesson Plan # 2—Sample Inclined Plane Data Analysis Chart 21
Lesson Plan # 2—Student Handout—Mathematical Analysis of Experimental Data 22
Lesson Plan # 3—Newton Makes a Grand Hypothesis 23
Lesson Plan # 3—Student Handout—Newton's Ideas About Gravity 27
Lesson Plan # 3—Student Handout—Rules for Writing Hypotheses 30
Lesson Plan # 3—Statements to Be Used on Concept Attainment Cards 31

2—WHAT IS SPACE? 33

Narrative 33
Lesson Plan # 1—What Is Space? 39
Lesson Plan # 1—Teacher Fact Sheet—What Is Space? 42

3—A SIMPLICITY OF PREMISES **43**

Narrative 43
Lesson Plan # 1—Principles of Relativity 51
Lesson Plan # 1—Student Handout—The Nature of Light 56
Lesson Plan # 2—Einstein's Special Relativity 58
Lesson Plan # 2—Teacher Sample—Graphic Organizer 69
Lesson Plan # 2—Student Handout—Graphic Organizer 70
Lesson Plan # 2—Student Handout—Simultaneity Experiment Involving
   Light on a Train 71

4—THE NEW GRAVITY **72**

Narrative 72
Lesson Plan # 1—Einstein's New Law of Gravity 77
Lesson Plan # 1—Student Worksheet—After the Play 80
Lesson Plan # 1—A Play About Gravity 81

5—THE ECSTASY **95**

Narrative 95
Lesson Plan # 1—The Problem of a Scientific Discrepancy 101
Lesson Plan # 1—Teacher Key—Graphic Organizer 105
Lesson Plan # 1—Student Handout—Graphic Organizer 107

6—AN ENIGMA **109**

Narrative 109
Lesson Plan # 1—Einstein's Dilemma 114
Lesson Plan # 1—Sample Synectics Progression 117
Lesson Plan # 2—Building Blocks of the Universe 119
Lesson Plan # 2—Student Handout—Dissecting Atoms 125
Lesson Plan # 2—Teacher Fact Sheet—Chemical Elements of the Human Body 129

7—BIRTH, DEATH, AND TRANSFIGURATION **130**

Narrative 130
Lesson Plan # 1—The Life Cycle of a Star 137
Lesson Plan # 1—Student Handout—Star Vocabulary 141
Lesson Plan # 1—Teacher Key—The Life Cycle of a Star 142
Lesson Plan # 1—Student Handout—The Life Cycle of a Star 143
Lesson Plan # 1—Role-Play Script—The Life Cycle of a Star 144

8—THE POINT OF NO RETURN 149

Narrative 149

Lesson Plan # 1—A Mysterious Encounter 155

Lesson Plan # 1—Teacher Fact Sheet—Black Holes 161

Lesson Plan # 1—Student Handout—Planning and Data Collection . . . 163

9—THE ULTIMATE FATE 166

Narrative 166

Epilogue 171

A Concluding Note to Teachers 173

Appendixes

    A—Newton Does a "Back of the Envelope" Check on His Postulates 175

    B—How to Weigh Earth 177

    C—Permittivity Defined 178

    D—Experimental Proof of Special Relativity 179

    E—The Momentous 43 Seconds 181

    F—The Origin of the Chemical Elements Needed to Make a Human Being 182

    G—Calculating the Gravitational Radius of Any Object 183

    H—Albert Einstein Opts for Closed Space 184

    I — Answers to Common Student Questions That Arose During Field Testing . . . 185

Selected Bibliography 189

    Internet Resources 191

References 193

Index 195

About the Authors 207

Preface and Acknowledgments

Upper elementary and middle school science curricula are notable for their omission of one of the greatest triumphs of science in the history of the world—Albert Einstein's revolutionary New Law of Gravity. Today our students are largely being taught science in a way that suggests that nothing has changed our understanding of gravitation since Newton published his *Principia* in 1687. But not so long ago, something did happen that profoundly changed our ideas about gravity, space, and time—Albert Einstein published his relativity papers. People with limited scientific knowledge are so "awed" by Einstein that they are convinced they could never understand him. Over the 90 years since the original publication of Special Relativity, the notion that these discoveries cannot be understood or taught has become legendary.

We are certainly not the first to claim that Einstein's work can be made clear to the general public. Einstein himself attempted several times to popularize his discoveries. The reason many popularizations of Einstein's Special and General Relativity fail is that they generally do not identify the foundation upon which the theory is based.

The purpose of this text is to present the evolution of scientific thought and scientific techniques from Aristotle to Stephen Hawking. Nestled in this framework, the discoveries of Albert Einstein figuratively fall into your lap. We wish to teach our students how true science works. The story of gravity is an ideal vehicle for this purpose.

The intent of this book is not to give quick packaged answers, but to expose students to engaging material that stimulates questions and motivates a desire to learn both content and processes. These lessons are designed with an eye on process-skill mastery, not necessarily on complete concept mastery.

As we wrote these lesson plans, we tried to avoid oversimplification of scientific concepts. We have all seen times when oversimplification leads to misinformation. However, we have attempted to provide analogies that give students something familiar as a starting point. These analogies are intended to help clarify new, unfamiliar, and seemingly unbelievable scientific ideas and principles. The lessons have been crafted with an eye on low-budget science departments. All of the experiments use low-budget supplies (e.g., rocks, leaves, water, eggs). The only laboratory supplies needed are gas discharge tubes and spectroscopes.

The technical content of the text is largely derived from the Misner, Thorne, and Wheeler textbook *Gravitation*. We are grateful to Professor Misner, who read and approved the technical content of an early draft of the book, and we thank him for encouraging us to continue working toward our goal of making Einstein's discoveries available to the lay reader.

Twelve lessons are presented here. All of the lessons are patterned at least in part after ten lesson models presented in *Models of Teaching,* 3d edition, by Bruce Joyce and Marsha Weil. Our intent has been to present as broad a range of teaching strategies as possible. This should enable the teacher to accomplish two goals: to reach the broadest possible range of student learning styles and abilities and to effectively teach science processes as well as science content.

The lessons were field tested in the fifth-grade classrooms at Central Elementary School in Simsbury, Connecticut, during the 1995–96 and 1996–97 school years. A total of 102 students that ranged in ability from "gifted and talented" to "inclusion" responded positively to the material. They showed excitement and enthusiasm as well as confidence that comes from understanding new material. We wish to thank William Marshall, principal, who believed in our project, encouraged our creativity, and allowed us to field test the lessons. We are grateful to Mr. Marshall for many hours spent discussing and debating the process of writing objectives and applying Bloom's taxonomy. We also want to thank Jane Mease, former principal of Cash Valley Elementary School in Allegany County, Maryland, who reviewed the lesson plans for clarity and accuracy.

We want to thank all the editors at Teacher Ideas Press that worked with us and especially Susan Zernial who recognized our purpose for writing this book and has been a constant source of encouragement. In addition, we thank Tony Dupee for his many suggestions on how to clarify our writing. And of course, Ismene, for her constant support and input from start to finish.

Finally, we must extend our deepest gratitude to John Smith. John's patience and sense of humor reminded us not to take ourselves too seriously, to enjoy our task, and to treasure each other. John's superior skills as a pilot brought us all together for this project and reminded us that no matter where we need to be, we can get there from here.

We hope that teachers, students, and parents will find the material we have presented to be accessible, exciting, and useful. If we have been successful in our endeavor, science teachers will be able to open doors to wonders of the world that their students never knew existed.

Introduction

This is a story about the history of our understanding of the strange force that simultaneously guides the raindrops in their fall from the clouds, keeps us from falling off Earth, keeps Earth in orbit around the Sun, and keeps all the billions of stars together in the Milky Way. This strange force, gravity, can rightly be called the glue of the universe. Without it, the universe would literally fall apart.

This book is founded on two premises:

1. You do not need to study advanced mathematics to grasp the concepts and implications of relativity. However, you do need to know how Einstein's ideas grew out of the work of those who preceded him. You must first learn about the great discoveries of Galileo, Newton, Faraday, Maxwell, and Riemann before attempting to study relativity.

2. Albert Einstein's relativity has altered forever our views of gravity, space, time, and how the universe works.

The book is comprised of two distinct formats. The first format is a narrative text section (the first part of each chapter) that details the history of scientific thought and the process of discovery on the subject of gravity. The second format (the second section of each chapter), consisting of a total of 12 lesson plans, is an instructional unit that uses the theme of gravity (and its ever-changing definition) as a vehicle to teach fundamental science concepts and processes. We strongly recommend that teachers who intend to use the lesson plans first read all nine chapters of the narrative text.

Chapter 1, The Antecedents, begins with the ancient Greek teacher, Aristotle, lecturing about gravity. We note that Aristotle's observational, common sense approach to the study of falling bodies can lead to unreliable conclusions. Two thousand years later, in Italy, Galileo uses a better approach—experimentation—to discover a simple but important mathematical relationship between the distance any object falls and the time of the fall. Then, one generation after Galileo, Isaac Newton, in England, asks and answers some crucial questions about gravity and the Moon that lead him to a powerful Law of Universal Gravitation.

Chapter 2 introduces our protagonist, space. Yes, empty space, the void, the vacuum, will become the most valuable player in the game. Space is the hero of our story, but please, don't expect us to give you any real insight into just what space *is*, not when our greatest scientists have, as yet, not penetrated the deepest mysteries of empty space. In this chapter we learn that Michael Faraday, James Clerk Maxwell, George Riemann, and Albert Einstein discovered that space is not *nothingness*, as was previously thought. Space has electrical and geometric properties that are real and measurable. Riemann, especially, saw the possibility that space can be an active participant in the drama. We find Einstein referring to gravity as a field in space. Gravitational fields, magnetic fields, electric fields, and electromagnetic fields are all made real. How one can actually see, hear, and feel the various fields is demonstrated.

In chapter 3, Einstein makes some startling discoveries about uniform motion through space. Expanding on Galileo's insights concerning the undetectability of uniform motion, Einstein asserts two simple postulates that launch his Special Theory of Relativity—a theory that unites space and time, but ignores gravity altogether. Many of the curious conclusions of this theory startled the scientific community (and everybody else that heard about them): There is a speed limit in the universe that simply cannot be exceeded; time does not flow uniformly for everyone; moving clocks keep slower time than stationary clocks; observers in relative motion will not agree on what is simultaneous; you can live your life in slow motion by taking a long trip in a very fast vehicle. All of these assertions are examined and explained in this chapter.

Two kinds of mass—gravitational and inertial—are described in chapter 4. Their incomprehensibly exact equality had been puzzling scientists for years. Einstein's resolution of the puzzle leads him to a New Law of Gravity—a law that supersedes, yet includes, Newton's law of gravity. Here we learn how to tell the difference between genuine advances in science and false advances proposed by "crackpots."

In chapter 5, several predictions of Einstein's New Law of Gravity are evaluated. Einstein wonders: Can the new law succeed where Newton failed? One glaring failure of Newton's Law of Universal Gravitation was its inability to account for the measured rotation of Mercury's orbit. To test the orbit prediction of his new law, Einstein solves a simple algebraic equation that—in one stroke—perfectly accounts for the measured rotation. Other predictions of his theory—the bending of starlight by the Sun and the retardation of clocks by gravity—are soon confirmed experimentally by other scientists. One prediction of the new law (the existence of gravitational waves) has not—to this day—been confirmed. Efforts currently under way to detect gravitational waves coming from distant catastrophic events in our galaxy are discussed.

The puzzle of why mathematical relationships, such as General Relativity, provide information on how the universe works is explored in chapter 6. We agonize with Einstein when he becomes aware of a serious contradiction between a prediction embedded in the mathematics of his new law and known astronomical observations. Twelve years later, a new, more powerful telescope helps an astronomer provide the resolution to the contradiction: Einstein's equations were correct all along! The chapter ends with a "film" showing the evolution of the universe from the time of the Big Bang to the birth of the first generation of stars.

In chapter 7, the commanding role of gravity in the life-history of stars is explored. We find that gravity controls every step of the birth, life, and death cycle of stars—from the ignition of their nuclear furnaces to the final cooling-down of the "corpses." We see the awesome power of gravity displayed most prominently during the death throes of massive stars. We witness dying stars being transformed into strange, compact objects.

Gravity's most fantastic creation—the black hole—is introduced in chapter 8. Einstein's New Law of Gravity dictates, in no uncertain terms, that dead stars whose mass exceeds a certain limit (after a portion has blown away during a violent explosion) *must* collapse into a black hole. The many weird attributes of black holes, the horizon where time stands still, the "singularity" where time comes to an end, the "law" that forbids us from seeing anyone (or anything) fall into the hole, are all described. We may be a bit startled to learn that such strange, unbelievable objects have been found in the Milky Way and in distant galaxies.

The final chapter of the narrative text examines how gravity dictates the ultimate fate of the universe. The equations in the new law of gravity are the "magic-like device"—the "crystal ball"—that reveal how one can calculate the path the universe will take as it continues its expansion. There are only two options for it: to continue to expand forever, or to expand to a maximum value, followed by a collapse to a singularity. Which path it takes depends solely on the total amount of matter in the universe. The text ends with a search for "missing" matter and a review of scientists' constantly changing estimates of the quantity of matter in the universe.

The curriculum material has been written with Professor George Eley Jr.'s (University of Maryland) five primary dimensions of science in mind (Eley 1987). The first of his dimensions is subject matter knowledge, a blend of history, mathematics, language, and scientific facts. The second dimension of science is process knowledge—the skill to follow generally accepted scientific procedures, such as carefully recording and reporting all results of experiments to ensure their repeatability by others. The third dimension is spirit, the values and attitudes of science—the assumptions that nature is orderly and its laws are discernible. The fourth dimension is science and society—the relationship between science and our everyday lives (e.g., the invention of the gasoline engine led to the development of the automobile, which in turn had a profound effect on how far we can live from our place of work). Eley's fifth dimension of science—nature and culture—embodies the idea that successful human cultural systems must also obey the natural laws that govern the universe. For example, if there is a universal speed limit, then all the human power *cannot* and *will not* enable us to exceed it.

Unit Goals

* To trace the changes in scientific thought that have led to our current understanding of gravity.

* To understand how attitudes toward science, scientists, and new ideas have changed throughout the ages (and affected the lives of scientists).

* To examine the multitude and variety of scientific techniques used by scientists from Aristotle to Stephen Hawking to perform experiments and gather information.

* To explore and evaluate the consequences (for our planet, the universe, and all living things therein) of knowing about and accepting Einstein's theories of Special and General Relativity.

These lessons were written with a 50-minute class in mind. Depending upon the length of your science classes, this entire unit can either be taught in as few as 15 class periods, or up to a maximum of 25 class periods. This makes the entire unit 3–5 weeks long if your students have science 5 days a week. The class periods during field testing were 30 minutes each. Classes this short are not ideal, but they are certainly manageable.

Because each lesson plan uses a different teaching model, the procedures vary. Each lesson contains a Teaching Model, Objectives, Vocabulary, Materials, and a detailed Procedure section. The key questions included with each lesson plan are designed to focus learning on key concepts. These questions are italicized for the teacher's convenience. Student handouts (reproducible pages) follow at the end of each lesson.

Supplementary material in the appendixes covers a range of both text and lesson-plan topics:

* How Newton checked the postulates for his Law of Universal Gravitation.

* How to use Newton's Law of Universal Gravitation to weigh the Earth.

* How to measure the electrical permittivity of space.

* How Special Relativity has been validated by scientists.

* How Einstein used General Relativity to account for the missing 43 seconds of arc in the advance of Mercury's orbit.

* The origin of the chemical elements needed to make a human being.

* How to calculate the gravitational radius of any object.

* Why Einstein favored a closed, finite universe.

* Answers to a compilation of student questions that arose during field testing at Central Elementary School in Simsbury, Connecticut.

Cast of Principal Characters

Aristotle	384 B.C.–322 B.C.
Galileo Galilei	1564–1642
Isaac Newton	1642–1727
Michael Faraday	1791–1867
George F. B. Riemann	1826–1866
James Clerk Maxwell	1831–1879
Albert Einstein	1879–1955
Stephen Hawking	1942–

Prologue

Before the curtain goes up, you might contemplate this:

> The laws by which mankind is supposed to live were said to have been clearly engraved by God on stone tablets and handed to Moses. The laws by which the universe lives—the laws of nature—were not so easily given.

It has been said that discerning the laws of nature is much like solving a murder mystery: you must first find the clues. One characteristic all great scientists have in common is a natural propensity to find the right clues. Once revealed, the clue may be maddeningly obvious. It may have been staring us in the face for years. Albert Einstein found one such clue in a well-known (and long-ignored) observation about the measurement of the mass of an object. In 1915, Einstein parlayed that clue into a remarkable new law of nature, a New Law of Gravity.

CHAPTER

The Antecedents

"We shall not obtain the best insight into things until we actually see them growing from the beginning . . ."

—Aristotle (330 B.C.)

You might ask: "How can students with no special talents for science understand Einstein?" The answer is that you do not need any special talents to understand what Einstein did—you only need a good teacher. Relativity can be meaningful and fascinating to anyone who is curious about our universe. We will discover that Albert Einstein gave us General Relativity, a "crystal ball" that gives us astounding insight into the workings of our universe, how it is evolving, and even how it will end. Journey back to 330 B.C. in Athens, Greece, at the Lyceum, where one can listen to Aristotle lecturing on gravity. It was in the Lyceum that Aristotle expounded some wrongheaded ideas on falling bodies that inadvertently laid the foundation for Albert Einstein's 1915 discovery of General Relativity.

Aristotle taught his pupils (including Alexander the Great) that "Earth things" such as clay and rocks fall down because they are trying to find their natural place at the center of Earth. Surprisingly, this statement is mostly correct. However, Aristotle also taught that it is obvious, from observation and common sense, that a large heavy stone must fall to the ground faster than a small stone. Aristotle's teaching may have been "obvious," and common sense, but nevertheless, it was wrong.

Two thousand years later (in 1638), Galileo exposed Aristotle's error by doing an experiment.

Of course Aristotle could have done the very same experiment, but he did not. Neither Aristotle nor his contemporaries ever did experiments. When performing an experiment, you are asking nature a question. Aristotle never thought to *ask* nature anything, he only observed nature. A scientist carefully designs every experiment to ask nature a very specific question. The experimental result is nature's answer.

Aristotle was confident that light objects fall to the ground more slowly than heavy objects because he had seen it with his own eyes. Certainly a leaf falls through the air more gently and more leisurely than a stone, but what you see can be misleading. Let us ask nature some questions: Is the air slowing the fall of the leaf? If the leaf were placed on top of the stone, would the stone cut a path through the air for both of them? If the leaf were riding on the back of the stone, would it keep pace with the stone all the way to the ground? Nature will quickly answer all of these questions—you need only do the experiment:

Take a flat stone about the size of the palm of your hand. Place a small leaf on top of the stone. Drop your hand quickly and observe the stone and leaf fall. Do it again—and again.

1

Conclusion: It was the air that slowed the leaf when it fell all by itself. Riding on top of the stone, the leaf fell just as fast as the stone, all the way to the ground.

Galileo came to much grief for daring to argue against Aristotle. It is curious but true: Aristotle's common sense logic was good, but his science was bad. He was totally unaware that common sense is a very unreliable tool to use in attempting to solve the riddles of the universe.

What does Aristotle's mistake about falling bodies have to do with Einstein's relativity? Einstein was well aware of Aristotle's mistake, and realized that beneath the experimental facts (about falling bodies) must lie the key to a deeper understanding of gravity. Einstein was puzzled as to *why* lead and wood fall to the ground with exactly the same acceleration. His solution to the puzzle (chapter 4) is now acknowledged to be the greatest single scientific contribution ever made to our understanding of the universe.

Galileo clearly described his work in determining experimental facts about falling bodies in his book *The Two New Sciences*. The book was published just five years after his infamous trial in Rome on June 22, 1633, where he was told to "abjure, curse, and detest" his errors and heresies. (de Santillana 1955) The experiment on the acceleration of falling bodies was ingenious in many ways. Galileo was confronted with several problems:

* How was he to measure the rate at which an object was moving as it was falling to Earth, when that rate was *changing* constantly as the object was falling?

* To get an accurate measure of the rate, he would have to drop the object from a great height, but how was he to measure this rate, when the object would be falling faster and faster as it approached the ground?

* How was he to accurately measure short intervals of time, when he had no clock?

Galileo solved the clock problem by using "a large vessel of water placed in an elevated position; to the bottom of this vessel was soldered a pipe of small diameter giving a thin jet of water,

which was collected in a small glass during each descent of the ball." (Knedler Jr. 1973) Thus, Galileo measured time by measuring the weight of uniformly flowing water.

Still, his "water clock" was really not adequate to measure the time of a freely falling object, which he knew fell with *increasing* speed (accelerated motion) as it approached the ground. Galileo solved the problem of timing a very rapidly moving object by avoiding it. He correctly concluded that he could use a ball rolling slowly down a smooth inclined surface without changing the free-fall relationship between the distance traversed by the ball and the time of travel:

A piece of wooden molding, about 12 cubits [about 18 feet] long, half a cubit [about 9 inches] wide and three finger-breadths thick was taken; on its edge was cut a channel a little more than one finger in breadth; having made this groove very straight, smooth, and polished and having lined it with parchment, also as smooth and polished as possible, we rolled along it a hard, smooth and very round bronze ball. (Knedler Jr. 1973)

Galileo measured the time for the ball to descend the full length of the channel, through one-half, two-thirds, three-fourths, and other fractions of the full length. Repeating the experiment 100 times, he always found that the distance traveled by the ball was proportional to the square of the time of travel, and that this relationship was true for all inclinations of the plane. Thus, Galileo knew that the relationship must also hold for a vertical plane, or free fall. The exact value of the acceleration of a body in free fall could not be determined by Galileo because he did not have a stop watch with which to measure it. We now know that any free-falling object on Earth accelerates 32 feet per second (every second it is falling) if air resistance is negligible. (Do you know how anyone could accelerate any automobile from 0 to more than 100 miles per hour in five seconds? Just push the car off the roof of a tall building and gravity's 32 feet per second every second will do the accelerating for you!)

Galileo had no knowledge of what caused the acceleration of falling bodies but was wise enough to know that the solution to the problem of how objects moved in free fall must precede the answer for why they move. "The present does not seem to be the proper time to investigate the cause of the acceleration of natural motion, concerning which various opinions have been expressed," he said. (Knedler Jr. 1973) The cause of the acceleration of natural motion was, however, to be investigated not long after Galileo's death.

The pace of our search for the origins of Einstein's Relativity now quickens. On Christmas morning 1642, less than one year after Galileo died in Arcetri, Italy, a remarkable baby was born to Hannah Newton in Lincolnshire, England. What was remarkable about this baby was not immediately obvious to his mother, or to anyone else. There was no way that they could have known that this baby, named Isaac after his father, who had died three months earlier, was gifted with a brain that was destined to carry forward Galileo's work and astound the world with new understanding of the universe. Isaac Newton was also destined to have a story about him bandied about concerning an apple that was said to have fallen on his head, which triggered his thinking about why objects fall to Earth. As far as can be determined from the writings of Isaac Newton, he was primarily interested in discovering the law of gravity that dictated exactly *how* (not why) an apple, or any object, falls to Earth.

In 1666, 24-year-old Isaac Newton wondered: Because gravity extends to the bottom of the deepest mines and to the top of the highest mountains, does it also extend to the Moon? If so, why does the Moon not fall to Earth? Could the motions of the Moon around Earth be accounted for with the same mysterious force that pulled an apple to the ground? Is it possible that every mass in the universe attracts every other mass with this same force? Could the motions of all of the planets be accounted for with this force? The answers to all of these questions were *yes*.

Newton answered these questions by postulating just three premises:

1. The force acting on the Moon is also acting on Earth.

2. The Moon orbits Earth only because this force constantly accelerates the Moon toward Earth. That is, the Moon is constantly trying to fall toward Earth. (See appendix A for Newton's "quick check" on this premise.)

3. The force decreases with the inverse square of the distance. (Thus, if at 1,000 miles from the center of Earth, the force is 1 unit strong, the force at 2,000 miles from the center of Earth is 1 over 2 squared, or $\frac{1}{4}$ unit strong. At 3,000 miles from the center of Earth, the force is 1 over 3 squared, or $\frac{1}{9}$ unit strong.)

With these three premises, Newton derived the Law of Universal Gravitation: *There is a power of gravity tending to all bodies proportional to the several quantities of matter they contain and inversely proportional to the square of the distance between them.* With this new law, to quote Steven Weinberg, "Mankind for the first time saw the glimpse of a possibility of a comprehensive quantitative understanding of nature." (Hawking and Israel 1987)

The tremendous power of the new law can be demonstrated by looking at its accomplishments. With this singular law, Newton was able to:

* Account for the motion of the Moon around Earth.

* Account for all of the known motions of the planets.

* Explain why the first day of spring does not arrive at exactly the same time every year (this delay in arrival was already known to the ancient Greeks, but had remained unexplained until Newton came along). (See fig. 1.1, p. 4.)

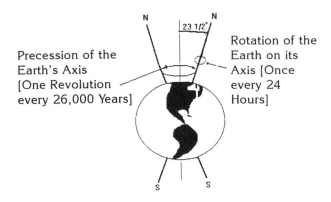

Fig. 1.1. Earth's north/south axis is not perpendicular to the plane in which Earth orbits the Sun. The Moon's gravity (and to some extent the Sun's gravity) pulls on the axis, trying to make it perpendicular. The result of this pull is that the axis moves (precesses) in a circle with a 23½-degree radius. It takes 26,000 years for the axis to make one trip around that circle. This slow motion of the axis causes the precession of the equinoxes. It is this precession that causes the first day of spring to arrive at a slightly different time every year.

• Account for the known 18-year cycle of total eclipses of the Sun.

• Solve the mystery of the comets by making them subject to the same law of gravity as the planets (thus enabling his friend Edmund Halley to calculate the orbit of a comet that appeared in the sky in the year 1682 and to predict its return 75 years later, which it did).

• Account for the tides in the lakes and oceans: as when the Sun or the Moon moves slowly over the body of water, its gravitational attraction pulls harder on the water than on the solid Earth below the water. The water responds by gradually leaving the shore and amassing in the center.

Fifty years after the death of Newton, Lord Cavendish again demonstrated the power of the Law of Universal Gravitation. Cavendish experimentally determined the numerical value of the proportionality constant in the law and then proceeded to calculate the weight of Earth! (See appendix B.)

Newton's Law of Universal Gravitation gave us a remarkable new understanding of the universe, a comprehensive and quantitative description of nature. In 1687, when his *Principia* was published, Newton was hailed far and wide as a genius without parallel.

However, there was one question concerning the force of gravity that puzzled Newton: How does the force get from the Sun to Earth, or from Earth to the Moon? There is nothing out there but empty space. Other forces must contact the objects they are affecting. A horse could hardly pull a carriage if it were not in contact with the carriage! How does the force of gravity travel through empty space? Isaac Newton never claimed to have found an answer to this question.

Two hundred years after Newton, Albert Einstein, using mathematical tools unavailable to Newton, was able to probe deeper and come up with a new explanation of gravity. Einstein said, in effect, let us try to answer all of Newton's unanswered questions about the way gravity works by redefining gravity. Maybe Newton's concept of gravity as an attraction of one body to another is not the entire truth. Maybe one has to dig deeper to get closer to the root of the concept. Einstein knew exactly what his challenge was: Replace the old idea of a force of attraction with a new concept that would retain all of the remarkable results that flowed out of Newton's Law of Universal Gravitation and simultaneously answer all of Newton's unanswered questions.

Einstein succeeded. With General Relativity, he retained every accomplishment of the Law of Universal Gravitation and opened up new vistas in our understanding of the universe. To understand Einstein's solution, we must first take a closer look at the one thing that gave Newton's force of gravity so much trouble—empty space.

"What is space? Here is the key to the whole riddle."

—Isaac Bashevis Singer (1970)

Chapter 1, Lesson Plan # 1

Aristotle's Ideas About Gravity

TEACHING MODEL

BSCS Style Invitation to Enquiry (with Small-Group Investigations)

OBJECTIVES

1. The students will investigate what Aristotle "knew" (believed) about gravity.

2. The students will design and execute experiments to scientifically test Aristotle's ideas.

3. The students will discover why it is important for scientists to do more than rely solely on their observations of the world and on their "common sense."

VOCABULARY

1. *Gravity* (according to Aristotle)—The force that keeps objects on our planet.

2. *Aristotle*—A famous teacher who lived in Athens, Greece, in the year 330 B.C.

3. *Common sense*—What people typically believe about the world around them, based on things they observe.

4. *"Earth things"*—Aristotle's term for objects found in or on Earth, such as clay, stones, and water.

5. *Weight* (according to Aristotle)—A measure of the heaviness of an object. The heaviness is caused by the attraction of Earth for the object.

6. *Bulk*—The size (volume) of an object.

7. *Galileo*—An Italian scientist living in Rome in the year 1633.

MATERIALS

*   Copy of "Student Handout—Aristotle's Ideas About Gravity" for each student

*   Leaf and stone for each group of students (the leaf must be smaller than the surface area of the stone)

From *Gravity, the Glue of the Universe.* ©1997 Harry Gilbert and Diana Gilbert Smith. Teacher Ideas Press. (800) 237-6124.

PROCEDURE

Introduction

1. Introduce the vocabulary list.

2. Pose the following question to the students: *Does gravity affect a light object, like a leaf, in the same way as it affects a heavy object like a stone? Why or why not?*

3. Brainstorm possible answers, and accept all responses.

Experiment 1

1. Divide the students into groups of two to five students each and pass out materials.

2. Have each group of students drop a leaf and a flat stone from an elevated location to determine which object will hit the ground first.

3. Have the students gather together and discuss as a class what they witnessed.

Discussion Questions

1. What did you observe?

2. What can you conclude about the effects of gravity based on what you observed?

3. Did each group observe exactly the same thing?

4. Can you account for any differences from group to group?

5. Can you think of any reason to suspect that what you observed may not have been good scientific evidence?

6. What natural factor may have affected your experiment for which we have not accounted? (airflow)

Aristotle, a famous science teacher in Athens, Greece, in the year 330 B.C., could have done this same experiment, but he never did it. He never did any experiments. He certainly observed leaves falling leisurely to the ground and stones falling rapidly to the ground. He concluded that this meant that a lighter body will always fall more slowly than a heavier body. He used his power of observation and his common sense! *He was wrong!* Can you redesign his experiment to account for the element that he overlooked—the effects of air currents on a falling leaf?

Experiment 2

1. Pose the following question to the students: *What would we need to do if we were going to adapt the experiment to account for airflow?*

2. Allow the groups time to design and to execute a new version of the experiment that accounts for airflow on the lighter object. The teacher may suggest the simple adaptation of placing the leaf on top of the stone and releasing them together. They must be released from waist high this time. (This helps to reduce accidental air currents.) Allow students to try other adaptations as they think of them.

3. Hold a class discussion on the results, and compare ideas to the ideas presented in the beginning of the lesson.*

Discussion Questions

1. Were your results the same or different from the first time?

2. Did each group have the same results?

3. What new conclusion can we draw about the effects of gravity on light and heavy objects?

4. How does our new conclusion compare to our original guesses at the beginning of class?

5. How does our conclusion compare to Aristotle's?

6. Why is it important for scientists to do more than just rely upon their observations of the natural world and common sense?

Almost 2,000 years after Aristotle, a famous Italian scientist, Galileo, came along and corrected Aristotle's mistake. The history of science is full of examples of one scientist coming along and correcting another scientist's mistakes. This is why you must always document exactly how you conducted an experiment, and exactly what you witnessed.

Reading Activity

Have the students read "Student Handout—Aristotle's Ideas About Gravity" and answer the review questions at the end.

---

*Note: When field testing this lesson, I discovered that my students would not believe that weight does not affect gravity. Their responses to the discussion questions that follow revealed that they were clinging tenaciously to Aristotle's common sense ideas. They told me, "A leaf and a stone are pretty close in weight." I overcame this problem by switching materials. I produced a 25-pound bag of clay and a skein of yellow yarn. The students could only just barely hold the clay long enough to drop it on cue. They also agreed that clay was an "Earth thing" and the yarn was a "non-Earth thing." When they got the same results with these new materials, they became convinced. I left the yarn and the clay on the science table all week. I noticed that every child ran the experiment again before or after class during that week. They had to try it themselves to be sure it was true.

Chapter 1, Lesson Plan # 1

Student Handout— Aristotle's Ideas About Gravity

In the year 330 B.C., in Athens, Greece, at the Lyceum, you could have listened to Aristotle teaching his students all about the universe. Well, you actually cannot go backward in time (more about time travel later), but you can read what Aristotle told his students. He was a prolific writer. You may protest, "Have not many of Aristotle's teachings been proven false?" Yes, Aristotle did proclaim that Earth was immobile. He did say that we have no reason to believe that Earth moves. All of our observations tell us Earth does not move! We do observe the Sun move. We observe the stars move. We see every night the planets move in the sky, but who has seen Earth move? Aristotle's clinching argument was his observation that a dropped stone hits the ground directly below the point of release. If Earth moved, the dropped stone would hit the ground ahead of, or behind the point of release. In conclusion, he told his students: "It is clear Earth does not move, and it must lie at the center of the universe." (McKeon 1966)

If you had been a student in his class at the Lyceum, could you have argued against his conclusion? Not many people did—not then, and not for almost 2,000 years. In 1633, Galileo came to much grief for daring to argue against Aristotle. It is curious, but true: Aristotle's common sense logic was good, but his science was bad. He was totally unaware that common sense is a very unreliable tool to use in attempting to solve the riddles of the universe.

Good science does penetrate the riddles of the universe. To gain an understanding of where science is today, you must study its beginnings. The roots of Einstein's relativity go all the way back to Aristotle's bad science. Using common sense derived from his keen observations, Aristotle said that "Earth things," such as clay and metal, fall down because they are trying to find their natural place. He distinguished between light and heavy objects by the speed of their fall to the ground: "by lighter or relatively light, we mean, one of two bodies endowed with weight and equal bulk which is exceeded by the other in the speed of its natural downward movement." (McKeon 1966)

Note that Aristotle did not do an experiment to find out if a lighter body would fall more slowly than a heavier body. He just used common sense—and he was wrong! In our universe, two bodies of equal bulk, like a two-pound stone and a one-pound block of wood, if released together, will hit the ground together.

Almost 2,000 years passed before Galileo came along and exposed Aristotle's error by doing an experiment. Aristotle could have done the very same experiment, but he did not. Neither Aristotle nor his contemporaries ever did experiments—they only observed nature. They never thought to ask nature a question, which is what all good scientists do. A scientist will carefully design an experiment to ask nature a very specific question. The experimental result is nature's answer.

Aristotle was confident that light objects fall to the ground more slowly than heavy objects because he had seen it with his own eyes. Certainly a leaf falls through the air more gently and more leisurely than a stone. But what you see may be misleading.

Let us ask nature some questions: Is the air slowing the fall of the leaf? If the leaf were riding on the back of the stone, would the stone cut a path through the air for both of them? If the leaf were placed on top of the stone, would it keep pace with the stone all the way to the ground? Nature will quickly answer all of these questions—you need only do the experiment:

> Take a flat stone about the size of the palm of your hand. Place a small leaf on top of the stone. Drop your hand quickly and observe the stone and leaf fall. Do it again—and again.

Conclusion: It was the air that slowed the leaf when it fell all by itself. Riding on top of the stone, the leaf fell just as fast as the stone, all the way to the ground.

Chapter 1, Lesson Plan # 1

Student Handout—
Aristotle's Ideas About Gravity

REVIEW OF WHAT WAS LEARNED

1. What conclusion did Aristotle reach about gravity by observing a falling leaf and a falling stone?

2. What method did Aristotle use to arrive at his conclusion about gravity?

3. What was the flaw in Aristotle's reasoning?

4. How did we use an experiment to eliminate Aristotle's flaw?

5. What was our conclusion about the effects of gravity on light and heavy objects?

6. Who was the famous Italian scientist who corrected Aristotle's mistake nearly 2,000 years later?

Chapter 1, Lesson Plan # 2

Galileo Asks Nature a Question

TEACHING MODEL
Small-Group Investigations

OBJECTIVES

1. The students will scientifically describe motion.

2. The students will construct, test, and use a Galilean scientific tool (water clock).

3. The students will re-create Galileo's experiment asking nature the question, How do objects move in free fall?

4. The students will draw their own conclusions about how objects move in the presence of gravity.

5. The students will uncover the mathematical relationship between the distance an object falls and the time it takes the object to fall that distance.

6. The students will compare Aristotle's and Galileo's experimental techniques.

VOCABULARY

1. *Gravity* (according to Galileo)—A force of attraction that pulls all objects toward the center of Earth.

2. *Free fall*—An object is said to be in a state of free fall when it is falling toward Earth without any slowing down due to the presence of air.

MATERIALS

Part 1

* Copy of "Student Handout—Galileo's Ideas About Gravity" for each student

* Empty 16-ounce coffee can for each group of students

* Hammer and a thin 1-x-18 wire brad for each group of students

* Empty beaker for each group of students

* Waterproof magic marker for each group of students

* Source of water

* Laboratory balance (or scale) for each group of students

Part 2

* Copy of "Student Handout—Experimental Data" for each group of students

* Copy of "Student Handout—Mathematical Analysis of Experimental Data" for each group of students

* A Galilean water clock and running supplies for each group, as built and tested in part 1

* Precut wooden channel* (as described on p. 2)

* Calculators for each group of students

* One marble for each group of students

* Meter stick or measuring tape for each group of students

* Book to prop up one end of each channel for each group of students**

PROCEDURE

Background Information

Galileo Galilei was a very well-respected scientist in Italy in the year 1633. Galileo spent his entire life studying to be a good scientist. He studied especially the writings and teachings of Aristotle. Unfortunately, as Galileo designed and carried out experiments to test commonly assumed "facts" about gravity, he began to understand that Aristotle was wrong. The writings of Aristotle were believed to be fact, and it was very difficult for Galileo to convince people that there could be something wrong with Aristotle's science. In fact, he was eventually sentenced to house arrest because people thought he was crazy to challenge Aristotle.

---

*Note: These channels are simple to build. Take 1-inch-wide by $1\frac{1}{2}$-inch-thick boards of scrap pine, each 5 feet long. Using a router (or $\frac{1}{2}$-inch router bit inserted into a drill press), cut a rough channel the full length of each board. Have the students use sandpaper to finish and polish the channels. Have the students measure the channels' length and mark them at $\frac{1}{4}$, $\frac{1}{2}$, and $\frac{3}{4}$.

**Note: All books must be identical in thickness. This is necessary to ensure that all of the channels are placed at identical angles.

Part 1—The Galilean Water Clock

Building a Galilean Water Clock

You will be simulating the same conditions within which Galileo Galilei worked. He had all the equipment and materials any good scientist had in 1633. Yet, it may interest you to know that you could re-create Galileo's laboratory in your own basement today. His laboratory was simple by today's standard. It had none of the modern conveniences that we take for granted (running water, electricity, and accurate clocks).

We are going to build one of the most important pieces of equipment Galileo had in his laboratory, a water clock. In fact, Galileo built this particular water clock. After we build our water clocks, we will take a closer look at exactly what Galileo thought about gravity and Aristotle.

1. Divide the class into groups of four to seven students each.

2. Take an empty coffee can and mark the can inside and outside with a waterproof magic marker halfway up the can.

3. Punch a small hole in the center of the bottom of the coffee can using a thin 1-x-18 wire brad and a hammer.

4. Explain how to use a balance scale, making sure that it is placed on a flat, stable surface and leveled prior to use. Weigh the empty beaker and record its weight before starting.

5. Pass out a copy of "Student Handout—Experimental Data" to each student. Review suggested jobs for team members. Individual tasks may be combined for small groups.

6. Demonstrate how to use the water clock. Tell the students that a water clock becomes less accurate as the water level drops. As the water level reaches the halfway mark, the water slows down too much to be a useful clock. The more constant the water level can be kept during the experiment, the more accurate will be the results.

7. To test the water clock, have each team practice determining how much water is collected while a person walks a fixed distance. The students should record the data for their practice on scrap paper or on the backside of "Student Handout— Experimental Data." (This practice time is extremely important.)

Using a Galilean Water Clock

1. Set up balance.

2. Weigh empty beaker.

3. Have ready a full bucket of water.

4. Fill water clock.

5. Position collection device for water.

6. Release water and start experiment.

7. Stop water.

8. Measure weight of beaker and water.

9. Subtract weight of empty beaker from weight of beaker plus water to obtain the weight of the collected water.

10. Record weight of collected water on chart.

11. Empty beaker.

12. Repeat steps 4–9.

Discussion Questions

1. Who was Galileo?

2. When and where did Galileo live?

3. Why was Galileo a very brave man?

4. What scientific instrument did we make and test in this experiment?

5. What materials did we need to build a Galilean water clock?

6. Describe the steps involved in building a Galilean water clock.

7. Why did Galileo not have an accurate clock in his laboratory?

8. What can a scientist do if the tools needed for an experiment are not available?

Part 2—Performing Galileo's Experiment

Introduction

1. Review the vocabulary terms *gravity* and *free fall*.

2. Discuss the following questions:
    * *If you were going to measure the effect of gravity, what would you use?* (water clock)

    * *What would you measure with the water clock?* (speed of falling objects)

* *What words can we use to describe movement?* (Take student responses here. These may include: fast, slow, smooth, jumpy, constant, variable, regular, erratic, accelerating, and decelerating.) Scientists often want to know the rate at which an object is moving (its speed). Then they ask if the rate is constant or not. If it is not constant, then it must be either accelerating or decelerating.

* *How was Galileo's scientific technique significantly different from Aristotle's?* (Galileo went a step beyond observing nature and recording his observations. He asked nature specific questions. He carefully designed and set up a repeatable experiment to capture nature's answer.)

Galileo knew a worthy experiment is one that can be repeated in laboratories all around the world, over and over again, with everyone finding the same results. Galileo knew he must design a simple, direct experiment to find his answer.

3. With the class, read "Student Handout—Galileo's Ideas About Gravity."

Experiment

1. Divide the class into groups of four to seven students each. Individual tasks may be combined for small groups.

2. Pass out a copy of "Student Handout—Experimental Data," a copy of "Student Handout—Mathematical Analysis of Experimental Data," and supplies to each group.

3. Measure the exact length of each channel and mark it off at $\frac{1}{4}$, $\frac{1}{2}$, $\frac{3}{4}$, and full length using exact measurements. To simplify data analysis later, all channels should be set at the same angle. Use the books to create an incline. Remember, each book must be the same thickness.

4. Have the students roll their marbles all the way down the wooden channel, use the water clock to measure the time of the marble's descent, weigh the water collected, and record the findings on the "Student Handout—Experimental Data" sheet.

5. Have the students repeat the procedure, rolling the marble from the $\frac{1}{4}$, $\frac{1}{2}$, and $\frac{3}{4}$ markers.

6. Fill in Class Results and Averages chart found at the top of "Student Handout—Mathematical Analysis of Experimental Data," as a class. Discuss the findings and the relationships indicated by the data. How would you describe the movement of the marble? Does it take the marble the same amount of time to travel each $\frac{1}{4}$ section of the channel? Can you spot any patterns in our data? If you do, it will be the mathematical relationship between the distance the marble traveled and the amount of water that you collected (the time).

Students may have a difficult time spotting the actual pattern here. It will suffice that the numbers progress logically from step to step. Reasonably, the accuracy of the water clock will be tenuous. Students may appreciate how difficult it is to find patterns using such crude instruments. However, there was nothing else available to scientists of this era.

Discuss how many times experiments had to be repeated to achieve reliable results. In spite of the shortcomings of this equipment, scientists were able to reach accurate conclusions that have stood the test of time.

Perhaps if we look at our data in a different way we will be able to see a pattern emerge. If we do discover a pattern in our numbers, we will be discovering a law of nature—the same law of nature that Galileo discovered in his laboratory so many years ago.

7. Fill in blank Inclined Plane Data Analysis chart with the students, at the bottom of "Student Handout—Mathematical Analysis of Experimental Data." Pass out calculators and have each group complete the chart using their experimental results. All of the numbers in the bottom row of the chart will be the same if the experiment has been precisely performed. (See "Sample Inclined Plane Data Analysis Chart.")

Are all of the numbers in your bottom row the same or nearly the same? What do the grams of water actually represent in this experiment? (Time passing) Using this table, we can say: Distance divided by time squared equals a constant (a number that is always the same), or $D/t^2 = C$. The appearance of this constant establishes a relationship between distance and time! This constant will change from experiment to experiment, only if the angle of the channel is changed. This relationship that we just discovered is identical to what Galileo discovered in his laboratory so many years ago.

We have better tools to measure time than Galileo had, but being older and wiser, he had better math skills than you do. Galileo figured out the precise relationship between the distance a falling object travels and the time of the fall. We now know that any free-falling object on Earth accelerates 32 feet per second every second it is falling (if air resistance is negligible). Do you know how anyone could accelerate any automobile from 0 to more than 100 miles per hour in five seconds? Just push the car off the roof of a tall building and gravity's 32-feet-per-second-per-second acceleration will do it for you.

Discussion Questions/Review of What Was Learned

1. What scientific instrument did we make today?

2. Why was Galileo a very brave man?

3. Why did Galileo not have an accurate clock in his laboratory?

4. What two questions did Galileo ask nature?

5. What conclusion did we draw about the mathematical relationship between the distance something falls and the time it takes for it to fall?

6. What is one possible method to get any car to accelerate from 0 to 100 miles per hour in just five seconds?

From *Gravity, the Glue of the Universe.* ©1997 Harry Gilbert and Diana Gilbert Smith. Teacher Ideas Press. (800) 237-6124.

Chapter 1, Lesson Plan # 2

Student Handout— Galileo's Ideas About Gravity

You may ask, what does Aristotle's mistake about falling bodies have to do with Galileo? Galileo went a step beyond observing nature. He asked nature two questions:

1. Is the effect of gravity measurable?

2. How do objects move as gravity is "pulling" them toward Earth?

Let us find out how Galileo determined the experimental facts about falling bodies. Galileo clearly described his work in determining experimental facts about falling bodies in his book *The Two New Sciences*. The book was published just five years after his infamous trial in Rome on June 22, 1633, where he was told to "abjure, curse, and detest" his errors and heresies. (de Santillana 1955) The experiment on the acceleration of falling bodies was ingenious in many ways. Galileo was confronted with several problems:

* How was he to measure the rate at which an object was moving as it was falling to Earth, when that rate was *changing* constantly as the object was falling?

* To get an accurate measure of the rate, he would have to drop the object from a great height, but how was he to measure this rate, when the object would be falling faster and faster as it approached the ground?

* How was he to accurately measure short intervals of time, when his clock was not accurate?

Galileo solved the clock problem by using "a large vessel of water placed in an elevated position; to the bottom of this vessel was soldered a pipe of small diameter giving a thin jet of water, which was collected in a small glass during each descent of the ball." (Knedler 1973) Thus, Galileo measured time by measuring the weight of uniformly flowing water.

Still, his "water clock" was really not adequate to measure the time of a freely falling object, which he knew fell with *increasing* speed (accelerated motion) as it approached the ground. Galileo solved the problem of timing a very rapidly moving object by avoiding it. He correctly concluded that he could use a ball rolling slowly down a smooth inclined surface without changing the free-fall relationship between the distance traversed by the ball and the time of travel:

> A piece of wooden molding, about 12 cubits [about 18 feet] long, half a cubit [about 9 inches] wide and three finger-breadths thick was taken; on its edge was cut a channel a little more than one finger in breadth; having made this groove very straight, smooth, and polished and having lined it with parchment, also as smooth and polished as possible, we rolled along it a hard, smooth and very round bronze ball. (Knedler 1973)

Galileo measured the time for the ball to descend the full length of the channel, through one-half, two-thirds, three-fourths, and other fractions of the full length. Repeating the experiment 100 times, he always found that the distance traveled by the ball was proportional to the square of the time of travel, and that this relationship was true for all inclinations of the plane. Thus, Galileo knew that the relationship must also hold for a vertical plane, or free fall. The exact value of the acceleration of a body in free fall could not be determined by Galileo because he did not have a stop watch with which to measure it.

Chapter 1, Lesson Plan # 2

Student Handout—
Experimental Data

Experiment on Effect of Gravity on Falling Objects Using a Galilean Water Clock

Date _____

Team Members:	Job:
	Hold can steady
	Control release of water
	Catch water
	Add water to top of can
	Walk during clock trials
	"Start"
	Record weight and do math calculations

Empty Weight of Beaker: _____

Distance of Roll	Weight of Water
¼	
½	
¾	
Full length	

Chapter 1, Lesson Plan # 2

Sample Inclined Plane Data Analysis Chart

Distance traveled	0.25	0.50	0.75	1.00
Grams of water collected	5.0	7.0	8.0	9.0
Grams^2	25	49	64	81
Distance/grams^2	0.01	0.01	0.01	0.01

Chapter 1, Lesson Plan # 2

Student Handout—
Mathematical Analysis of Experimental Data

Class Results and Averages

Team	¼ Length	½ Length	¾ Length	Full Length
Total				
Average				

Inclined Plane Data Analysis

Distance traveled	0.25	0.50	0.75	1.00
Grams of water collected				
Grams^2				
Distance/grams^2				

Chapter 1, Lesson Plan # 3

Newton Makes a Grand Hypothesis

TEACHING MODEL
Concept Attainment

OBJECTIVES
1. The students will identify the major attributes that make a statement a hypothesis.

2. The students will distinguish between hypotheses and other statements presented in the lesson.

3. The students will formulate original hypotheses.

4. The students will name three premises behind Newton's Law of Universal Gravitation.

5. The students will distinguish between Newton's, Aristotle's, and Galileo's ideas about gravity.

VOCABULARY
1. *Hypothesis*—A tentative scientific statement that may or may not be true. A statement that clearly predicts that something specific will happen under specific conditions.

2. *Gravity* (according to Newton)—The force of attraction between all masses.

3. *Tangent line*—A straight line that touches a curve at only one point but does not intersect the curve.

4. *Universe*—All existing things, including Earth, all celestial bodies, and all of space.

5. *Planet*—A sphere of rocks (like Earth) or a sphere of gas (like Jupiter) orbiting a star.

6. *Star*—A sphere of hydrogen and helium gas hot enough to continuously emit light.

7. *Premise*—A statement that may or may not be true and makes no predictions about anything else. Example: *All ravens are black.*

8. *Postulate*—A tentative scientific statement assumed, without prior proof, to be true.

9. *Acceleration*—An object continuously moving faster and faster.

10. *Phenomenon*—Anything that you can see, touch, smell, hear, or taste.

11. *Comet*—A chunk of powdery minerals and ice orbiting the Sun.

12. *Infinite*—Immeasurable and without end.

13. *Matter*—Anything that occupies space.

14. *Mass*—The quantity (amount) of matter.

15. *Attribute*—A quality that defines an object.

MATERIALS

* Copy of "Student Handout—Newton's Ideas About Gravity" for each student.

* Copy of "Student Handout—Rules for Writing Hypotheses" for each student.

* Concept Attainment Cards (see "Statements to Be Used on Concept Attainment Cards")

PROCEDURE

This lesson is designed following the Concept Attainment model. (Joyce and Weil 1986) Therefore, the format is somewhat different from a Direct Instruction lesson. This lesson style provides several excellent opportunities to use a "wait-time" technique called Think-Pair-Share. This technique was developed by Frank Lyman Jr., Professional Development Center Coordinator, Howard County Schools and the University of Maryland, in 1978. The following are the components of Think-Pair-Share:

* Students **listen** while the teacher poses a question.

* Students are given quiet time in which to **think** of a response.

* Students **pair** with a neighbor and discuss their responses.

* Students are invited to **share** their responses with the entire group.

A time limit is set for each step in the process. Many teachers use cueing devices such as bells, pointers, hand signals, or cubes to move students through the cycle. Students may be asked to write or diagram their responses while in the Think and/or Pair modes. (Lyman 1987)

1. In this exercise you will be prompting the students to discover the attributes of hypotheses. Label two columns on the blackboard: A and B (representing hypotheses and non-hypotheses). Do not reveal the true titles of these columns at this time. Place two examples (Concept Attainment Cards) under each column, and ask the students: *What rules am I using to place these statements in these two different categories?*

2. Encourage students to **think** about the possible "rules" and to work in **pairs** to decide under which category to place additional Concept Attainment Cards. Finally, invite the students to **share** their rules with the entire group.

3. Add more examples (Concept Attainment Cards) to the proper categories, and allow the students to modify their rules for placement as more examples are given.

4. When the students are confident that they have the rules correct, have them test their rules by generating examples of their own for each category.

5. Confirm the students' examples and state the complete rules used for placement of cards in each category. Pass out a copy of "Student Handout—Rules for Writing Hypotheses" to each student.

6. Have the students generate new examples based on the complete rules. Each student generates an original hypothesis, and together the class checks them for adherence to the rules.

7. Ask the students the following question: *In doing an experiment, if you find that your hypothesis was wrong, has your experiment failed?* (No! Your experiment only fails if a) you used sloppy procedures, or b) your experiment cannot be repeated by another scientist. [This means that another scientist following your instructions cannot get the same results as you.])

8. Introduce the vocabulary for the lesson.

9. Sir Isaac Newton wondered about the following questions: *Because gravity extends to the deepest mines and to the top of the highest mountains, does it also extend to the Moon? If so, why does the Moon not fall to Earth?* Discuss these questions with the class.

10. Read part 1 of "Student Handout—Newton's Ideas About Gravity" as a class, and discuss how Newton's ideas differ from Aristotle's and Galileo's ideas. Point out that Newton's Law of Universal Gravitation is actually a hypothesis. Have the students recite the three premises behind Newton's Law of Universal Gravitation.

11. Read part 2 and part 3 of "Student Handout—Newton's Ideas About Gravity" as a class, and discuss how Newton and, later, Lord Cavendish proved Newton's hypothesis (his Law of Universal Gravitation).

REVIEW QUESTIONS

1. What attributes separate a hypothesis from an ordinary statement?

2. How would you know your experiment had failed?

3. Name the three premises behind Newton's Law of Universal Gravitation.

4. Explain in your own words Newton's Law of Universal Gravitation.

5. How did Newton explain the fact that the Moon has not fallen into Earth?

Chapter 1, Lesson Plan # 3

Student Handout—
Newton's Ideas About Gravity

Part 1

On Christmas morning of 1642, less than a year after Galileo died in Arcetri, Italy, a remarkable baby was born to Hannah Newton in Lincolnshire, England. What was remarkable about this baby was not immediately obvious to his mother, or to anyone else. There was no way that they could have known that this baby, named Isaac after his father (who had died three months earlier), was gifted with a brain that was destined to carry forward Galileo's work and astound the world with new discoveries on how the universe works. Isaac Newton was also destined to have a story bandied about concerning an apple that was said to have fallen on his head, which triggered his thinking about why objects fall to Earth. Well, as far as one can determine from the writings of Isaac Newton, he was primarily interested in discovering the law of gravity that dictated exactly *how* (not why) an apple, or any object, falls to Earth.

In 1666, 24-year-old Isaac Newton wondered: Because gravity extends to the bottom of the deepest mines and to the top of the highest mountains, does it also extend to the Moon? If so, why does the Moon not fall to Earth? Could he account for the motions of the Moon around Earth with the same mysterious force that pulled an apple to the ground? Is it possible that every mass in the universe attracts every other mass with this same force? Could he account for the motions of all of the planets with this force? The answers to all of these questions were *yes*, he could! That is, a natural-born genius like Isaac Newton could do it.

Newton did it by postulating just three premises:

1. The force acting on the Moon is also acting on Earth.

2. The Moon orbits Earth only because this force constantly accelerates the Moon toward Earth. That is, the Moon is constantly trying to fall toward Earth.

3. The force decreases with the inverse square of the distance. (Thus, if at 1,000 miles from the center of Earth, the force is 1 unit strong, then at 2,000 miles from the center of Earth, the force is 1 over 2 squared, or $\frac{1}{4}$ unit strong. At 3,000 miles from the center of Earth, the force is 1 over 3 squared, or $\frac{1}{9}$ unit strong.)

Using those three premises, Newton derived the Law of Universal Gravitation: *There is a power of gravity tending to all bodies proportional to the several quantities of matter they contain and inversely proportional to the square of the distance between them.* With this new law, to quote Steven Weinberg, "Mankind for the first time saw the possibility of a comprehensive quantitative understanding of nature." (Hawking and Israel 1987)

Part 2

The tremendous power of the law can be demonstrated by looking at its accomplishments. With this singular law, Newton was able to:

* Account for the motion of the Moon around Earth.

* Account for all of the known motions of the planets.

* Explain why the first day of spring does not arrive at exactly the same time every year. (This delay in arrival was already known to the ancient Greeks, but had remained unexplained until Newton did so.)

* Account for the known 18-year cycle of total eclipses of the Sun.

* Solve the mystery of the comets by making them subject to the same law of gravity as the planets (thus enabling his friend, Edmund Halley, to calculate the orbit of a comet that appeared in the sky in the year 1682 and to accurately predict its return 75 years later).

* Account for the tides in the lakes and oceans. As the Sun or the Moon moves slowly over the body of water, the gravitational attraction pulls harder on the water than on the solid Earth below the water. The water responds by gradually leaving the shores and amassing in the center of the body of water. The surface of the water is closer to the Sun or the Moon than the land beneath the water.

Fifty years after the death of Newton, Lord Cavendish again demonstrated the power of the Law of Universal Gravitation. Cavendish experimentally determined the numerical value of the proportionality constant in the law and then proceeded to calculate the weight of Earth! (See appendix B.)

Newton's Law of Universal Gravitation gave us a remarkable new understanding of how the universe works. This was a comprehensive and quantitative description of nature never before attained. In 1687, when his *Principia* was published, Newton was hailed far and wide as a genius without parallel.

However, even geniuses have their limits. There was one question concerning the force of gravity that puzzled Newton: How does the force get from the Sun to Earth, or from Earth to the Moon? There is nothing out there but empty space. Other forces must contact the objects they are affecting. A horse could hardly pull a carriage if it were not in contact with the carriage! How does the force of gravity travel through empty space? Isaac Newton never claimed to have found an answer to this question.

Part 3

Two hundred years after Newton, Albert Einstein, using mathematical tools unavailable to Newton, was able to probe deeper and come up with a new explanation of gravity. He said, in effect, let's try to answer all of Newton's unanswered questions about the way gravity works by redefining what gravity is. Maybe Newton's concept of gravity as an attraction of one body to another is not the whole truth. Maybe one has to dig deeper to get closer to the root of the concept.

Einstein knew exactly what his challenge was: Replace the old idea of a force of attraction with a new concept that would retain all of the remarkable results that flowed out of Newton's Law of Universal Gravitation, and simultaneously answer all of Newton's unanswered questions.

With his new concept, General Relativity, Einstein retained every accomplishment of the Law of Universal Gravitation, and in addition, opened up new vistas in our understanding of the entire universe.

How did Albert Einstein do that? We will tell you how he did it, but first, we must take a close look at the one thing that gave Newton's force of gravity so much trouble—*Empty Space.*

"... What is space? Here is the key to the whole riddle."

—Isaac Bashevis Singer (1970)

Chapter 1, Lesson Plan # 3

Student Handout—
Rules for Writing Hypotheses

1. A hypothesis predicts that something will happen.

2. A hypothesis contains an "if . . . then" statement.

3. A hypothesis is not something already known or previously proven to be true.

4. A hypothesis is not a personal opinion statement.

5. A hypothesis that has a long list of predicted items that actually come true is the best (strongest) hypothesis.

From *Gravity, the Glue of the Universe.* ©1997 Harry Gilbert and Diana Gilbert Smith. Teacher Ideas Press. (800) 237-6124.

Chapter 1, Lesson Plan # 3

Statements to Be Used on Concept Attainment Cards

HYPOTHESES

1. If light-colored liquids cool faster than dark-colored liquids, then I will find that hot milk cools off faster than hot cocoa.

2. If a dropped ball never bounces all the way back to where it started, then when the ball hits the ground, it must lose energy.

3. If shaking cream in a jar turns the cream foamy, then I can make whipped cream by putting cream into a partially empty jar and shaking it.

4. If Earth pulls "Earth things" back with a stronger force than "non-Earth things," then a dropped Ping-Pong ball will fall more slowly than a big rock.

5. If a fire needs oxygen to keep burning, then cutting off the supply of air will put out the fire.

6. If this metal is a magnet, then it will pick up a paper clip.

7. If I give my dad a 100-pound weight to lift, then he will do it.

8. If I pour water into two cups (one containing sand and one containing marbles), then the cup with the sand will hold more water.

9. If Sam and Joe race to the edge of the field, then Sam will get there first.

10. If space is real, then it must be measurable in some way.

NON-HYPOTHESES

1. The population of Chicago is greater than the population of Simsbury (may substitute any small town name). [*This is a known fact.*]

2. Sam is faster than Joe. [*This is either an opinion statement or a known fact.*]

3. If I put a dime into a machine, then I will get candy. [*This is a known fact.*]

4. If I hit you with a water balloon, then you will get wet. [*This is previously proven.*]

5. If I hit my thumb with a hammer, then it will hurt. [*This is previously proven.*]

6. If I fight in school, then I will get a detention. [*This is previously proven.*]

7. If I study, then I am more likely to pass the test. [*This is previously proven.*]

8. If the dog hears a noise, then it will bark. [*This is either a known fact or an opinion statement.*]

9. If the electricity is off, then the electric refrigerator won't work. [*This is a known fact.*]

10. My dad is stronger than your dad. [*This is an opinion statement.*]

11. My magnet will pick up all metals. [*This is false. Also incorrect form.*]

12. My magnet will pick up aluminum foil. [*This is false. Also incorrect form.*]

13. The 1928 New York Yankees ball club could beat any of today's teams. [*This is an opinion statement that is not provable.*]

14. If at sea level I heat a pan of water to 100°C, then the water will boil. [*This is a known fact.*]

What Is Space?

"From whence did you come?"
"From space, from space, Sir. Whence else?"
"Pardon me, my Lord, but is not your Lord already in space?"
"Pooh! What do you know of space? Define Space."
"Space, my Lord, is height and breadth indefinitely prolonged."
"Exactly, you see, you do not even know what space is!"

—Edwin A. Abbott (1880)

The above conversation took place in Abbott's book *Flatland.* The first speaker is a "Flatlander," a two-dimensional creature. The second speaker is from our world, a three-dimensional creature. The confusion about "what is space" continues to this day. The consensus of modern scientists is that there is a lack of any deep understanding about the nature of empty space.

"How much space does a man need?" asked Tolstoy in a similarly titled short story, which touches upon the physical reality of space. This old Russian tale tells of a peasant who lost an opportunity to become the owner of a tract of land. The deal offered to the peasant is simple: He can have all the land that he could mark off by walking, starting out at sunrise, provided that he returns to his starting point by sunset. If he returns after sunset, he loses everything. The greedy peasant stakes out a tremendous stretch of land and arrives back at his starting point only to collapse in a heap. They buried him under six feet of ground.

To the Russian peasant, space meant land—acres of land. What if an army of bulldozers dug out of his land a canyon 100 feet deep? Would not the *space* of his original acreage still *exist*? What

if the canyon were filled with water to make a beautiful lake? The peasant would have acres of water, but what about the space? What is space?

Aristotle claimed that he was the first person to ponder over this question at length. He spoke of space as "place" and "void." He said that "place" is "the innermost motionless boundary of what contains"—his exact words as translated from the Greek. He said that void "does not exist . . . unless one is willing to call the condition of movement void, whatever it may be." (McKeon 1966) Two thousand years after Aristotle, Isaac Newton spoke of space as "eternal, infinite, uncreated, uniform throughout, not mobile, nor capable of inducing change of motion in bodies." (Westfall 1980) This is incorrect, however, because space *does* affect the motion of all bodies (see chapter 4). An attempt to define space was made by the Scientific and Technical Information Division of NASA (National Aeronautics and Space Administration). Because they were administering space, they felt they had an obligation to define it: "Space is that part of the universe between celestial bodies." (Glasstone 1965) You can search far and wide for a clear definition of space. Why? We use the word *space* without hesitation (i.e., "space travel," "spaceships," and "air space"). However, we find it difficult to define space because it cannot be felt, smelled, tasted, or weighed. We cannot measure its movement or destroy it, yet we are forever immersed within it.

Most astonishingly, we, who move about in space, are mostly empty space! Our flesh and blood and bones are all made up of atoms (carbon, hydrogen, oxygen, etc.). And all atoms are mostly empty space. The atoms that make up our bodies and Earth and the Sun are not rigid, solid spheres. The ground you are standing on is not as solid as you may think.

"How can that be? Is the Empire State Building, and the ground it is standing on, made up of empty space?" Well, no, they are made up of atoms and all atoms are made up of electrons, neutrons, and protons. If you could take all the atoms in the Empire State Building, as well as all the atoms in *all* the buildings on Manhattan Island, and squeeze them together until all the electrons are pushed into all the protons, you would be left with enough solid material to fill up just *one teaspoon*! (That is not a misprint!) Under certain circumstances, gravity can indeed squeeze all the space out of atoms (see chapter 7).

If we pump all the air out of a steel tank, what is left in the tank? Space. Can we remove the space from inside that tank? No, it could not be pumped out, and space cannot be moved from one place to another (just as Newton said). The absence of space cannot even be imagined. Perhaps this is why scientists from Aristotle to Einstein struggled with the meaning of space.

One thing we can do with space is examine its properties. One need only look up at the stars on a clear night to become aware that space is fabulously transparent to light (i.e., light moves through space). Stars that are 1 quadrillion (1,000,000,000,000,000) miles from Earth are easily visible. Using a pair of ordinary binoculars, one can see stars whose light has traveled 30,000 light-years of space to reach us (1 light-year is 5.8 trillion miles). Even without binoculars it is possible to see the light from an entire galaxy of stars called Andromeda, situated 2 million light-years from Earth. On a winter night in 1964, Maarten Schmidt used a 200-inch telescope on Mt. Palomar in California to photograph a quasar, an old galaxy—7 billion light years from Earth—that looks like a star.

Astronomers tell us that Earth has made about 4.5 billion trips around the Sun without any signs of slowing down. From this we can infer that space offers no resistance to a massive object (any object that has mass) moving through it. What else moves through space? The force of gravity, too, must move through space. It must move from the Sun to Earth, from Earth to the Moon, and from any object that has mass to any other object that has mass. How else could Earth respond to the Sun's gravity, and the Moon to Earth's gravity? (Einstein will tell us "how else"—see chapter 4.)

In summary, there are three items that move through space without resistance:

1. All forms of light, including visible light, radio waves, X-rays, and infrared light.

2. Massive objects (any object that has mass), these include stars, planets, comets, and meteorites.

3. Newton's force of gravity.

If massive objects, the force of gravity, and light can all move through space without hindrance of any sort, can we not just as well declare that space is "nothing"? "Nothing" would allow movement without hindrance.

Scientists say that a thing is real if you can measure it. Space cannot be weighed, nor can its flow be measured (as you would measure the flow of water). Distance of space can be measured, but this is of no help because one could just as well say that there is nothing between Earth and the Moon as say that there are 238,800 miles of space between them. So, what properties are left?—electrical and magnetic properties! There is a very important property of space that can be measured: its electrical permittivity (see appendix C). Thus, empty space must be a real entity because its electrical properties can be measured very precisely in well-defined experiments that can be repeated in any physics laboratory in the world—and no other substance has exactly the same properties as empty space.

Are there any other properties of space that can be measured? What about a geometric property, such as shape? It was Euclid, a contemporary of Aristotle, who first implied in 300 B.C. that space has a definite shape. Euclid did not come out and say "space is flat" (it would have been impossible in his time to make sense of these words), but his mathematics implied such a property. He talked about spatial relations between objects. Space, as an arena where all objects existed, did not figure in Euclid's mathematics.

The concept of space as an arena was first introduced in about 1630 by the French mathematician and philosopher René Descartes. He described all points as being located in three-dimensional space. Euclid gave us a flat space with his axiom that parallel lines may run for infinite length and still remain perfectly parallel. Few seriously doubted Euclid until 1854, when George Riemann said (in a lecture to the faculty of the University of Göttingen): "The properties that distinguish [our] space from other conceivable [spaces] are only to be deduced from experience." (Misner 1973) With these words, Riemann opened up the Pandora's Box of possible spaces in which parallel lines may *not* remain parallel forever. Euclid had to postulate his axiom; he assumed that his axiom was correct solely on the basis of common sense. He could not prove that parallel lines will remain parallel upon infinite extension in our space. Many mathematicians expended tremendous efforts trying to prove this axiom by deducing it from other axioms. Mathematicians now realize that Euclid's axiom cannot be proved.

Riemann recognized that one could imagine spaces where initially parallel lines would eventually cross each other because the space is warped. Riemann understood that the only way to determine how parallel lines behave in our space is to perform the experiment ("deduce it from experience"). Excepting a few mathematicians, nobody paid much attention to Riemann. He died of tuberculosis in 1866 at the age of 40. He left physicists "far removed from such a way of thinking; space was still for them, a rigid, homogeneous something, susceptible of no change of conditions. . . . Riemann, solitary and uncomprehended, [had] a new conception of space, in which space was deprived of its rigidity and in which its power to *take part in physical events was recognized as possible*" (emphasis added) (from an essay by Albert Einstein on the "Problem of Space, Ether, and the Field in Physics").

In 1915, 61 years after Riemann's lecture at the University of Göttingen, Albert Einstein published his paper on General Relativity, in which he took the giant step of "endowing space with physical qualities" and proving mathematically that gravity was a manifestation of the *geometry* of space. Einstein demonstrated that a geometric property, the gravitational field, was the most important property of space. The concept of a gravitational field has its basis in the concepts of magnetic and electric fields, originated in 1851 by Michael Faraday and put into elegant mathematical form by James Clerk Maxwell in 1865 (with his publication of *A Dynamical Theory of the Electromagnetic Field*).

If you have ever played with bar magnets, you know how a magnetic field "feels." When you try to push the "north" or "south" ends of two bar magnets together, you feel that there is "something" just ahead of each magnet keeping them from touching each other. You can actually visualize a magnetic field if you have a sheet of glass or a cardboard, a bar magnet, and iron filings.

Tape the magnet to the underside of the glass or cardboard. Sprinkle the iron filings at random over the top of the surface. The iron filings form a pattern of lines emerging from the magnet that seem to be reaching out into space (see fig. 2.1, p. 36). Faraday called this pattern "the lines of force of the magnetic field surrounding the bar magnet." (Wightman 1953)

Magnets were known to the ancient Greeks who discovered the strange iron ore (lodestone) that was capable of physically attracting pieces of iron. However, nobody knew the mechanism of this attraction until Faraday suggested that there are invisible lines of force coming out of the magnet that represent the field surrounding the magnet at all times, as shown in figure 2.1.

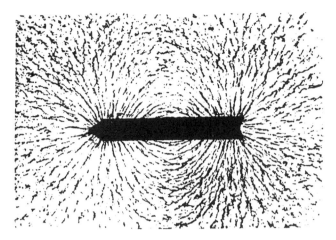

Fig. 2.1. An invisible magnetic field surrounding a bar magnet is made visible by iron filings.

The beginning of our understanding of electricity is generally attributed to William Gilbert, the 16th-century Englishman who was the first to show that static electricity can be generated by vigorously rubbing together pairs of 20 different substances. Gilbert, however, had no idea there is an electric field surrounding all charged objects.

The shape of the electric field present between two objects of equal but opposite charge is shown in figure 2.2.

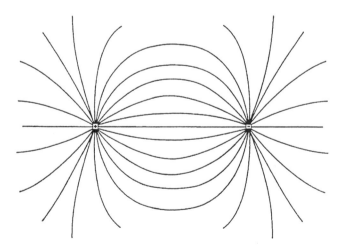

Fig. 2.2. The electric field existing between two objects of equal but opposite charge is idealized by drawn lines.

Faraday and Maxwell spoke of stresses in the immediate surroundings of magnetic poles and electric charges. These stresses in turn produce stresses in ever widening circles, diminishing in strength with distance from the source. *These stresses are the fields.* They exist in empty space, and they have "a life of their own," so to speak—they can break away from the magnet or electric charge and travel off into space at 186,000 miles per second.

Maxwell deduced that the stresses that break away from the magnets and from the electric charges are actually identical. They represent a strange marriage of electricity and magnetism. Maxwell showed that what was traveling off into space at 186,000 miles per second from either the magnet or the electrical charge was an *electromagnetic field:* oscillating electric and magnetic stresses each spontaneously generating the other, spreading out into space at the speed of light.

If one could shake a common bar magnet fast enough, an electromagnetic field would shake loose. An easier magnet to agitate is an electromagnet. (An electromagnet can be built by winding a coil of insulated wire around an ordinary iron bar. Attach one end of the wire coil to the negative terminal of a battery and the other end to the positive terminal—the iron bar immediately becomes a strong magnet.)

In 1888, Heinrich Hertz used an electromagnet to verify that fields can be shaken loose. He actually caught the fields when they arrived at an isolated single loop of wire with a very tiny gap between the two ends of the wire. Hertz isolated this loop of wire in a closed darkened room. In an adjoining room, he placed a battery-powered electromagnetic spark generator. He turned on the spark generator, closed the door, and went into the dark room with the isolated loop of wire. (See fig 2.3.) "It was not without astonishment," Hertz said, when he saw sparks jumping across the tiny gap in the isolated loop of wire. The battery-generated sparks were continuously sending out (shaking loose) an electromagnetic field (radio waves), which traveled through the wooden door

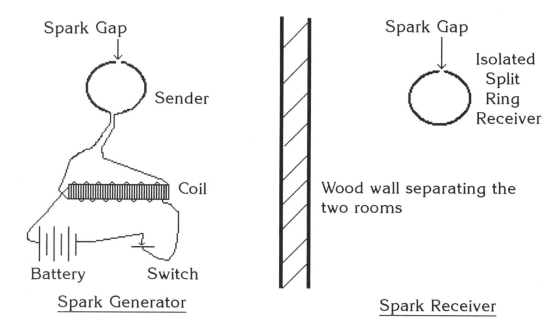

Fig. 2.3. The laboratory setup used by Hertz to shake loose an electromagnetic field. The switch is continually opened and closed to induce sparks in the gap in the split ring sender.

and into the room with the isolated loop of wire. The sparks appeared in the isolated loop because the traveling electromagnetic field caused electric currents to flow within the wire, and the current then jumped across the gap between the two ends of the wire. (One can see a "giant" spark during any thunderstorm, when a bolt of lightning leaps from cloud to cloud. The Faraday electromagnetic field generated by the lightning can easily be detected as a loud crackle of "interference" on any AM radio—FM radios suppress this interference.)

Such a "shaken loose" magnetic field moving through space, not anchored to any electric charges or magnets, is called an electromagnetic wave. Hertz deduced the velocity at which these waves traveled from one room to the other by measuring their wavelength and frequency. He found the velocity to be as Maxwell's equations had predicted: 186,000 miles per second (the velocity of light).

In principle, visible light could be produced by shaking a magnet, but at a rate of 500 trillion

(500,000,000,000,000) oscillations per second. We now know that the tiny current loops (electrons) inside individual atoms are able to oscillate fast enough to produce visible light. White light pours out of an electric lightbulb because the atoms of tungsten in the filament are just hot enough to generate the required frequency (see table 2.1, p. 38). The identification of light with an electromagnetic field in motion was the culmination of the Faraday-Maxwell teamwork. Einstein called the Faraday-Maxwell discoveries "the most profound and fruitful change in our concept of reality since Newton." (Einstein 1934)

Today, "Faraday's field is very busy," to quote J. Robert Oppenheimer. "It transmits light, it transmits heat; it transmits all the waves that feed the television sets and radios all over the world." (Oppenheimer 1964) (See table 2.2, p. 38.)

In the next chapter we will meet a young boy who had the imagination to wonder how the world would look to someone riding on a beam of light.

Table 2.1
How to Generate Faraday's Electromagnetic Fields

Common Name	Rate of Electron Oscillations Needed (cycles/second)	Type of Device Needed
Gamma Rays	1×10^{20}	Radioactive atoms in an excited state, or an atomic bomb
X-rays	1×10^{18}	Abruptly stopped stream of electrons using a metal plate (X-ray tube)
Visible Light	5×10^{14}	A hot wire (tungsten lightbulb), a laser, or a chemical reaction (firefly)
Infrared Light	1×10^{14}	Anything at all, because all atoms emit infrared light when slightly warm
Microwaves	1×10^{12}	Electrons excited by an electromagnetic field (a magnetron tube)
Radio Waves (AM)	1×10^{6}	A resonant inductance/capacitance circuit, or any spark generator

Table 2.2
The Electromagnetic Spectrum

Common Name	Wavelength (centimeters)	Energy/Photon (electron volts)	Passage Through the Atmosphere? (if arriving from outer space)
Gamma Rays	less than 1×10^{-8}	greater than 1×10^{5}	No, blocked by nitrogen, oxygen, and ozone in upper atmosphere
X-rays	1×10^{-8} to 1×10^{-6}	1×10^{3} to 1×10^{5}	No, blocked by ozone
Ultraviolet Light	3×10^{-6}	100	No, blocked by ozone
Visible Light	4×10^{-5} to 7×10^{-5}	7 to 10	Yes
Infrared Light	0.0035 to 7×10^{-5}	0.01 to 7	No, blocked by water
Microwaves	0.3 to 0.0035	0.01 to 0.0001	No, blocked by water
Radar	30 to 0.3	1×10^{-5} to 1×10^{-4}	Yes
Television Waves	300	1×10^{-7}	Yes
Radio Waves (FM)	400	5×10^{-7}	Yes
Radio Waves (AM)	30,000	1×10^{-8}	No, blocked by ionosphere

Notes:
One electron volt is equivalent to 1.6×10^{-19} joule of energy. One joule per second will deliver enough power to light a one-watt lightbulb.

The ionosphere is a region of Earth's atmosphere extending from 30 miles to 250 miles above the surface of Earth. The atoms in the ionosphere are highly ionized by solar radiation. An ionized atom is an atom that has lost one or more of its electrons. Atoms with their normal complement of electrons are electrically neutral. Losing even one of its electrons makes the atom electrically charged.

Chapter 2, Lesson Plan # 1

What Is Space?

TEACHING MODEL
The Classroom Meeting (modified version)

OBJECTIVES
1. The students will name various contemporary meanings and uses of the word *space*.

2. The students will use classroom meeting rules and procedures to discuss and analyze historical ideas about space.

3. The students will identify and label the properties of space.

4. The students will attempt to construct a verbal/visual model of space.

5. The students will formulate a scientific, consensus definition of an ordinary word, *space*.

VOCABULARY
1. *Astronomer*—A person who studies the sky, Sun, stars, planets, and so on.

2. *Interior decorator*—A person who decorates the inside of a home.

MATERIALS
There are no specific materials required for this lesson. The teacher may wish to have on hand a collection of art supplies that the children can use to construct three-dimensional models of space.

PROCEDURE

1. Set up or review Classroom Meeting guidelines and procedures, and introduce vocabulary.*

2. Use the following questions to begin a discussion of the word *space*.

   * *What are some common phrases using the word* space*?* (I need space. He's spaced out.)

   * *What is the definition of space implied by each of these uses?* ("space" signifies "room"; "spaced out" signifies "his mind is far away")

   * *Compare the definitions of space used by different types of people; how does an interior decorator's space compare to an astronomer's space?*

   * *What is air, and how does air differ from space?*

3. Use "Teacher Fact Sheet—What Is Space?" to trace the historical ideas about space with the students. Encourage the students to ask questions and to debate among themselves their reactions to these ideas about space.

4. Have each student write a paragraph answering the question, *What is space?* before proceeding with step 5. Depending upon the length of your class period, this may be a good stopping point.

5a. Have the students share their responses to the question in step 4. Divide the class into small groups. Direct the groups to attempt to create a verbal/visual model of space using the following guidelines.

---

*Note: Traditionally, the Classroom Meeting has been used as a format for discussion of social issues relevant to classroom dynamics. In this lesson we use this format to discuss the multiple meanings of the word *space*. If your students are already familiar with one format for a Classroom Meeting, use what they already know. If you have never used a Classroom Meeting, the setup and rules can range from extremely simple to rather complex. (Joyce and Weil 1986) The most important elements in the Classroom Meeting are: everyone sits in a circle, one person speaks at a time, and everyone must have an opportunity to speak. The teacher may impose any manner and variety of rules and guidelines to ensure that the shyest students get a chance to speak and that the boldest students do not dominate the discussion. The most useful technique we used during the field testing of this lesson was having the students call on other students to speak after they were finished. When discussion slowed down, or began to stray off topic, we introduced a new question and called upon someone who was holding back to begin the responses.

5b. Guidelines for Creating a Model of Space

* Begin with ideas discussed in the Classroom Meeting.

* Add ideas and thoughts of the members of your group.

* Ask each other clarifying questions.

* Try to reach a consensus on what is space.

* Use words, pictures, diagrams, three-dimensional models, exemplars, and non-exemplars to create a model of space.

Example:

What is an orange?

An orange is a small round sphere with a rough outer skin and a sweet edible inside layer. (Is this enough to distinguish an orange from a kiwi?) The inside layer is soft and juicy and comes apart in sections. (Is this enough to distinguish an orange from a tangerine?)

6. Have the students share their completed models of space and continue the discussion of space. Compare models group to group and class models to historical models and concepts.*

7. Have the students formulate a consensus statement about the definition and properties of space.

---

*Note: You may videotape these presentations to develop an assessment from year to year documenting how different groups define space. Also, this affords the students an opportunity to learn about public speaking by analyzing their video performances.

Chapter 2, Lesson Plan # 1

Teacher Fact Sheet— What Is Space?

1. Tell the story of the Russian peasant. (See narrative on p. 33.)*

2. If we went to your house with an army of bulldozers and dug out a canyon 100 feet deep, would the space of your yard and house still exist? What if it rained and the canyon became filled with water? Would the original space still exist?

3. Aristotle said, "Space is the innermost, motionless, boundary of what contains." (See narrative on p. 33.)

4. Newton said, "Space is eternal, infinite, uncreated, uniform throughout, not mobile, nor capable of inducing change of motion in bodies."

5. NASA said, "Space is that part of the universe between celestial bodies."

6. All atoms are mostly empty space. If you could take all of the atoms in the Empire State Building, plus all the atoms in all the buildings on Manhattan Island, and squeeze them together until all the electrons are pushed into all the protons, you would be left with only enough solid material to fill one teaspoon. (See narrative on p. 34.)

7. A mathematician in 300 B.C., Euclid, developed mathematics for an axiom that implies a flat space. The axiom is that parallel lines will always be parallel no matter how far they run. (See narrative on p. 35.)

8. René Descartes (1630), a French philosopher, described all points as located in three-dimensional space.

9. In 1854, German mathematician George Riemann said, in effect, that space might be warped or curved like a tennis ball and it might be flexible like play dough, in which case parallel lines would eventually cross each other. (See narrative on p. 35.)

*Note: See the narrative text in chapter 2 for elaboration of several of these topics (i.e., pages 1, 3, 6, 7, 9).

A Simplicity of Premises

"How can one really know a great moment unless one has first felt a great disappointment?"

—an old Jewish saying

"A theory is the more impressive, the greater
the simplicity of its premises, and
the more extended its area of applicability."

—Albert Einstein (1907)

"Hurtling, rattling rolling round the sky
. . . .
Faster and faster, up and up they soar
Till time stands still. . . ."

—C. F. Ramuz (1918)

The final leg of our journey in search of the genesis of relativity takes us to Zurich, Switzerland. The year is 1900. A young Jewish boy has just graduated from the Swiss Federal Institute of Technology (a typical European technical college). His one ambition is to continue his studies at his alma mater as a professor's assistant and work toward a Ph.D. degree. For six of his classmates, it had been easy—they applied for assistantships and they received them. For Albert Einstein, it worked out otherwise—he was refused. He was also refused assistantships by Wilhelm Ostwald, a famous chemist, and by Kammerlingh Onnes, a famous physicist. He was, however, accepted in 1902 as Technical Expert, Third Class, by the Swiss Patent Office, where he had plenty of spare time to think about the Faraday-Maxwell electromagnetic field, to read all the current literature on

research in physics, and to contemplate his happy teenage days spent with his family in Milan, Italy: He was 16 years old and free as a bird—free to let his imagination soar. "What would the world look like if I rode on a beam of light?" he asked himself one day. (Schilpp 1949) He knew that light traveled at 186,000 miles per second (in 1675 a Danish astronomer, Oli Roemer, determined the speed of light), and Einstein puzzled about whether anything else could move that fast.

What does it mean to move through space at 186,000 miles per second? It means that the NASA *Apollo* moon rocket would have reached the moon in $1\frac{1}{3}$ seconds rather than the three days it actually took to get there—at a speed of 6.8 miles per second. It means that a jet airliner could leave New York's Kennedy International Airport traveling due east, fly all the way around the world, and return to Kennedy from the west $\frac{1}{7}$ of a second later.

Einstein did not know about airplanes or rocket ships in 1895, but he did know that it takes light from the nearest star, Proxima Centauri, more than four years to travel the 23 trillion miles to Earth. Astronomers long ago (in the 1920s) decided it was too cumbersome to deal with distances in the universe using the mile or the kilometer as the unit of measure. They needed a measure that was more appropriate to the distances involved when dealing with the stars. The "light-year"—the distance that light travels in one year (5.8 trillion miles)—was chosen as the measure. If Proxima Centauri should explode tonight (chapter 7 discusses the explosion of stars), there would be no way we could know about the explosion until four years from tonight.

But Albert Einstein, Technical Expert, Third Class, was not thinking about exploding stars. Rather, he was thinking usefully about how the world would look to a boy riding on a beam of light, traveling at 186,000 miles per second. Through his acquired knowledge of physics and personal experience, he had no problem reasoning how the world would look to someone moving much more slowly than the speed of light. He quickly found several inconsistencies in the then-current theories of physics that blocked his understanding of what it means to travel at the speed of light. He soon understood that the old theories had to be rewritten. Einstein focused his attention on relative motion. He, like other physics students, had learned that no mechanical experiment can establish that some *one* object is absolutely motionless.

Imagine you are the pilot of a spaceship. You are lost. Your radio is dead. Your windows are frosted. The first thing you want to do is stop and somehow get your bearings. You turn off all the rocket's engines. Will you know when you have stopped moving? You had better face reality: There is no way to establish that your spaceship is absolutely motionless—unless you can look out of your window and *relate* to another object (but your windows are frosted)!

Here on Earth we usually measure motion relative to the ground upon which we are traveling. When traveling in an enclosed compartment, such as an airplane or train, passengers relate the motion of their bodies to the compartment. When flying in an airplane, we "sit still" or "walk to the rear," relating our motion to the cabin of the airplane. There is no need to know whether the plane's speed is 300 miles per hour or 600 miles per hour (so long as it is constant; i.e., the plane is neither accelerating nor decelerating) before pouring a drink or buttering a roll. If permitted, children could play catch in the aisles using the same motions and reactions learned from playing catch on the ground. The plane's velocity, while constant, is unnoticed and not measurable by anyone who does not look out of a window.

Perceptions of airplane motion caused by "air pockets," takeoffs, landings, and any increases or decreases in speed are certainly evident inside the cabin, but these reflect *changes* in motion. A change in motion is easily detected. Uniform motion in a closed system is undetectable.

The undetectability of uniform motion was not known to the ancient Greeks. In 300 B.C., Aristotle felt confident that Earth was immobile because he could not detect any motion. Can you, the reader, detect the motion of Earth as a body (excepting earthquakes)? You have often been told that Earth orbits the Sun, but have you ever felt this movement?

Galileo, in 1632, was well aware of the undetectability of uniform motion. In his book *Dialogue Concerning Two New Sciences*, he tells of many delightful mechanical experiments that anyone can perform:

> Shut yourself up with some friend in the main cabin below decks on some large ship, and have with you there some flies, butterflies, and other small flying animals. Have a large bowl of water with some fish in it; hang up a bottle that empties drop by drop into a wide vessel beneath it. With the ship standing still, observe carefully how the little animals fly with equal speed to all sides of the cabin. The fish swim indifferently in all directions; the drops fall into the vessel beneath; and, in throwing something to your friend, you need not throw it more strongly in one direction than another, the distances

being equal; jumping with your feet to-gether, you pass equal spaces in every direc-tion. When you have observed all these things carefully (though there is no doubt that when the ship is standing still every-thing must happen in this way), have the ship proceed with any speed you like, so long as the motion is uniform and not fluctuating this way and that. You will discover not the least change in the effects named, nor could you tell from any of them whether the ship was moving or standing still.

Each one of Galileo's mechanical experiments on the boat proved that uniform, absolute motion is undetectable.

The Galilean principle of relativity,

The results of any *mechanical* experiment are independent of the state of uniform motion of the laboratory. (Misner 1977)

was a familiar (though unnamed) part of physics in the year 1905, when Albert Einstein was work-ing out his theory of relativity. So, what was Einstein's contribution? Einstein convinced him-self that a more powerful "principle of relativity" must be at work in the universe. In a persistent line of thought that followed his question about riding a beam of light, Einstein decided:

The results of *any* experiment whatever must be independent of the state of uniform motion of the laboratory. (Misner 1977)

Notice how Einstein's principle differs from the Galilean principle of relativity. Einstein's prin-ciple boldly includes *any* experiment (electrical as well as mechanical). The Galilean principle applied only to ordinary objects, but Einstein rec-ognized that light (electromagnetic waves) must be included.

With a dogged logic that could not be thrown off the track by unexpected conclusions, Einstein saw one crucial test for his expanded principle of relativity. The test would be to measure the veloc-ity of light inside uniformly moving objects. Then, unlike all other measured velocities, the

velocity of light would be absolute. Scientists were much dismayed as the results of one experi-ment after the other reached the same conclusion:

The velocity of light in no way depended on the velocity of the emitter of the light. (Einstein 1950)

They desperately tried to find devious explana-tions for their surprising results—surprising, be-cause the scientists knew that if the velocity of light were truly independent of source or ob-server, they could never measure light traveling at greater than 186,000 miles per second. How could that be? What if we were moving in the opposite direction to the light at 93,000 miles per second; would not the light go past us at $1\frac{1}{2}$ times 186,000 miles per second? We know that kind of calculation would be true for wind, or *anything at all going past us in the opposite direction.* Ein-stein listened to the scientists and replied that we should not seek explanations but rather accept—as a law of nature—the concept "the velocity of light is absolute." This is just the way the universe is. Thus one need not say "relative to the velocity of the emitter of the light or to the velocity of the observer," because in any laboratory, whatever its uniform velocity, light will be found to move at 186,000 miles per second.

Einstein had answered his question about riding a beam of light. The answer was simple: He could not ride a beam of light because he could never catch up to one. No matter now fast he pursued it, the light would be moving away from him at 186,000 miles per second. Does that sound like nonsense? Such apparent nonsense must be accepted if it leads to conclusions that can be verified by laboratory experiments! Einstein's search for conclusions led to many that were in-deed startling and unexpected, but not one has conflicted with actual experimental results. Today all scientists believe the predictions of Einstein's Special Theory of Relativity because, during the past 90 years, so many of them have been experi-mentally validated (see appendix D).

In 1905, however, hardly any experiments were available. It took the inspired insight of Einstein's great imaginative mind to give him the confidence that he was on the right track. In fact, Einstein describes only one simple experiment that he considered a key to Special Relativity:

———

Connect a *stationary* loop of wire to an electric meter (to record any electric current in the loop). Move a bar magnet through the loop:

> **Result:** The meter records a flow of current the moment the magnet enters the loop.

> **Explanation:** The electric current appeared in the coil because a moving magnet generates an electric field in the neighborhood of the magnet.

Move the same loop (connected to an electric meter) toward a *stationary* magnet:

> **Result:** Exactly the same as above.

> **Explanation:** There was no electric field in the neighborhood of the stationary magnet, but the electrons in the coil of wire start to move the instant the coil moves through the stationary magnetic field.

———

Einstein wondered, why should we need two different explanations for what is, after all, the very same experiment? He realized that the two explanations make an unwarranted distinction between rest (the stationary loop of wire) and uniform motion (the moving bar magnet)—implying that uniform motion is detectable. The Galilean principle of relativity states that you cannot make an experimental distinction between rest and the uniform motion of *mechanical* objects (recall Galileo's elegant boat experiment). Electricity is not a mechanical object, so Einstein (with experimental validation) expanded the Galilean principle of relativity to include electricity and magnetism, thereby requiring only one explanation for the loop of wire/magnet experiment.

In 1905, the year Albert Einstein completed his Ph.D. thesis on a new way to count molecules, he used his expanded principle of relativity, along with his new law of nature concerning the velocity of light, as the foundation to derive his Special Theory of Relativity. The derivation of the theory required only two postulates:

1. The results of any experiment (mechanical or electromagnetic) are independent of the state of uniform motion of the laboratory—meaning there is no distinction between rest and uniform motion; in other words, absolute rest does not exist in the universe.

2. It is a law of nature that the velocity of light is absolute—meaning the velocity of light in empty space is always 186,000 miles per second, regardless of its direction or the observer's state of motion relative to the light.

A rather startling conclusion was immediately drawn by Einstein from the two postulates: The age-old notion that time is absolute had to be discarded! The Special Theory of Relativity implies that the two ideas "light is absolute" and "time is absolute" cannot coexist in our universe. Before Special Relativity, everyone assumed that the concepts "a moment in time," "earlier," "later," and "simultaneous" must be the same for all people everywhere. After Relativity, that assumption was no longer tenable.

The idea that time "flows" independently of all observers had to be abandoned. According to relativity, time, which is, after all, just the measure of the duration between events, is inexorably linked to space. Events separated in space may be simultaneous to one observer in that space, but these same events will appear sequential to a second observer who is in motion relative to the first observer.

Imagine an Einstein-style thought experiment:

A train is moving past a station platform, but not stopping. A person standing in the middle of one car pushes a button that sets off two flash bulbs—one at the front and one at the back of the car—at the moment the car passes the platform. The person who pushed the button, of course, sees both flashes simultaneously. However, there is another person standing on the station platform. What does he see? He sees the flash at the back of the car first, then the flash at the front. Why do they see the very same events differently? They see them differently because the flash at the back of the moving car reaches the person on the platform ahead of the flash at the front of the moving car. The flash at the back of the car is moving toward the platform, the flash at the front of the car is moving away from the platform.

If the man on the platform had really been far away from the passing train, the time interval between flashes could have been very long indeed.

Roger Penrose, professor of mathematics at the University of Oxford, in his book *The Emperor's New Mind,* provides another example:

Imagine two people (anywhere on Earth) slowly walking past each other in the street. Events on a planet in Andromeda galaxy situated 2 million light years from Earth, judged by our two walkers to be exactly simultaneous with the moment they walk past each other, could amount to a difference of several Earth-days! For example, as far as *one* of the walkers could know, a space fleet launched from a planet in Andromeda with the avowed intent of wiping out life on Earth is already on its way; the *other* walker's information received from the same source in Andromeda says that the very decision to launch the fleet will not be made for several days.

Penrose's curious scenario is possible because Einstein teaches that each person carries his own simultaneous space as he moves about. Simultaneous space is defined as a sort of "slice of space" in any one past instant of that person's life. The news about all events that occur in this "slice of space," traveling at the speed of light, will reach

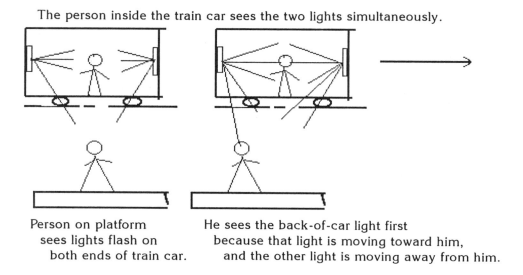

The person inside the train car sees the two lights simultaneously.

Person on platform
sees lights flash on
both ends of train car.

He sees the back-of-car light first
because that light is moving toward him,
and the other light is moving away from him.

Fig. 3.1. A thought experiment involving two views of the same event when one viewer is in motion relative to the other viewer.

him simultaneously. The news must reach him through light signals, radio signals, or any other form of photon traveling at 186,000 miles per second—the universal speed limit. In Penrose's scenario, the messages arriving from Andromeda will take a long time indeed to reach Earth—traveling at 186,000 miles per second, they will take about 2 million years. The farther away the source of the message, the greater the discrepancy in time between messages received by any two people moving past each other. The lesson we learn from Penrose's example is that easily measurable differences in time sequences will occur for events happening at a great (astronomical) distance from two observers who are moving at even slightly unequal velocities (their actual velocities do not matter). It is important that they are moving relative to each other; thus, their velocities will be unequal.

However, we are not yet finished with Relativity surprises. Our common sense notion of time was further jolted when Einstein announced that the rate at which a perfectly normal clock will tick off seconds is dependent on the state of motion of the clock! Time can be "stretched out" by going on a journey. To quote Einstein:

> If one of two synchronous clocks at "A" is moved in a closed curve with constant velocity until it returns to "A," the journey lasting "t" seconds, then by the clock that has remained at rest, the traveled clock on its arrival at "A" will be ½ times "t" times its velocity squared divided by the velocity of light squared second slow. (Lorentz 1952)

Suppose these two clocks are next to each other on a circular track. They are reading exactly the same time, synchronized to the split second. One clock remains at rest along the track. The other clock goes for a trip around the track at a uniform speed and returns to its starting point. If the two clocks are compared, the traveled clock will be slow exactly the amount predicted by Einstein! If

time were truly absolute, this result would be sheer nonsense. Yet repeated experiments show that, indeed, Einstein was correct. For example, atomic particles (called muons) moving at 99.7 percent of the speed of light live 12 times longer than slow-moving particles. One must conclude that motion through space has an effect on time that defies common sense (recall that Aristotle was fooled by the common sense notion that heavy objects must fall faster than light objects). The construction of the universe is evidently much more subtle than common sense can discern. You may protest that you have never observed clocks to behave in the strange way that Einstein describes, but this is true only because you have never seen a clock that has moved at very high speeds (several thousand miles per second). The Einstein "stretch-out" of time is only noticeable at speeds approaching the speed of light.

Notice that Einstein does not specify the type of clock moving on the closed curve. It can be a spring clock, a quartz crystal clock, an atomic clock, a radioactive clock, or *the heartbeat of a human being*—all will go out of synchronization with an "at rest" or "stay-at-home" clock after a trip at a very high uniform speed. Observe how precisely Einstein stated it—he tells you *exactly* how much slower the traveling clock will be when it returns to its starting point. All experimental results are in precise agreement with Einstein's equations. Here is the beauty of Einstein's theories! Here is the difference between Einstein and so many science fiction writers. Anyone could have written about distortions in time, but only Einstein gives you the exact mathematical relationships involved in the distortions. All of Einstein's conclusions are verifiable by experiment—which means, the equations truly describe the workings of the universe!

Imagine you have a twin brother (or sister) and you would like to prove to your twin that any traveling clock, even a human "clock," runs slower than a stay-at-home clock:

Buy yourself passage on a rocket ship headed for a star about 7 light-years distant. Tell the astronauts piloting the ship that they must maintain a speed equal to 96 percent of 186,000 miles per second, round-trip, because you can only afford to be away from home for 14 years. To assure your stay-at-home twin that you will be gone for only 14 years, take along a 14-year supply of food and water, and a very accurate clock to keep track of time.

When you land on Earth after 14 years of travel, be prepared for a shock when you meet your twin at the spaceport. You will find that Earth has gone around the Sun 50 times since you left home! Your twin will be 50 years older than he or she was the day you left on your trip. You will be 14 years older than you were on the day you left on your trip. Fifty minus 14 equals 36; thus, you will be 36 years *younger* than your twin! How is this possible?

It is possible because, while moving at 96 percent of the speed of light, the traveling twin's heartbeat, metabolism, and thought processes were slowed down compared to that of the stay-at-home twin. If there had been a pregnant woman aboard the same rocket ship (traveling 14 years at 96 percent of the speed of light), her 9-month term would have lasted 9 x 3.57, or 32 months (as measured by Earth time). Multiply 9 months by 3.57 because 3.57 is the Einstein "stretch-out" time factor for any clock moving at 96 percent of the speed of light. Her term as measured by clocks aboard the rocket ship would have been 9 months, and she would have in no way realized that 32 months had passed on Earth during her pregnancy!

Did the traveling twin find the long-sought fountain of youth? He did arrive home to find he was 36 years younger than his twin. The "price" he paid for those 36 years was a 14-year trip in a rocket ship. It was a 14-year stretch-out of time into 50 Earth years. But he was not at all aware of the stretch-out during the trip. His body aged the normal 14 years that it would have aged in 14 years if he had never gone on the trip. So what did he gain? What did Rip Van Winkle gain? In effect, the traveling twin "slept" for the 36 years gained on his stay-at-home twin! Actually, he lived in slow motion during his 14-year trip in the rocket ship. If this is the kind of fountain of youth you want, you can have it as soon as rocket ships can be built to travel at speeds approaching the speed of light.

The twin paradox shows that time is not absolute, that clocks moving at speeds approaching the speed of light do tick off time much more slowly than clocks at rest. If a clock could move at the speed of light, it would not note the passage of time at all because time stands still at the speed of light! This is the way the universe works.

Imagine the reaction to Einstein's Special Theory of Relativity as word spread throughout the scientific community about this bold attempt to confront established, age-old ideas, not to mention common sense. In 1911, W. F. Magie, a professor of physics at Princeton University, called Special Relativity "a great and serious retrograde step in the development of . . . physics." (Williams 1968) In 1912, the American physicist L. T. More became so emotional in denouncing Special Relativity that he attacked the entire German nation: "Undoubtedly the German mind is prone to carry a theory to its logical conclusion, even if it leads to unfathomable depths—Anglo-Saxons are apt to demand a practical result, even at the expense of logic . . ."

In spite of Magie and More, the speed of light (186,000 miles per second) is a kind of barrier velocity or speed limit that cannot be equaled or exceeded by any moving object in the universe. Repeated attempts in laboratories all over the world to accelerate objects to the speed of light have always met with failure. Not even very tiny objects such as atoms or parts of atoms (protons, electrons) can catch up to a ray of light—no matter how much energy is supplied to them. In our universe, two clocks will go out of synchronization if one is moving relative to the other, *and* time would stand still for you just as it does for a photon, if you could travel at 186,000 miles per second.

You cannot blame Einstein for the clock paradox any more than you can blame him for a snowflake melting in your hand! If your hand is at a temperature greater than 0°C (32°F), the snowflake *must* melt just as surely as a fast-traveling clock *must* keep slow time. Einstein's theory led inexorably to further conclusions: If an object with mass were accelerated to the speed of light, not only would its "time-keeping" become infinitely slow, but its mass would become infinitely great, and its length would shrink to zero!

What kinds of objects *can* travel at the speed of light in empty space? Only objects with *zero mass* and *zero length* when they are stationary: the photon, the neutrino, and the graviton. I call these the three "Messengers of the Universe," because they bring us news of distant events occurring in other galaxies. We say the photon, neutrino, and graviton have zero rest mass, meaning that *if* one stopped moving, it would have zero mass. However, photons, neutrinos, and gravitons cannot survive a halt in motion. You can easily stop a photon—your body stops billions of them every second—but these photons are instantly transformed into other forms of energy. Hold your hand near a lightbulb—the heat you feel is the instant energy generated by photons stopped by your hand. Look up at the stars tonight and your eyes will stop photons that have been traveling in empty space for many years. These "star-born" photons will "die" on your retina and their energy will instantly cause a chemical reaction to occur in your eye, which will enable you to see the star.

In summary, Einstein's Special Theory of Relativity states:

- The speed of light is absolute; time is not.

- The flow of time is dependent upon the state of motion of the clock. A traveling twin will come home to find himself younger than his birth twin.

- The speed of light in empty space cannot be reached or exceeded by any massive object in the universe.

Are these statements nonsense? Each one is a conclusion that flowed from Special Relativity.

Anyone can challenge Special Relativity. Over 90 years have elapsed since Einstein published his theory. No one has found an experimental result that vitiates the validity of the postulates or contradicts any of the conclusions drawn from them—conclusions that depend only on rigorous mathematical reasoning. (See appendix D for a scientific consensus on Special Relativity.)

Einstein's greatest achievement was yet to come. Its seed was planted in the Relativity Principle. Recall the restriction, ". . . the state of *uniform* motion of the laboratory." Einstein was convinced that there must be a way to formulate physical laws that would be valid for observers in non-uniform (accelerated) motion. This was the spur that drove Einstein to formulate a new theory of gravitation (General Relativity) in which there appear many startling predictions—including the existence of an invisible boundary to an unearthly object where time appears to stand still (chapter 8).

In the next chapter, Einstein discovers the Principle of Equivalence and announces his New Law of Gravity.

Chapter 3, Lesson Plan # 1

Principles of Relativity

TEACHING MODEL
Inductive Thinking (Classification)

OBJECTIVES

1. The students will sort, classify, and label a given set of exemplars.

2. The students will analyze the continued validity of categories after the introduction of more exemplars.

3. The students will give examples to prove that all of the following are relative: viewpoint, size, sound level, distance, and motion.

4. The students will name a series of extremely large numbers.

5. The students will define light and identify the speed of light and the distance light travels in one year.

6. The students will discuss and demonstrate an understanding of Galileo's principle of relativity and his experiment on the relativity of motion.

VOCABULARY/BACKGROUND MATERIAL

1. *Numbers*—Scientists, especially astronomers and physicists, often work with extremely large numbers:

hundred	2 zeros	quintillion	18 zeros
thousand	3 zeros	sextillion	21 zeros
million	6 zeros	septillion	24 zeros
billion	9 zeros	octillion	27 zeros
trillion	12 zeros	nonillion	30 zeros
quadrillion	15 zeros	decillion	33 zeros

2. *Relative*—Something is relative to something else if the two objects are connected in some way (not always a physical connection). We use the term *relative* when comparing something to something else.

3. *Mechanical experiment*—A mechanical experiment is an experiment that can be set up using objects with moving parts.

4. *Accuracy*—A measurement is said to be accurate if it is very close to the true value of the item. For example: If you want to determine the length of a given piece of wood, you can use a common yardstick, which would give you the answer to about $\frac{1}{8}$ of an inch. Or, you could use a precision ruler, which would give you the answer to $\frac{1}{32}$ of an inch. An accurate measurement involves using both the proper instrument and doing careful work while making the measurement. Accuracy applies to all measurements (length, weight, volume, etc.).

5. *Uniform motion*—An object is in uniform motion when it is moving at a constant (unchanging) speed. A car driven at a constant 50 miles per hour along a freeway is in uniform motion. An object drifting through empty space is in uniform motion because there is no friction to slow it down and no fuel to speed it up.

MATERIALS

Part 1—Numbers and Light

* Copy of "Student Handout—The Nature of Light" for each student.

* Piece of string or twine for demonstration about light.

* Prism

Part 2—Relativity

* An index card (3" x 5") for each group of students.

* A box or bag for each group of students, containing a set of objects to be sorted. Following is a list of items that work well; they are common to many classrooms. The items should lend themselves to relative grouping. See note at step 1 of part 2 of Procedure section (see p. 54).

    plastic tangram triangles (all same color, different sizes)

    Cuisenaire rods (all different sizes and colors)

balls of different sizes (try to avoid balls too easily identified with specific sports)

skulls of various sizes (skeleton pieces can be obtained from
biological supply companies)

model cars of various sizes (same type would be best, e.g.,
all cars, or all trucks, or all vans)

balance weights (gram stackers) of various sizes

Note: For use in part 2, step 4, of the lesson, withhold one exemplar that is
clearly "out of scale"—comparatively too large or too small (e.g., a triangle
that is so big it makes all of the other triangles look small, or a ball so tiny
it makes even the smallest ball in the box look big)—from each set of items.

PROCEDURE

Part 1—Numbers and Light

1. Introduce the names of large numbers (see vocabulary).

2. Pass out "Student Handout—The Nature of Light." Read the
   passage together and demonstrate and discuss the following
   concepts as they arise.

   * A light-year is a unit of measure marking how far light
     travels in one Earth year.

   * A prism splits apart a beam of light into "pieces" of varying
     length (similar to splitting a piece of twine into individual
     strands).

   * Light traveling through a prism generates a rainbow of
     colors as the different wavelengths of light separate from
     each other.

   * All visible light is a small part of the electromagnetic
     spectrum (refer to table 2.2, p. 38).

   * All light is composed of millions of tiny particles called
     photons.

   * Photons die when they hit things, and photons release
     energy (in the form of heat) when they die.

   * Reflected light is actually new photons generated by the
     energy released by the original photons as they smash into
     the surface of the mirror.

   * Photons are emitted ("sweated out") by excited (hot)
     electrons.

Key Questions About Numbers and Light

1. *What is light?*

2. *What is a light-year?*

3. *How far does light travel in one year?*

4. *How fast does light travel?*

5. *What is the name of the tiny packages of energy that make up all light?*

6. *If photons always die when they hit a surface, how can an object like a mirror reflect light?*

7. *Where do photons come from?*

8. *Why is looking up at the stars in the night sky like looking into a history book?*

9. *What name do we give a number with 12 zeros after it?*

Part 2—Relativity

1. Divide the class into small lab groups of three to six students per group. Give each group a box of exemplars to sort and classify.*

2. Have each group sort the contents of their box into logical categories; write down the rules for membership in each category on an index card, and name or label each category.

3. Have each group share their objects, categories, and rules with the entire class.

4. Introduce the additional "out-of-scale" exemplar (previously withheld from the box) to each box of exemplars. (See note, p. 53.)

5. Lead a class discussion of the term *relative* (see vocabulary). Discuss the idea of relativity of viewpoint (front, back, right, left); size (big, little); distance (near, far); speed (fast, slow); sound volume (loud, soft); and measurement (long, short). Be sure to distinguish between relative and *accuracy* (see vocabulary). Relative does not mean a lack of accuracy.

---

*Note: In the Materials section we have listed items common to many classrooms: tangram triangles, Cuisenaire rods, balls, gram stackers, and skulls. *Any* set of objects may be used for this activity. Even pictures of objects may be used.

Items should be easily classified by either size, weight, or speed. Be careful to avoid distracting features such as mixed colors or mammals versus reptiles. If students do classify the objects or pictures according to categories inappropriate to the lesson (non-relative groupings), simply ask them to find another way to classify the objects before proceeding with the lesson. This trial-and-error process is part of the Inductive Thinking model of instruction.

Key Questions About Relativity

1. *What do we mean when we say that sound volume is relative?*

2. *Give an example of something other than sound that can be measured relatively.*

3. *Explain how motion is relative.*

4. *How does the term* relative *differ from the term* accurate?

Part 3—Uniform Motion and Galileo

1. Review the vocabulary words *mechanical experiment* and *uniform motion.*

2. Introduce and discuss Galileo's experiment on the relativity of motion (see narrative on p. 44) and Galileo's Principle of Relativity (see narrative on p. 45).

Key Questions About Uniform Motion and Galileo

1. *What is uniform motion?*

2. *Describe Galileo's experiment on motion.*

3. *Restate Galileo's Principle of Relativity.*

Chapter 3, Lesson Plan # 1

Student Handout— The Nature of Light

The speed of light in empty space is 186,000 miles per second. This means that if you were able to travel on a beam of light, you would reach the Moon in $1\frac{1}{3}$ seconds rather than the three days it takes us by rocket ship. It means that a jet going at the speed of light would travel once around the world in $\frac{1}{7}$ of a second. However, as we shall see later, nothing can travel at the speed of light except light itself.

A light-year is the distance that light travels in one year. If you think about how fast light travels, you will guess that light travels a very great distance in one year. (Light is not like a car. It does not go slow at first and faster later on. Light travels at exactly the same speed all of its life.) A light-year is 5,800,000,000,000 miles, or five trillion eight hundred billion miles. The star closest to our Sun, Alpha Centauri A, is 4 light-years away. In other words, the light we see from stars in the night sky is history. The light has been traveling a long time, and it has come a very long way. Looking up into the star-filled night sky is like reading a history book. We see the star Alpha Centauri A tonight as it was four years ago.

What exactly is light? Visible light is actually a small part of the electromagnetic spectrum. A light beam is like a piece of twine. It looks solid, but it is really a bundle of different strands. When a beam of light goes through a prism, the prism breaks the light into its individual threads. The difference between a beam of light and a piece of string is that when the beam of light splits up, it breaks into pieces of all different lengths. Each length of light is seen by the eye as a different color.

When a beam of light goes through a prism, the prism splits the beam of light into various lengths called wavelengths. What, then, makes up a wavelength? A wavelength of light is actually a bundle of tiny particles called photons. Where do these photons come from? Most photons in our universe are emitted by excited electrons. An electron is a small particle that orbits the nucleus of an atom. (We will learn more about electrons in chapter 6.) The most common way to excite an electron is to heat it up. When electrons get very hot they jump around. While they are jumping around they continuously "sweat" photons. Unbelievably, electrons have an unlimited supply of photons that they can "sweat" when they are hot. When hot, you also sweat; except your sweat is just water, and you do not have an unlimited supply. You also do not light up when you sweat, but an electron does.

A photon is a tiny package of energy that has zero mass. It must always be moving. It can never stop and rest. It does not even slow down as it comes to a stop. If it stops, it immediately releases its energy in the form of heat. For example, when you hold your hand in the sunlight, you stop millions of photons with your hand. What you feel is the heat released by the dying photons as they hit your hand.

If photons always die when they hit a surface, how can an object like a mirror reflect light?

Let us follow the photons in their journey from the lightbulb. The photons are "sweated out" by excited electrons in a lightbulb. They then proceed toward the mirror. When they reach the mirror they pass right through the transparent glass surface of the mirror and smash into the silver coating at the back of the mirror. The photons die as they stop moving. As the photons die, they release energy into the electrons in the silver coating at the back of the mirror. The silver electrons get hot and excited after being smashed by the dying photons, and they "sweat out" new photons. These new photons travel on the reflected path, and they are seen by us as reflected light.

Chapter 3, Lesson Plan # 2

Einstein's Special Relativity

TEACHING MODEL
Advanced Organizer

OBJECTIVES
1. The students will list, define, and give examples of the three types of scientific experiments: physical, thought, and mathematical.

2. The students will use a graphic organizer (an outline) to organize data from experiments relating to Albert Einstein's Special Relativity.

3. The students will formulate conclusions based on experimental data.

4. The students will distinguish when changes in wording significantly affect the meaning of a statement.

VOCABULARY
1. *Equation*—The left side of the equality symbol must equal the right side. (Examples: $2 + 2 = 4$, $6 + 4 = 8 + 2$)

2. *Physical experiment*—An experiment that can be set up and performed (a "traditional" experiment).

3. *Thought experiment*—An experiment that can only be done in the mind (or perhaps by drawing pictures and diagrams, but the experiment is impractical or impossible in a laboratory).

4. *Mathematical experiment*—An experiment in which numerical data or information is arranged into mathematical relationships to find numerical patterns.

5. *Uniform motion*—Motion that is constant (unchanging), such as a car moving down the road at a steady 55 miles an hour.

6. *Light-year*—The distance that light travels in empty space in one year (5.8 trillion miles).

7. *Simultaneity*—When two events occur in the same instant of time.

From *Gravity, the Glue of the Universe.* ©1997 Harry Gilbert and Diana Gilbert Smith. Teacher Ideas Press. (800) 237-6124.

8. *Photon*—The elementary particle that makes up all electromagnetic fields (light, radio waves, etc.).

9. *Infinite*—Immeasurable and without end.

MATERIALS

* Copy of "Teacher Sample—Graphic Organizer," for teacher reference

* Copy of "Student Handout—Graphic Organizer" (blank) for each student

* Copy of "Student Handout—Simultaneity Experiment Involving Light on a Train" for each student

* Copy of the diagram describing the Simultaneity Train Experiment on a chart, overhead transparency, or chalkboard

PROCEDURE

Review of Prior Learning

Set the stage for the day by reviewing the definition of *uniform motion* and *light-year*. It may be confusing to the students that *light-year* is a term that measures a distance in terms of time. Point out that we do sometimes measure distance with time when we say, for example, "New York is one hour's train ride from my house." Review the definitions of: *equation*, *simultaneity*, *photon*, and *infinite*.

Setting the Purpose

1. Write on the chalkboard or overhead projector the following statements:

    Galileo's Principle of Relativity—The results of any mechanical experiment are independent of the state of uniform motion of the laboratory.

    Einstein's Principle of Relativity—The results of any mechanical or any electromagnetic experiment are independent of the state of uniform motion of the laboratory.

2. Guide the students in a comparison of Galileo's Principle of Relativity and Einstein's Principle of Relativity. Look at the wording. How are they alike? How are they different? State that the goal for the day has two parts. First, to understand why and how the addition of these words could make any significant difference in the meaning of such a statement. Then we will look at three *Truths* that Albert Einstein uncovered when he added these three words to Galileo's statement.

From *Gravity, the Glue of the Universe.* ©1997 Harry Gilbert and Diana Gilbert Smith. Teacher Ideas Press. (800) 237-6124.

3. Write on the chalkboard or overhead projector the following statements:

> The results of throwing a surprise party for my sister are independent of whether it rains on that day.

> The results of throwing a surprise swimming party at the lake for my sister are independent of whether it rains on that day.

Ask the students to examine these two sentences. How are these sentences alike? How are they different? Does it change the meaning of the first statement in any significant way to add those four extra words? Can you explain why or how these words make a difference? (The addition of the four extra words changes a true statement into a false statement.)

4. Guide the students to look back at Galileo's and Einstein's statements. Which words have been added by Einstein? ("or any electromagnetic") What would we need to check if we wanted to decide if the addition of these three words constitutes a significant change? (We would need to determine if there is any real difference between Galileo's mechanical experiments and electromagnetic experiments.)

Background (Electricity)

Static electricity was known in ancient times, but our ability to harness electricity and to control its movement through wires was not discovered until the 1800s. Around 1870, James Clerk Maxwell discovered a set of rules of nature that he said govern electromagnetism. These rules make up the foundation of all that we know about electricity today.

There was, however, a small flaw in what Maxwell and all of his contemporaries assumed about light (electromagnetism). Early on, everyone assumed that the speed of light would measure differently depending upon whether you were standing still or moving when you took the measurement. For example, imagine Galileo's boat (see page 44 in the narrative text). We flash a beam of light in through a porthole in the front of the boat and out through a porthole at the rear of the boat. Maxwell assumed that if the boat were standing still, the measurement of the speed of light as it traveled through the boat would be 186,000 miles per second. If the boat were moving forward, the speed of the light would be greater than 186,000 miles per second. He would add the speed of the moving boat to the speed of light. This meant that Galileo's Principle of Relativity did *not* apply to light.

So, according to Maxwell, the three words Einstein added to Galileo's statement *do* make a significant difference. Einstein studied the works of both Galileo and Maxwell. He couldn't accept the idea that light could be the only stuff in the universe that did *not* follow Galileo's Principle of Relativity. He found a way to include light.

Background (Albert Einstein)

In 1905, Albert Einstein published a scientific paper that revolutionized scientific thought. This paper (which has come to be known as the paper on Special Relativity) was based on two ideas. First, Einstein said that Galileo's relativity principle must be expanded to include more than mechanical experiments. Second, Einstein formulated his newly discovered law of nature concerning the velocity of light. The end result of this was the addition of the three words to Galileo's Principle of Relativity ("or any electromagnetic").

Clearly, Albert Einstein understood that adding these three words to Galileo's Principle of Relativity was a significant change. The general public and the portion of the scientific community who were so quick to dismiss Einstein as a "crackpot" must have understood that this was a significant change to Galileo's ideas. We, too, are in agreement that these three words change Galileo's ideas significantly (see p. 45 in the narrative for elaboration).

Exploration of Einstein's Truths

1. Introduce and discuss the vocabulary words: *physical experiment*, *thought experiment*, and *mathematical experiment*.

2. Introduce the truths about the universe that Einstein uncovered. Pass out a copy of "Student Handout—Graphic Organizer" (blank) to each student. Use the chalkboard or an overhead projector to model filling in the graphic organizer. Have the students fill in their graphic organizers as you explain the following concepts and experiments.

Here is the first truth Einstein uncovered as he was thinking about Galileo and Maxwell and their ideas about light and the relativity of motion.

I. There is a Universal Speed Limit That Nothing in Our Universe Can Exceed.

Over the past 90 years, thousands of experiments have been done in laboratories all over the world. Every one of these experiments has proven that Einstein was correct when he announced that the speed of light in a vacuum, 186,000 miles per second, is the universal speed limit. In every accelerator laboratory all over the world, no matter how much energy was supplied to a particle, the operators were not able to get the particle to travel at the speed of light. Remarkably, they are able to attain speeds of 99.99999 percent of the speed of light! The physicists are now convinced that not even all the energy in the universe would get their particles to travel at the speed of light! (See p. 45 in the narrative for elaboration.)

A. Experiment Description: Worldwide Experiments in Acceleration.

1) Type of Experiments: Physical experiments.

2) Notes: Acceleration experiments have been attempted in New York, Japan, Switzerland, Illinois, China, and Russia. Each experiment has proven that Einstein was correct about this truth.

The second truth Einstein uncovered has to do with time and motion of clocks.

II. Time Is Linked to Space (this means that the passage of time varies with the state of motion of the clock).

A. Experiment Description: Simultaneity Experiment Involving Light on a Train.

Suppose you have a person standing in the middle of a boxcar on a train. The boxcar has several special features: The sides are made of glass, there is a camera flash unit located at each end of the boxcar, and the boxcar is traveling past a station at nearly the speed of light. The person standing in the middle of the boxcar is holding a button that can make both cameras flash at the same time.

Imagine that you are standing on the station platform as the speeding glass boxcar rolls past. The person inside the boxcar pushes the flash button at the exact moment that he passes you and your eyes meet. Will you both see the same event in the next instant? What will *you* see?

Here is how Einstein would explain what happens. The person inside the boxcar will see the lights at both ends of the boxcar flash simultaneously. However, you (on the platform) will see the light at the back of the boxcar flash first and the light at the front of the boxcar will flash a fraction of a second later. Why do you think this happens? How can this single event be simultaneous for one person yet not simultaneous for another person? (See p. 47 in the narrative for elaboration.)

Of the three types of experiments, physical, thought, and mathematical, which type of experiment would you say this is?

1) **Type of Experiment: A thought experiment.**

2) **Notes: Simultaneous events are only simultaneous to two observers who are not in motion relative to each other. Either both observers must be motionless or both must be moving at exactly the same speed in the same direction.**

Let's look at the next experiment Einstein conducted to prove this truth.

B. Experiment Description: Experiment with a Clock Moving Around a Circular Track.

Suppose two clocks are next to each other on a circular track. They are reading exactly the same time, synchronized to the split second. One clock remains at rest along the track. The other clock goes for a trip around the track at a uniform speed and returns to its starting point. If the two clocks are compared, the traveled clock will be slow by exactly the amount predicted by Einstein! If time were truly absolute, this result would be sheer nonsense. Yet experiment after experiment has shown that, indeed, Einstein was correct. For example, atomic particles (called muons) moving at 99.7 percent of the speed of light live 12 times longer than slow-moving particles. One must conclude that motion through space has an effect on time that defies common sense (recall that Aristotle was fooled by the common sense notion that heavy objects must fall faster than light objects). The construction of the

From *Gravity, the Glue of the Universe*. ©1997 Harry Gilbert and Diana Gilbert Smith. Teacher Ideas Press. (800) 237-6124.

universe is evidently much more subtle than common sense can discern. You may protest that you have never known clocks to behave in the strange way that Einstein describes, but this is true only because you have never seen a clock that has moved at very high speeds (several thousand miles per second). The Einstein "stretch-out" of time is only noticeable at speeds approaching the speed of light.

Notice that Einstein does not specify the type of clock moving on the closed curve. It can be a spring clock, a quartz crystal clock, an atomic clock, a radioactive clock, or *the heartbeat of a human being*—all will go out of synchronization with an "at rest" or "stay-at-home" clock after a trip at a very high uniform speed. Observe how precisely Einstein stated it—he tells you *exactly* how much slower the traveling clock will be when it returns to its starting point. All experimental results are in precise agreement with Einstein's equations. Here is the elegance of Einstein's theories! Here is the difference between Einstein and science fiction writers. Anyone could have written about distortions in time, but only Einstein gives you the exact mathematical relationships involved in the distortions. All of Einstein's conclusions are verifiable by experiment—which means, the equations describe the workings of the universe.

This experiment is a mathematical experiment. Einstein did the math to show *exactly* how much the traveling clock would be slowed. (See p. 48 in the narrative for elaboration.)

1) **Type of Experiment: A mathematical experiment.**

2) **Notes: Time is constant only if both clocks are moving at the same speed. This difference is detectable only at extremely high speeds.**

Could we do this type of experiment using different types of clocks? What do you think we would find?

The third experiment is a thought experiment that addresses these questions.

C. **Experiment Description: Experiment Involving Identical Twins.**

1) **Type of Experiment: A thought experiment.**

Suppose you have a twin brother (or sister) and you would like to prove to your twin that any traveling clock, even a human "clock," runs more slowly than a stay-at-home clock:

Buy yourself passage on a rocket ship headed for a star that is about 7 light-years distant. Tell the astronauts piloting the ship that they must maintain a speed of 96 percent of 186,000 miles per second, round-trip, because you can only afford to be away from home for 14 years. To assure your stay-at-home twin that you will be gone for only 14 years, take along a 14-year supply of food and water, and a very accurate clock to keep track of time.

When you land on Earth after 14 years of travel, be prepared for a shock when you meet your twin at the spaceport. You will find that Earth has gone around the Sun 50 times since you left home! Your twin will be 50 years older than he or she was the day you left on your trip. You will be 14 years older than you were the day you left on your trip. Thus, you will be 36 years *younger* than your twin!

Consider the following example. Say you and your twin are 10 years old when you leave on your trip. You travel for 14 years. Calculate how old you will be at the end of your trip (10 + 14 = 24 years old). For your stay-at-home twin, 50 years have passed while you were away. Calculate how old your twin will be when you return home (10 + 50 = 60 years old). Now calculate the difference between your age and the age of your *identical* twin (60 – 24 = 36). When you return from your 14-year trip, you will be *36* years younger than your identical twin!

How is this possible? Because, while moving at 96 percent of the speed of light, the traveling twin's heartbeat, metabolism, and thought processes were slowed down compared to the stay-at-home twin.

Did the traveling twin find the long-sought fountain of youth? He did arrive home to find he was 36 years younger than his twin. The "price" he paid for those 36 years was a 14-year trip in a rocket ship. It was a 14-year stretch-out of time into 50 Earth years. But he was not at all aware of the stretch-out during the trip. His body aged the normal 14 years that it would have aged in 14 years if he had never gone on the trip. So what did he gain? In effect, the traveling twin lived in slow motion for 36 years while aging only 14 years. If this is the kind of fountain of youth you want, you can have it as soon as rocket ships can be built to travel at speeds approaching the speed of light.

The twin paradox shows that time is not absolute, that clocks moving at speeds approaching the speed of light do tick off time much more slowly than clocks residing on Earth. If a clock could move at the speed of light, it could not note the passage of any time at all because time stands still at the speed of light!

This means that photons, which are particles of light and which move at the speed of light, never age. Think about your digital alarm clock. Imagine it flashing 12:00 midnight in the middle of the night. These photons leave the clock and travel out into space. Some of them hit your eye and die on contact, but others continue to travel out the window and beyond. For these photons it will always and forever be 12:00 midnight. This is the way the universe works.

2) Notes: The fast-traveling twin was in slow motion for 14 years.

There is one more type of experiment we could do to prove this truth about time, space, and motion.

D. Experiment Description: Experiment Involving the Length of a Woman's Pregnancy.

1) Type of Experiment: A mathematical experiment.

Recall the rocket ship with the traveling twin. If there had been a pregnant woman aboard the same rocket ship (traveling 14 years at 96 percent of the speed of light), her 9-month term would have lasted 9 x 3.57, or 32 months (as measured by Earth time). Multiply 9 months by 3.57 because 3.57 is the Einstein "stretch-out" time factor for any clock moving at 96 percent of the speed of light. Her term as measured by clocks aboard the rocket ship would have been 9 months, and she would have no way to realize that 32 months had passed back home on Earth during her pregnancy!*

2) Notes: Time is not absolute. Time is relative to the movement of the clock.

This brings us to the third and final truth that Einstein uncovered in Special Relativity.

---

*Note: This experiment is being classified as a mathematical experiment because its value as a teaching tool is mathematical. Have the students do the math. A pregnancy on Earth lasts 9 months. The number 3.57 is the time dilation factor obtained from Einstein's Special Relativity equations for a 14-year trip. It is connected to the actual speed of the rocket ship in which she is traveling. The students multiply the normal length of pregnancy by this number (3.57) to get the length of the traveling pregnancy. (9 x 3.57 = 32) This idea can be extended by taking other Earth animals (dogs, elephants, whales, cats, etc.) and having the students calculate the traveling pregnancy lengths.

III. As an Object's Speed Increases, Its Mass Increases.

   **A. Experiment Description: Experiments Involving
   Fast-Moving Electrons.**

   1) Type of Experiments: Physical experiments.

Every day physicists working in laboratories all over the world take note of the fact that as accelerating atomic particles are pushed faster and faster, the experimenter must supply a greater amount of energy to obtain the next small increment in acceleration. (See appendix D.) Before Einstein, nobody anticipated this strange behavior of the accelerating particles. Prior to Special Relativity, there was no explanation. Einstein's theory says you must supply a greater amount of energy to obtain the next increment in acceleration because the mass of the particle is increasing as the speed of the particle is increasing.

We can look at this in a slightly different way. The mass increase with speed idea actually helps the universal speed limit idea make sense. As any object moves faster and faster, it takes more and more energy to make it accelerate. More gasoline is used during acceleration from 60 to 70 mph than going from 50 to 60 mph. If an object is becoming heavier the faster it moves, it follows logically that it will take ever-increasing amounts of energy to keep moving the object faster and faster. If an object keeps getting heavier the faster it travels, then it follows that there must be some speed at which the object would get so heavy that not all the energy in the universe could make it move any faster. It just so happens that in our universe this speed is the speed of light, 186,000 miles per second. As an object approaches this speed, it becomes infinitely heavy, and it can never achieve the speed of light.

What do you suppose makes the photon so special that it can travel 186,000 miles/second? Because the photon has no mass to begin with, it can travel extremely fast without gaining any weight. (See "Student Handout—The Nature of Light.")

   **2) Notes: At extremely high speeds, the faster an object is
   moving, the heavier it becomes. Thus, more energy is
   required to accelerate the object to a greater speed.
   Hence, an object would have infinitely heavy mass as
   it approaches the speed of light.**

Key Questions for Review of Learning

1. *Is there any significant difference between Galileo's mechanical experiments and electromagnetic experiments introduced by Einstein? Why or why not?*

2. *Name the three different types of experiments we examined in this lesson.*

3. *Why do you suppose there is a speed limit in the universe?*

4. *What enables a photon to be able to travel at 186,000 miles/second?*

5. *Explain why the two people in the train experiment see the cameras flash at different times.*

6. *In the experiment with a clock moving around a circular track, does it matter what type of clock is used?*

7. *What did the traveling twin gain?*

8. *What would happen to time if we could travel at the speed of light?*

Follow-Up Assignments

1. Write an essay on this topic: How will the new ideas we have talked about change your life or the lives of all people in the future?

2. Write a short essay (one or two paragraphs) answering this question: If you were Albert Einstein, would you have the courage to stand up for your convictions if you had discovered these startling new facts?

3. Write an imaginary essay (based on scientific facts): What would the world and the things in it look like if you could ride on a beam of light?

Chapter 3, Lesson Plan # 2

Teacher Sample— Graphic Organizer

Special Relativity, by Albert Einstein (1905)

I. There is a Universal Speed Limit That Nothing in Our Universe Can Exceed.
  A. Worldwide Experiments in Acceleration.
    1) Physical experiments.
    2) Notes: Acceleration experiments have been attempted in New York, Japan, Switzerland, Illinois, China, and Russia. Each experiment has proven that Einstein was correct about this truth.

II. Time Is Linked to Space (this means that the passage of time varies with the state of motion of the clock).
  A. Simultaneity Experiment Involving Light on a Train.
    1) A thought experiment.
    2) Notes: Simultaneous events are only simultaneous to two observers who are not in motion relative to each other. Either both observers must be motionless or both must be moving at exactly the same speed in the same direction.
  B. Experiment with a Clock Moving Around a Circular Track.
    1) A mathematical experiment.
    2) Notes: Time is constant only if both clocks are moving at the same speed. This difference is detectable only at extremely high speeds.
  C. Experiment Involving Identical Twins.
    1) A thought experiment.
    2) Notes: The fast-traveling twin was in slow motion for 14 years.
  D. Experiment Involving the Length of a Woman's Pregnancy.
    1) A mathematical experiment.
    2) Notes: Time is not absolute. Time is relative to the movement of the clock.

III. As an Object's Speed Increases, Its Mass Increases.
  A. Experiments Involving Fast-Moving Electrons.
    1) Physical experiments.
    2) Notes: At extremely high speeds, the faster an object is moving, the heavier it becomes. Thus, more energy is required to accelerate the object to a greater speed. Hence, an object would have infinitely heavy mass as it approaches the speed of light.

Chapter 3, Lesson Plan # 2

Student Handout—
Graphic Organizer

I. Truth: _____

  A. Experiment Description: _____

    1) Type of Experiment: _____

    2) Notes: _____

II. Truth: _____

  A. Experiment Description: _____

    1) Type of Experiment: _____

    2) Notes: _____

  B. Experiment Description: _____

    1) Type of Experiment: _____

    2) Notes: _____

  C. Experiment Description: _____

    1) Type of Experiment: _____

    2) Notes: _____

  D. Experiment Description: _____

    1) Type of Experiment: _____

    2) Notes: _____

III. Truth: _____

  A. Experiment Descriptions: _____

    1) Type of Experiments: _____

    2) Notes: _____

Chapter 3, Lesson Plan # 2

Student Handout—
Simultaneity Experiment Involving
Light on a Train

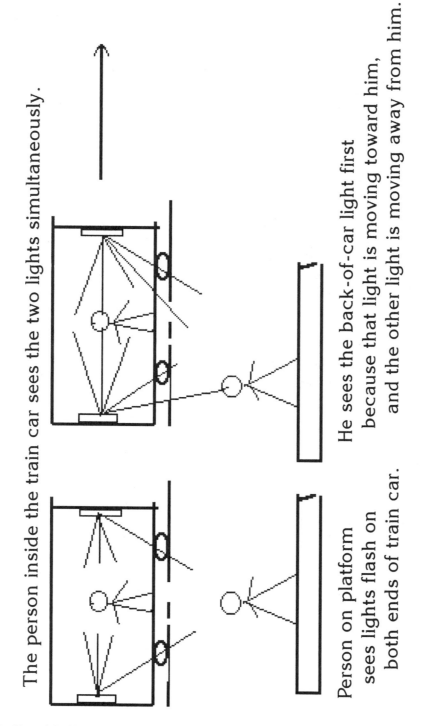

The person inside the train car sees the two lights simultaneously.

He sees the back-of-car light first because that light is moving toward him, and the other light is moving away from him.

Person on platform sees lights flash on both ends of train car.

From *Gravity, the Glue of the Universe.* ©1997 Harry Gilbert and Diana Gilbert Smith. Teacher Ideas Press. (800) 237-6124.

CHAPTER

The
New Gravity

"The identity of [inertial mass and gravitational mass] is fundamental and forms a new and essential clue leading to a more profound understanding. This was, in fact, one of the most important clues from which General Relativity was developed."

—Albert Einstein (1938)

"[T]owards the end of the last century it became evident to several men of science that there must be something "fishy" about a theory which ascribes to the same stuff the complete inability to alter its own state of rest or motion, together with the power to affect, apparently instantaneously, the motion of other matter even millions of miles away."

—W. P. D. Wightman (1953)

Do you have seven coins and some masking tape? If so, we will do a Max Born gravity experiment. U.S. quarters will be just fine.

Stack six coins into a cylinder and wrap them with masking tape. Place the wrapped coins in the palm of your outstretched hand. Place one "bare" coin in the same hand and compare their weights. Do you feel the six coins pressing against your palm about six times as strongly as the one? Slowly lower your hand. The six coins continue to press harder than the one. Put your hand straight out in front of you, then suddenly swing your hand rapidly straight down and pull your hand back, letting the coins fall to the floor. The six coins and the one coin hit the floor at the same time, just as Galileo would have expected.

Yet the six coins *pressed* against your hand much stronger than the one coin. What happened to all that pressing force when you suddenly pulled your hand away from the coins?

Think about instant replay on television. We will stop the action at the instant you pulled your hand rapidly down; the six coins and the one coin become suspended in space, ready to start their journey downward. Your support is now gone and they are on their own. Now we run the camera in slow motion and see the six coins and the one coin advancing toward the floor in unison, at a faster and faster pace, moving like two well-drilled soldiers running exactly together. They accelerated at exactly the same rate (32 feet per second every second). Why did they move at all? According to Newton, because the force of gravity had pulled them downward, toward the center of Earth. If there were no gravity, the coins would

72

have remained suspended in space when your hand was removed. We know there is gravity, and we know the stacked coins weigh six times more, or are six times more *massive* than the one coin—so why did they move in unison? Why did they accelerate toward the floor exactly at the same rate?

If a heavy and a light object have equal acceleration, the heavy object must have been given more energy than the light object. It takes a larger engine and more gasoline to accelerate a 4,000-pound truck from 0 to 60 miles per hour than it takes to give a 1,000-pound sports car the same acceleration. Evidently, gravity is pulling six times harder on the six coins than on the one coin—this is why they fall in unison.

Newton's law tells us that *the force of gravity between two objects is proportional to the product of the masses of the objects.* We know that the mass of Earth is constant. We observed the heavy object accelerate in unison with the lighter object. Therefore, the force of gravity *must* pull harder on the heavy object. This is the conclusion that must be drawn.

Enter another scientific advance made by Newton—the concept of *inertia.* Newton defined inertia as the "inherent tendency of all bodies to resist acceleration." In other words, an object at rest tends to remain at rest, and an object in motion tends to stay in motion in a straight line, unless disturbed by an outside force. All objects do not have the same inertia. A heavy stone has more inertia than a light stone. Pushing a wagon on a level sidewalk is easier when empty than when someone is sitting in it. It occurred to Newton that one could, in fact, measure the mass of any object by measuring its inertia. Newton reasoned this way:

> If the same force acts on two different stationary objects, the resulting velocities will depend upon the inertial mass of each object—the smaller mass will attain the greater velocity or speed. (Born 1965)

In the Max Born experiment, we said that the six coins were six times more massive than the

one coin. How did we determine their mass? We could have used a calibrated spring scale and simply placed the coins on the scale pan. The scale works very well because the objects on the scale pan are being pulled down by the force of gravity. In fact, the mass determined on the scale is called the *gravitational mass* of the object.

We know that spring scales are utterly useless in the absence of gravity. An astronaut in a space ship far from Earth, where gravity is zero, could not measure the gravitational mass of the coins with a spring scale, but he could determine their *inertial mass* by Newton's method. Inertial experiments can, in principle, be run anywhere in the universe (inertial mass is not in any way dependent on gravity). Would an astronaut, using Newton's method of measuring inertia, get the same value for the inertial masses of the coins as would be obtained on Earth using a spring scale? *Yes.* A more practical example of an astronaut encountering inertia occurred recently when the Hubble space telescope was being repaired. The astronauts complained about the considerable physical effort that was required to move the metal boxes into position—even though the boxes, the telescope, and the astronauts were all in a zero-gravity environment.

The inertial mass of any object turns out to be identical to its gravitational mass. From 1687 to 1915, this equality was considered accidental or curiously coincidental. The equality of the mass of an object determined by two different measurements was not anticipated. There was no apparent reason why the gravitational and inertial masses should be equal, as they are determined independently of each other. To Einstein, the equality of the two masses was a key to a deeper understanding of the universe. It was one of the important clues that led him to derive his New Law of Gravity.

There were other troublesome things about Newton's Law of Universal Gravitation. The power of the Sun to control the motion of Earth and all the planets and comets through millions of miles of empty space was curious indeed. How did the force of gravity travel 93 million miles from the Sun to Earth? Newton puzzled over this question but never did find an answer. In 1692, he wrote to a friend:

> That gravity should be innate, inherent, and essential to matter, so that one body may act upon another at a distance through a vacuum without the mediation of anything else . . . to convey the force from one to another, is to me so great an absurdity that I believe no man . . . can ever fall into it. (Wightman 1953)

There was something odd about a theory of gravity that said the Sun could precisely dictate the motion of all distant planets but gave no hint of how the Sun managed to exert its control.

Einstein knew there must be a better, more intuitive way to explain gravity, and he had real motivation to find it. Einstein's Special Theory of Relativity had dealt only with laboratories in uniform motion. It excluded gravity and all accelerations. He wanted desperately to expand Special Relativity to include *all moving systems*, regardless of whether they were accelerating, decelerating, or maintaining a constant velocity. Einstein's Principle of Relativity was limited to systems in *uniform* motion.

For 10 years Einstein struggled toward a new theory of gravity that would start from a general principle and develop as the simplest possible representation of our world and universe. After several false starts (and at least once convincing himself it was a hopeless task), Einstein startled the scientific world in 1915 with his paper on General Relativity. He had indeed found a new way to look at gravity—in fact, a New Law of Gravity. Gone was Newton's mysterious force that traveled through space attracting all bodies exactly in proportion to their inertial masses.

Are all the predictions of Newton's Law of Universal Gravitation gone as well? *No.* Einstein's new law included Newton's Law of Universal Gravitation within its framework as a *limiting case* when the velocities are small and gravity is weak. Einstein went beyond, yet encompassed Newton's law.

There you have the most important clue for distinguishing a true advance in science from a false advance. A new theory must somehow include all that was true in the old; if not, it is more of a useless sidetrack than an advance. The ancient Greeks who had theorized that Earth was a sphere had to explain why it appeared to be flat as far as anyone could see. When Copernicus theorized that the planets revolved around a *stationary* Sun, he had to explain why everyone could *see* the sun daily moving along a very definite path in the sky. One must be suspicious of any new theory that "makes hash" out of old observations! More commonly, a "crackpot" theorist will simply ignore the need to explain all the usual old experiments that simply do not interest him. He will not be concerned with preserving all of the hard-won successes of the past.

Einstein knew the tremendous value of Newton's Law of Universal Gravitation—and he made sure his General Relativity included Newton "in the limit" (when gravitation was weak). As Professor Misner said,

> The rich interconnection of General Relativity with Newton's theory, and with Special Relativity, is in fact, a fundamental basis for the widespread acceptance of it. . . . The unity of science is maintained by a network through which simpler theories maintain their vitality by links to more sophisticated, but more accurate theories. (Yourgrau 1977)

The key to Einstein's "break" with Newton is the necessity that gravity should be described as a *field in space* rather than a strange property of matter. Newton's force of attraction was just by chance exactly proportional to inertial mass. Einstein understood that gravity was somehow a *property of space*. Just as the magnetic and electric fields of Faraday and Maxwell continuously diminish in strength as they move away from the magnet into empty space, gravity too, diminishes in strength with distance from the source.

Is it possible to visualize a gravitational field in the same way a magnetic field can be visualized with iron filings? Yes, and you have probably seen it many times without recognizing it. If you have ever watched a steady downpour of rain on a calm, windless day, you have *seen* the gravitational field of Earth. Just as surely as iron filings outline the magnetic field of a magnet, the falling raindrops outline Earth's gravitational field. Each raindrop falls along a path predetermined by the gravitational field. The field is always present, whether it is raining or not, because it is the result of an interaction between Earth and the space around Earth.

To understand what determines the strength of a gravitational field, Einstein said one must first ask if it is possible that gravity is altogether the result of an *interaction between matter and space*—between Earth and the space immediately surrounding Earth. If so, could this explain how Earth finds its very specific path through space around the Sun? With General Relativity, Einstein shows one can best understand how Earth finds its way around the Sun by studying the interaction between Earth and the *space surrounding* Earth at every instant of its travel. He was not concerned with one object in space "attracting" another object in space. So, what happened to the force of attraction? Let's just say it is no longer needed. Einstein "did away" with attractions when he formulated his Principle of Equivalence.

To understand the "magic" of Einstein's Principle of Equivalence, imagine being a passenger in a rocket ship in outer space. You are moving along at a uniform speed and completely weightless. Every object not tied down in your cabin is floating. This is the normal zero-gravity situation that you are familiar with from watching astronauts on television. Suddenly, your pilot decides to play a trick on you by accelerating the rocket ship at a steady 32 feet per second every second. Everything that was floating around the cabin suddenly moves to the back of the cabin. You, too, find yourself pressed against the aft end of the cabin. You stand up (with the aft end as your "floor"), take a deep breath, and realize that this is just like being back home on Earth—gravity has been restored to your spaceship. If a passenger in the accelerating rocket ship were to take a heavy (lead) object and a light (wooden) object in his hand and perform the Max Born experiment, what would happen? Both objects would fall to the floor in unison, just like on Earth. This was Einstein's famous "thought experiment" (although he

used a box moving in space instead of a spaceship). A steadily accelerating spaceship imitates the force of gravity in every detail. In fact, there is no way to distinguish between gravitational forces and the forces observed inside an accelerating object. This Einstein called the Principle of Equivalence.

There is absolutely no way to tell from *inside* the rocket ship just what is causing you to feel yourself and every object, light or heavy, pulled to the floor. Is your rocket ship on the launch pad on Earth, or is it accelerating in space at 32 feet per second every second? If you had no windows, you could not devise an experiment to tell you what was generating the "normal weight" inside the spaceship.

Einstein had solved the puzzle about objects of different weights falling to the ground in unison: They must fall to the ground in unison because they are following a path predetermined by the space in which they are falling. The space in the vicinity of Earth must be distorted (curved) by the very presence of Earth. Simply stated: *Gravity is curved space.*

Isaac Newton had never imagined that space could play a role in gravitation. Newton adopted a strange force of attraction between massive objects to account for the paths of the planets around the Sun, because it never occurred to him that the space around the Sun could possibly do anything. Albert Einstein looked at the planets and asked, what is there immediately surrounding the planets that makes them move in precisely elliptical paths around the Sun? What he found around the planets was space. If you asked why a river follows a particular twisting and turning path on its way to the ocean, Einstein would answer that the only way the river can get to the ocean is to follow the dictates of its twisting and turning shoreline.

The relativity field equations (the magic that Einstein gave us) describe the intimate relationship between space and massive objects situated in that space. Einstein's equations say that the gigantic Sun curves (distorts) the space in which the Sun is situated, and the curved space "tells" the planets and comets exactly how they must move, just as surely as the Churchill Downs racetrack tells the horses the path they must follow when running the Kentucky Derby.

It is difficult to imagine a curved three-dimensional space, but one can easily visualize a curved two-dimensional space: Take a sheet of paper, which represents two-dimensional space, and crinkle it. The bent piece of paper represents curved space. One can see how massive objects will distort three-dimensional space: Cover the top of a large cooking pot with plastic wrap. Tape the plastic wrap around the sides of the pot so that the surface of the film is taut. Place a small object at the center of the plastic wrap. The heavier the object, the more distortion you will see.

You may have never noticed any effects of the space around *you* being distorted. *True.* Yet also, you have never been aware of Newton's contention that *every* massive object attracts *every* other massive object. We cannot be aware of the distortion in space around us because the amount of distortion around such masses (100–200 pounds) is utterly trivial. A massive object such as Earth (13 septillion pounds [13 followed by 24 zeros]) or the Sun (4 nonillion pounds [4 followed by 30 zeros]) is required to feel the gravitational effects of bent space. Earth, with all of its septillion pounds of matter, is just *barely*

able to hold on to you (how much effort does it take for you to walk or jump?).

Riemann, the mathematician, said our space might be curved, and Einstein said our space *is curved* in the presence of matter. It is not necessary to "imagine" a curved three-dimensional space to examine the consequences that could necessarily follow if one lived in a severely curved space: Distortion of vision is one effect of strong space curvature. An experiment you can do to assure yourself that the space surrounding Earth is only very slightly curved, is to walk in a straight line away from a tall building and periodically check to see if the building is still directly behind you. If the space you are walking in were severely curved, the entire building would gradually seem to move to the right or to the left of your line of vision as you receded from it. You would know you were in severely curved space if after a two-mile walk in a straight line the building had disappeared from your clear view. More importantly, you would never be able to get back to where you started, no matter how hard you tried (just such a situation is discussed in chapter 8).

In the next chapter we will see how some of the predicted consequences of Einstein's equations were experimentally verified.

Chapter 4, Lesson Plan # 1

Einstein's New Law of Gravity

TEACHING MODEL

Role Play (with demonstrations, explanations, and discussions)

OBJECTIVES

1. The students will use knowledge of gravity and the famous scientists Aristotle, Galileo, Newton, and Einstein to enact a play about gravity.

2. The students, playing selected roles, will debate the validity of various scientific points of view about gravity.

3. The students will demonstrate experiments supporting scientists' views of gravity.

4. The students will distinguish between a real advance in scientific thinking and a "crackpot" idea.

5. The students will recite Albert Einstein's New Law of Gravity.

VOCABULARY

1. *Weight*—A measure of how strongly Earth's gravity "pulls" an object.

2. *Mass*—The quantity of matter in an object. A measure of how much matter an object contains.

3. *Inertial mass*—The mass of an object as measured by its resistance to a change in its motion (anywhere in the universe). How hard you have to "push" to move something (an alternative way to distinguish heavy and light—pushing rather than lifting).

4. *Gravitational mass*—The mass of an object as measured on an equal-arm balance or a spring balance (on the surface of Earth). An object's weight on Earth.

From *Gravity, the Glue of the Universe.* ©1997 Harry Gilbert and Diana Gilbert Smith. Teacher Ideas Press. (800) 237-6124.

5. *Newton's Law of Inertia*—An object at rest tends to stay at rest unless it is moved by the addition of energy (a push or a pull), and an object in motion tends to stay in motion at a constant speed unless it is slowed down, sped up, or stopped by an outside force (friction, extra energy, a wall).

MATERIALS

* Copy of "A Play About Gravity" for each student
* Copy of "Student Worksheet—After the Play" for each student
* Flat stone, about the size of the palm of your hand, and a leaf, slightly smaller than the stone
* Skein of yarn
* 25-pound bag of art clay
* Notebook for the character Newton
* Seven quarters
* Masking tape
* Seven identical textbooks
* Twine
* Empty table
* Diagram of matter curving space
* Spring scale
* Optional: costumes for each character and a set for the play

PROCEDURE

1. Go over the first four vocabulary words, and demonstrate the differences and similarities between inertial mass and gravitational mass using a spring scale. You may also wish to briefly discuss why a balance scale is more often used in science than a spring scale (it is more accurate).

2. Introduce Newton's Law of Inertia and explain it briefly.

3. Pass out a copy of "Student Worksheet—After the Play" to each student and review all questions as a class. Tell the students that they will be expected to know the answers to these key questions after the play.

4. Pass out a copy of "A Play About Gravity" to each student. Assign roles. Note that the scientists have longer speaking roles and the assistants have more interesting "doing" roles. Assign two students to each character. You should have the class *read* the play at least twice to give everyone a chance to play a part. Even on a read-through, the students should get up to demonstrate the experiments called for in the script.

5. After the play has been read through, ask the students for questions. You may either discuss questions 6–11 in class immediately following the play, or you may wish to assign them for homework and discuss them the next day. Questions 1–5 should be completed at home when the students have had a chance to carefully study the play and think about their character. These are good actor preparation questions if you plan to enact this play for an audience. You may also use questions 1–5 as an audience viewing guide when you perform the play (have each audience member choose a character to watch carefully during the performance).

Chapter 4, Lesson Plan # 1

Student Worksheet— After the Play

1.   What are your character's beliefs and understandings of gravity as the play opens?

2.   How does your character react to the new information received about gravity during the play?

3.   What examples or experiments does your character use to convince the other characters about the nature of gravity?

4.   What part of the play did you understand the most and why?

5.   What part of the play did you understand the least and why?

6.   What is Newton's Law of Inertia?

7.   What is inertial mass?

8.   What is gravitational mass?

9.   What distinguishes a real advance in science from a "crackpot" idea?

10.   What is Albert Einstein's definition of gravity?

11.   Why do falling objects follow a predetermined path to the ground?

Chapter 4, Lesson Plan # 1

A Play About Gravity

CHARACTERS

(Note: The students who are reading the parts of Teacher and Assistants can fill in their own names if they so desire.)

Sir Isaac Newton	Newton's Assistant	Galileo
Albert Einstein	Einstein's Assistant	Aristotle's Assistant
Max Born	Judge	Galileo's Assistant
Astronaut	Aristotle	Teacher

SETTING

A modern classroom, anywhere in the modern world.

(All characters enter the classroom and take seats as students would. The Teacher takes his/her place at the front of the classroom.)

TEACHER:

Welcome to today's science class. I think we should begin by going around the room and giving introductions. Give us your name, date of birth, where you live, and what you do. I'll start. I am Mrs. Smith, and I was born in 1962. I am a science teacher. I am also the teacher for today's lesson.

NEWTON:

Hello. I am Sir Isaac Newton. I was born on December 25, 1642, in Lincolnshire, England. I am a mathematician and a scientist.

ALBERT EINSTEIN:

Hello. I am Albert Einstein. I was born on March 14, 1879, in Ulm, Germany. I am also a scientist and a mathematician.

MAX BORN:

Hello. I am Max Born. I was born on December 11, 1882, in Breslan, Poland. I am a physicist.

ASTRONAUT:

Hello. I am Sally Jones. I was born in 1951 in California, USA. I am an astronaut.

NEWTON'S ASSISTANT:

Hello. My name is John. I was born in 1660 in England. I am an assistant to Sir Isaac Newton. I help him with his experiments.

EINSTEIN'S ASSISTANT:

Hello. My name is Hansjorg. I was born in 1890 in Germany. I am Dr. Einstein's assistant. I help him with his experiments and calculations.

JUDGE:

Hello. My name is John Upright. I was born in 1940 in New York. I am a judge. I am an expert on making sure rules are being followed.

ARISTOTLE:

Hello. I am Aristotle. I was born in 384 B.C. in Athens, Greece. I am a teacher. I teach my students everything they need to know about the whole universe. They learn about art, literature, plays, how to think, and the laws of nature.

ARISTOTLE'S ASSISTANT:

Hello. My name is Paul. I was born in 360 B.C. in Athens, Greece. I am one of Aristotle's students. I have learned many things from my teacher.

GALILEO'S ASSISTANT:

Hello. My name is Anthony. I was born in 1580 in Rome, Italy. I am Galileo's assistant. I help him with his laboratory experiments. I also bring him food every day, and I help to keep the house clean, as he cannot leave the house. As you may know, Galileo has been placed under house arrest by the authorities in Rome.

GALILEO:

Hello. I am Galileo Galilei. I was born on February 15, 1564, in Pisa, Italy. I am a scientist.

TEACHER:

Welcome again, everyone. Now that we know a bit about everyone, let's get on with today's lesson. The topic of today's lesson is gravity. How many of you know what gravity is? *(Everyone raises a hand.)* Good. Aristotle, will you please tell us what gravity is?

ARISTOTLE:

Certainly. Gravity is Earth reaching up and pulling back to it "Earth things." You see this happen all the time. Just think about how quickly a stone falls back to Earth. The stone is made of Earth, and Earth wants it back. So Earth pulls the stone back quickly. Now think of a leaf. The leaf is from a tree. Earth has no interest in the leaf. The leaf falls slowly and lazily down until it rests on Earth.

JUDGE:

Wait a minute, Aristotle. I don't mean to be disrespectful, but did you ever do an experiment to verify your facts about gravity?

ARISTOTLE:

An experiment? No. Why should I do an experiment? Why should I go to all the trouble of setting up an experiment about something that is as plain as day? Everyone knows a stone falls faster than a leaf. It is plain common sense!

JUDGE:

Well, it does make sense the way you explain it. I just thought maybe . . . I mean I am wondering . . . If we asked a question . . . Do *all* non-Earth things fall more slowly than Earth things? This yarn is non-Earth and this clay is Earth. Will the yarn fall more slowly than the clay?

ARISTOTLE:

Of course it will! I don't need any experiment to know the answer to your question. Earth will pull the clay back to it. Earth will ignore the yarn. It's quite simple.

GALILEO:

Aristotle, I believe that if we try this experiment, you will be quite shocked by the result.

ARISTOTLE:

Preposterous, rubbish!!!

GALILEO:

May I borrow your assistant for a few moments, please?

ARISTOTLE:

Yes. (*Motions with annoyance for his assistant to go to Galileo's side.*)

GALILEO:

(*Addressing both his assistant and Aristotle's assistant.*) Now, one of you take this yarn, and one of you take this 25-pound bag of clay. Hold them above Earth at exactly the same height. Judge, please come over here. I want you to watch this procedure very closely, and to tell everyone what you see. When I give the signal, drop the clay and the yarn. If they are *not* dropped exactly together, it won't count because one object will have a head start. Are you ready? Okay, 1 . . . 2 . . . 3 . . . DROP! (*Clay and yarn hit the ground together.*)

JUDGE:

Hey! They hit the ground at exactly the same time!

ARISTOTLE:

No they didn't! You must have released the yarn ahead of the clay! You clumsy assistant! Give me the yarn. I can do it correctly!

GALILEO:

Okay. Ready? 1 . . . 2 . . . 3 . . . Drop.

JUDGE:
They hit the ground together again!

ARISTOTLE:
I've never seen anything like this! This is astonishing! We really must do this again!

GALILEO:
Okay. Ready? 1 . . . 2 . . . 3 . . . Drop.

JUDGE:
The same result!

TEACHER:
Galileo, will you share with all of us your definition of gravity, please?

GALILEO:
Certainly. *(Galileo motions for the assistants to put away the clay and the yarn.)* Mr. Aristotle, for 2,000 years people believed exactly what you said about gravity. Gravity was Earth pulling back to it things that had been taken away from it. It occurred to me that perhaps there could be a different explanation of gravity. I discovered, and did experiments to prove, that gravity is a force deep inside Earth that pulls all things toward the center of Earth. *All* objects fall toward Earth with the same steadily increasing speed. The farther they fall, the faster they travel. The only reason your leaf appears to fall more slowly than the rock is that the air slows down the leaf. If my assistant would place the leaf on top of the stone, you will see that they hit the ground together. *(Galileo motions for his assistant to do the experiment.)*

JUDGE:
They do hit the ground together!

ARISTOTLE:
Assistant, you try it please. *(Aristotle's assistant tries the experiment.)*

JUDGE:
They still hit the ground together.

ARISTOTLE:
Simply amazing! So you say that the farther an object falls, the faster it will be traveling as it falls?

GALILEO:
Yes, I've done experiments to prove it. After class, if you'd like to come over to my house, I'll show you.

ARISTOTLE:

Yes, I'd like that very much.

TEACHER:

Sir Newton, you look a bit uncomfortable with all of this. Is there something you'd like to say about gravity?

NEWTON:

Yes, thank you. You may already know this, but in 1666 I formulated the Law of Universal Gravitation, which truly settles this matter once and for all. In the Law of Universal Gravitation, I say gravity is *not* an Earth-based phenomenon. Every object with mass has gravity, and the greater the mass of the object, the stronger its gravity. Also then, every object in the universe attracts every other object with this force called gravity. And furthermore, this gravity decreases the farther apart the objects are from each other. Earth's gravity is attracting the Moon, but the Moon is just far enough away and moving in its orbit fast enough not to be pulled straight in. Instead, the Moon continually falls partway and then recovers. This force of gravity actually pulls the Moon around Earth! So you see, everything has gravity, but the more massive objects have more gravity.

GALILEO:

But I know I am correct about the speed of falling objects! Where does that fit into your fancy Law of Universal Gravitation?

JUDGE:

Galileo is correct. If your Law of Universal Gravitation is good science and not just stuff and nonsense, you *must* account for the good ideas that came before you. Galileo acknowledged Aristotle's observations about the leaf and the stone. Galileo discovered that Aristotle had not accounted for the interference of air upon the leaf. How do you, Sir, account for Galileo's ideas in your *new* law of gravity?

NEWTON:

Hold your horses! Give me a chance to answer the question before you get so suspicious! I only practice good science, Sir! First of all, my Law of Universal Gravitation does *not* say Galileo was wrong! I began with the belief that Galileo was correct. Then I looked up at the Moon. Because gravity extends to the bottom of the deepest mines and to the top of the highest mountains, could it be possible that gravity also reaches to the Moon? If gravity reaches the Moon, why doesn't the Moon fall crashing into Earth? My Law of Universal Gravitation (and my mathematical calculations that prove it) agree perfectly with Galileo's acceleration results, but they also go further. I've taken gravity *outside* Earth. My Law says that Galileo can do his same experiments on the Moon or on Mars, and he will get similar (though not exactly the same) results.

JUDGE:

I must say, it certainly sounds like you follow good scientific procedure. You did account for Galileo in your work.

NEWTON:

Thank you, Sir. Now Galileo, come Sir, you challenged Aristotle in your day. Is it not possible for you to admit that I may have stumbled upon an answer to a question that you did not even ask? Without your ideas I could never have asked my question about the Moon, and without your information on the acceleration of falling bodies, I could never have completed the math to prove my Law of Universal Gravitation. I am forever in your debt, Sir, but I hope you can open your mind to these ideas.

GALILEO:

Very well, but I'd like to see your mathematical calculations.

NEWTON:

Here, I have them in my notebook.

TEACHER:

Excuse me, Gentlemen, I really must insist that you continue this inquiry after class. Now, Sir Newton, if you would please, I believe that you made some astonishing discoveries about the nature of objects with mass. Would you share these with us?

NEWTON:

Certainly. You are, I believe, referring to inertia. Inertia is the tendency of any object to resist acceleration (or movement). In other words, an object at rest, like a box, tends to stay at rest unless it is acted upon by an outside force, like a push.

ARISTOTLE:

That sounds quite reasonable.

NEWTON:

Thank you. Now it also follows that an object in motion will tend to stay in motion in a straight line and at a steady speed, unless it is disturbed by some force.

ARISTOTLE:

That, too, seems quite reasonable.

NEWTON:

Thank you again. Now, all objects do not have the same inertia. A heavy stone has more inertia than a light stone. Have you ever pushed a wagon on a level sidewalk? Then you must have noticed that it moves a lot faster and easier when empty than when full.

ARISTOTLE:

I see what you mean. It certainly takes fewer horses to pull a one-man chariot than it takes to pull a King's chariot.

NEWTON:

Yes! My explanation for this difference in inertia is simply that the one-man chariot has *less mass* than the larger, King's chariot. We can actually measure the inertial mass of an object by recording how much force it takes to move it.

GALILEO:

Very well. But tell me, can you measure this inertia only on Earth, or does inertia also extend beyond our planet?

NEWTON:

Oh yes! Inertia works the same everywhere in our entire universe.

ASTRONAUT:

Boy, we sure found that out when we went to repair the Hubble space telescope! You might think it would be a breeze to move all of those large parts around out in space where gravity is very weak. No way! It was extremely hard work. Those are *large massive* parts, and they sure had inertia. It took a lot of force to get them to move!

TEACHER:

Max, you look like you might have something to add to this discussion.

MAX BORN:

Yes, yes. Thank you. I have an experiment we can do that may help tie all of this together. Do you have seven quarters and some masking tape? Please, assistant to Sir Newton, will you step up here a moment? *(Newton's assistant steps forward.)* First stack six of these coins into a neat cylinder; then wrap them with masking tape. *(Assistant does as directed.)* Now place the wrapped coins in the palm of your outstretched hand. Place the one bare coin in the same hand so you can compare their weights. What do you feel?

NEWTON'S ASSISTANT:

I can feel the package of six coins pressing against the palm of my hand much more than the single coin. In fact, I'd have to say it feels like they are pressing *six* times as strongly as the single coin.

MAX BORN:

Good. Now, very slowly lower your hand toward the ground. Do the six coins continue to press harder than the single coin?

NEWTON'S ASSISTANT:

Yes, they do.

MAX BORN:

Judge, please come forward to observe this next step. *(To Newton's assistant.)* Now, put your hand straight out in front of you, then suddenly swing your hand rapidly straight down and back. *(Newton's assistant does as directed and the coins crash to the floor.)* *(To the Judge.)* What happened when the coins hit the floor? Did you hear only *one* crash or two?

JUDGE:

I heard only one crash. The package of six coins and the single coin hit the floor together, just as Galileo said they would.

GALILEO:

What is the point here—I thought my clay and yarn experiment demonstrated this same idea quite nicely.

MAX BORN:

But wait, the package of six coins *pressed* against your hand much more strongly than the single coin, correct?

NEWTON'S ASSISTANT:

Correct.

MAX BORN:

Then what happened to all that pressing force when you suddenly pulled your hand away from the coins? *(A moment of thoughtful silence.)*

TEACHER:

Let's watch what happened on instant replay. We will stop the action at the instant you pulled down your hand rapidly. We see the package of six coins and the single coin suspended in space, ready to start their journey downward. Your support is now gone. The coins are on their own. Now we run the camera in slow motion and see the package of six coins and the single coin advancing toward the floor in unison, at a faster and faster pace. They move like two well-drilled soldiers running exactly together.

GALILEO:

They accelerate at exactly the same rate, which happens to be 32 feet per second every second.

TEACHER:

Yes. Now why are they moving at all?

NEWTON:

The force of gravity is pulling them toward Earth.

ASTRONAUT:

If there were no gravity, the coins would remain suspended in space when your hand was removed.

ARISTOTLE:

We know there is gravity and we know the stacked coins weigh six times more, or are six times more *massive*, than the single coin. So why are they moving in unison? Why are they accelerating toward the floor exactly at the same pace?

NEWTON:

If a heavy and a light object have equal acceleration, the heavy object must have been given more energy than the light object.

ASTRONAUT:

I know it takes a larger engine and more gasoline to accelerate a 4,000-pound car from 0 to 60 miles per hour than it takes to give a 1,000-pound sports car the same acceleration.

MAX BORN:

Evidently, gravity is pulling six times harder on the package of six coins than on the single coin. That is the answer to *why* the two items are moving in unison.

JUDGE:

Newton's Law of Universal Gravitation tells us that the force of gravity between two objects is proportional to the product of the masses of the objects. We know the mass of Earth is constant. We observed the heavy object accelerate in unison with the lighter object. Therefore, we must conclude that this strange force of gravity *must* pull harder on the heavy object! Gravity does not pull equally on all objects!

TEACHER:

Dr. Einstein, you've been quite silent through our discussion. Can you think of anything to add? Do you have any questions about what we have been discussing?

ALBERT EINSTEIN:

Why is it that the inertial mass of an object (which you already said is not dependent on gravity) is identical to the gravitational mass of the same object on Earth?

GALILEO and NEWTON:

(*In unison.*) It is accidental. Just a curious coincidence.

ALBERT EINSTEIN:

How does the force of gravity travel 93 million miles through mostly empty space from the Sun to Earth? Sound does not move through empty space. A horse cannot pull a carriage if there is not a rope or a beam of wood between them.

From *Gravity, the Glue of the Universe.* ©1997 Harry Gilbert and Diana Gilbert Smith. Teacher Ideas Press. (800) 237-6124.

NEWTON:

I don't know how gravity gets from the Sun to Earth. I have thought about this, though, and I have come to the conclusion that we may never find the answer to that question.

JUDGE:

Wait . . . I feel a challenge in the air here. Before we go any further with this discussion, Dr. Einstein, I want you to consider something very carefully. Here is the most important clue for distinguishing a real advance in science from a false advance. A new theory must somehow include all that was true in the old, else it is not an advance, but rather a useless sidetrack. The ancient Greeks who theorized that Earth was a sphere had to explain why it appeared to be flat as far as anyone could see. When Copernicus theorized that the planets revolved around a *stationary* Sun, he had to explain why everyone could *see* the Sun daily *moving* across a very definite path in the sky. You must be very suspicious of any new theory that "makes hash" out of old observations! More commonly, a "crackpot" theorist will simply ignore the need to explain all the usual old experiments that don't interest him. He will not be concerned with preserving all of the hard-won successes of the past.

TEACHER:

All right, Dr. Einstein, keeping the Judge's comments in mind, will you tell us your ideas about gravity?

ALBERT EINSTEIN:

Let's begin by backing up. A few minutes ago we were discussing inertia. Judge, you have announced that the force of gravity *must* be pulling harder on heavier objects than it is on light objects.

JUDGE:

This is certainly true, based on the results of Mr. Born's coin experiment.

ARISTOTLE:

You know, I didn't want to say this, but because you brought this up again, I will. If gravity is pulling harder on some objects than it is on others, doesn't it seem like perhaps I was correct about gravity in the first place?

ALBERT EINSTEIN:

Please, Sir, hold that thought for a moment and follow what I am saying closely. Let's try another experiment. *(Einstein motions for his assistant to join him at the front of the class.)* For this experiment I will need seven textbooks and some twine. *(Assistant gathers supplies and follows the instructions as given.)* Stack six of the books in a pile, and tie them together with string. Now tie a string around the single remaining textbook. Attach a pulling string to both bundles. Place the two bundles on a flat surface; this table will do. Now pull both bundles toward you. Think—do you have to

From *Gravity, the Glue of the Universe.* ©1997 Harry Gilbert and Diana Gilbert Smith. Teacher Ideas Press. (800) 237-6124.

pull harder on one bundle? Don't answer yet! Now let's have all of the assistants come forward to try this experiment before we discuss the results. *(All assistants step forward and pull the bundles. Albert Einstein's assistant fixes the bundles between trials.)* Now, did you have to pull harder on one bundle than the other?

ASSISTANTS:

(In unison.) Yes, we had to pull harder on the stack of six books than on the single book.

ALBERT EINSTEIN:

How much harder did you have to pull?

ASSISTANTS:

(In unison.) Six times harder.

ALBERT EINSTEIN:

Does this experiment remind you of any other experiment you've done lately?

ASSISTANTS:

(In unison.) Yes, it is just like the coin experiment.

ALBERT EINSTEIN:

Ah, but is it? What force was pulling on the coins?

ASSISTANTS:

(In unison.) Gravity.

ALBERT EINSTEIN:

What force is acting on the books on the table? Surely it is not gravity.

ASSISTANTS:

(In unison.) No, it isn't gravity. It is Sir Newton's force of inertia.

ALBERT EINSTEIN:

So what you are telling me, then, is that this inertia required six times more energy to move six books than to move one book. And earlier we determined that gravity pulls six coins six times harder than it pulls one coin.

ASSISTANTS:

(In unison.) Yes, that is correct.

NEWTON:

We have already said that this equivalence is just a curious coincidence. It is neither possible nor necessary to explain this observation.

ALBERT EINSTEIN:

With all due respect, Sir Newton, you are quite wrong. Not only is it possible, it is extremely necessary to explain this equivalence. Please, everyone take a seat and let me explain my Principle of Equivalence. *(Everyone sits down.)* Suppose you are a passenger in a rocket ship in outer space. You are moving along at a uniform speed and completely weightless. Every object not tied down in your cabin is just floating in air.

ASTRONAUT:

This is exactly what it is like when you are drifting through space in a spaceship.

ALBERT EINSTEIN:

Suddenly your pilot decides to play a trick on you by *accelerating* the rocket ship at a steady 32 feet per second every second. Now everything that was just floating around the cabin suddenly moves to the back of the cabin. You find yourself pressed against the aft end of the cabin. You stand up, take a deep breath, and realize it is just like back home on Earth. Gravity has been restored to your spaceship. There is absolutely no way to tell from *inside* the rocket ship just what is causing you to feel yourself and every object, light or heavy, pulled to the floor. Have you landed on Earth, or is your rocket ship accelerating in space at 32 feet per second every second? If you had no windows, you would not be able to determine the answer. If you conducted either Galileo's gravity experiments or Max Born's coin experiment, you would find that the results matched exactly the results you would get on Earth. A steadily accelerating spaceship imitates the force of gravity exactly in every detail! There is no way (from the inside) to distinguish between the inertial force of a steadily accelerating object and gravitational forces.

NEWTON:

Okay. I follow you. But I still do not have a clue where this will lead you. What does this thought experiment tell us about gravity that we did not already know?

ARISTOTLE:

Are you saying, Dr. Einstein, that we could create our own gravity in a spaceship far away from Earth?

GALILEO:

Yes he is, and, if I am correct, he is also about to tell us that we are all overlooking something about the force of gravity.

ALBERT EINSTEIN:

And I am going to follow all of the Judge's guidelines for good science. I am going to preserve all your observations and hard-won discoveries. Just as each of you has stepped one or two steps beyond those who came before you, I am preparing to take the next logical step—A New Gravity.

Except for Aristotle, none of you have attempted to explain how this mysterious force, gravity, travels through empty space. You all claim that gravity is a property of matter. Things have gravity. Earth has gravity. The Sun has gravity. Let's agree to put aside all of these previous ideas about gravity temporarily. When I am finished, you may come back to these ideas if you so wish. *(Everyone nods in agreement.)*

Let's assume that gravity is a property of space. Think about what we know about magnetic fields and electric fields. Both forces diminish in strength as we move away from the source into empty space. Newton has correctly calculated that gravity, too, diminishes in strength as we move away from objects. So let us then say that all objects have a gravitational field around them much like a magnet has a magnetic field around it.

Furthermore, we can see this gravitational field every time it rains. Falling raindrops outline Earth's gravitational field. Each raindrop falls along a path predetermined by the gravitational field. And the field is there whether it is raining or not. The field always surrounds Earth because it is the result of an interaction between Earth and the space around Earth.

Falling bodies reach the ground together, no matter whether they are made of lead or wood, because they are following a path predetermined for them by the space in which they are falling. The space in the vicinity of Earth must be distorted (curved) by the presence of Earth. To put it in plain English, *gravity is just curved space.*

NEWTON:

Wait a minute! Are you saying that the empty space that surrounds our planet and the Sun actually creates gravity?! How can *empty* space do that?! I thought empty space could do nothing!

ALBERT EINSTEIN:

What is present immediately surrounding the planets that makes them move in a precisely elliptical path around the Sun?

ASTRONAUT:

The only thing surrounding the planets is empty space.

ALBERT EINSTEIN:

Let's remember a couple of things. First of all, empty space is *not* nothingness. Also, these ideas I am presenting to you are ideas that I have "proven" mathematically with my now-famous relativity field equations.

Imagine a box that has been strung with rubber bands going across from each inside surface to the surface directly across from it. Let this web of rubber bands be space itself. While the box is empty, the rubber bands are straight and flat. (Remember Euclid, who said space was flat?) If I put a tennis ball inside the middle of the box, what happens to the rubber bands?

GALILEO:

They will bend around the ball. They will no longer be straight and flat. The rubber bands near the ball will be curved. In fact, they will push against the ball in an attempt to return to their original position.

NEWTON:

And the farther away from the tennis ball we look, the less curved the rubber bands will be. If the box is large enough, we may even see that the rubber bands at the edge of the box are not affected at all by the tennis ball.

ARISTOTLE:

So, gravity, then, is actually space pressing against objects that are within it!

JUDGE:

Wait! I have never noticed any effects of the space around *me* being distorted.

ALBERT EINSTEIN:

True, and you also have never been aware of Newton's contention that "every mass attracts every other mass" either! We cannot be aware of the distortion in space around us because the amount of distortion around small masses like us (100 to 200 pounds) is utterly trivial. You need a great mass like Earth (13 septillion pounds or 13 with 24 zeros) or the Sun (4 nonillion pounds or 4 with 30 zeros) to become aware of the gravitational effects of space. Earth, after all, with all its septillion pounds of matter, is just barely able to hold on to you! (How much effort does it take for you to walk or jump?)

JUDGE:

Well, what you are saying sounds quite reasonable, but it will take some time for us to check out the situation. We must be certain that all of our old conclusions fit into this new definition of gravity.

ALBERT EINSTEIN:

Take all of the time you like. As long as you do not call me a "crackpot" or dismiss me as crazy, I welcome your help in making sure that I have followed all the rules.

TEACHER:

Well, class, we have come a long way today in our understanding of gravity. It may interest you to know that for the past 80 years, scientists and mathematicians have been studying Albert Einstein's notes and equations and calculations. To this day, no one has found any flaws in his New Law of Gravity. Class dismissed.

The Ecstasy

"If there is any hope of finding a deviation from Newton's law, the greatest chance is in the case of Mercury (which is closest to the Sun where the gravitation is strongest). Imagine my joy at the result that the equations yielded the correct motion of Mercury. I was beside myself with ecstasy for days."

—Albert Einstein (1916)

Newton's Law of Universal Gravitation states that if there is just one planet orbiting a star such as our Sun, the path will be a perfect ellipse, and that the planet will repeat that same path forever (as long as the star and the planet retain their original masses). If there are several planets orbiting the star, each planet will disturb the motion of the others in such a way as to induce a slow rotation, or change of the position, of the orbit around the star (see fig. 5.1).

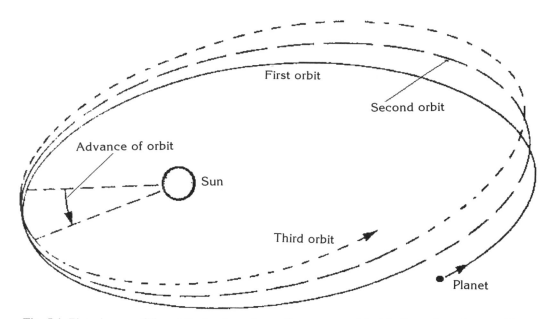

Fig. 5.1. The advance of the orbit of a planet is greatly exaggerated in this figure (e.g., for an orbit advancing at a rate of 43 seconds of arc per 100 years, the cycle is approximately 3 million years).

Because the power of gravity belongs to all bodies, not only does the Sun attract the planets, but each planet attracts every other planet. The resultant forces between the planets continually disturb their orbits so the path traced out each year is slightly shifted from the previous year's path. However, one lone planet orbiting a star will show zero shift of its orbit from year to year, according to Newton.

In 1840, long before Einstein, astronomers noted a rotation of the planet Mercury's orbit around the Sun. Using Newton's equations, the extent of the influence upon Mercury's orbit by the other planets had been laboriously calculated. Astronomers were certain that Mercury's orbit should advance exactly 531 seconds of arc every 100 Earth years. (Astronomers measure angular distances in the sky in units of degree, minutes, and seconds of arc. An advance of 1,800 seconds of arc of a planet's orbit would equal the diameter of the full Moon.) The 1840 very precisely *measured* advance of Mercury's orbit was found to be 574 seconds of arc every 100 Earth years. But the *calculations* called for 531 seconds of arc. The measured value was only 43 seconds of arc too much. The astronomers were exceedingly unhappy with the 43-second discrepancy. They knew 43 was way beyond any errors they could have made in their measurement.

If only there were another planet close to the Sun, scientists could explain their result. If Mercury had a close companion planet (and its mass were just right), it would disturb Mercury's orbit an additional 43 seconds of arc, and thus account for the discrepancy. Some astronomers were so confident that there *must* be another planet near Mercury that they named it—Vulcan, a proper name for a planet close to the Sun. The astronomers never found Vulcan, though their telescopes were quite good enough to spot it, had it been out there.

In 1915, Einstein gave the planet Vulcan "a decent burial" when he announced to the scientific world that his equation and his New Law of Gravity neatly accounted for Mercury's extra 43 seconds of arc. This was the first "much more" that General Relativity had to offer over and above Newton's Law of Universal Gravitation.

Einstein's equation for the orbits of the planets is not quite the same as Newton's. The new equation said that the path of each and every planet around the Sun is indeed an ellipse but that the ellipse itself rotates, regardless of the presence of other planets—the closer the planet is to the Sun, the faster the rotation. In other words, even if there were only one planet in the solar system, its elliptical orbit would slowly rotate. The ellipse traced out by a planet (such as Mercury) rotates independently of any disturbance from other planets. The presence of other planets *adds* additional motion to the path.

Einstein reasoned, if his New Law of Gravity were correct, then the rotation of the elliptical orbit of Mercury must calculate out to be 43 seconds of arc per 100 Earth years, if Mercury were the only planet in the solar system. Mercury's actual measured value of 574 seconds of arc per 100 Earth years in the real solar system would then come from 531 seconds of arc due to disturbances from the other planets, plus 43 seconds of arc due to the natural rotation of Mercury's orbit.

When Einstein completed the lengthy calculation, the rotation turned out to be exactly 43 seconds of arc! Einstein was "beside himself with ecstasy for days" when the number 43 "fell out" of his calculation.

A curious thing about General Relativity is that although its basic math is complex, the math in the last steps of a direct calculation of a specific effect (such as the rotation of a planet's orbit) may be on the level of high school algebra. If you are not intimidated by very large numbers, and can work with exponents, you may glimpse a bit of the excitement that Einstein felt when he calculated those momentous 43 seconds (see appendix E for details of the calculation).

Einstein had been searching for 10 years for a mathematical description of the interaction of matter with space. In this one equation, he achieved a result that surely justified all his labors: The 43-second discrepancy in Mercury's orbit had been neatly explained, and the search for the planet Vulcan could be quietly abandoned.

Not everyone could accept his General Relativity as the New Law of Gravity. In 1915, very few scientists were ready to embrace Einstein's

New Law of Gravity on the basis of the 43-second result. However, civilization had progressed somewhat since the days of Bruno and Galileo—and at least no one suggested that Einstein be burned at the stake, or recant his outrageous theory. That is, no one until Stalin and Hitler arrived on the scene. In the 1930s, Russian scientists proudly denounced Einstein and proclaimed Relativity to be a false theory. In 1933, the Germans, under Hitler, burned Einstein's books in their notorious bonfires—with the acquiescence of at least one world-renowned physicist who chose to stay at the University of Göttingen during the Hitler years. The German authorities called Relativity a Jewish theory, unworthy of being taught in their schools.

Undaunted by his critics, Einstein had another "ace" to put on the table: His new law predicted the bending or deflection of starlight by the warp in space near the Sun. What did he mean by the bending of starlight? If you stand on Earth and look up at a star in the vicinity of the Sun when the Sun is shining, Einstein's law predicted that the star you would be "seeing" would actually be 1.75 seconds of arc away from where you saw it (see fig. 5.2).

Because one cannot see the stars when the Sun is shining, Einstein suggested that astronomers measure the deflection of light from stars that would become visible during the next eclipse of the Sun. It is only during the darkness that

descends with a total eclipse of the Sun that one is able to see the background stars in relation to the Sun. We seldom think about it, but the sky is really full of stars day and night. The Sun's brilliant light totally overwhelms the feeble light of other stars.

The task Einstein set for the astronomers was to photograph the stars that become visible during an eclipse and measure their apparent displacement due to the bending of the starlight as it passed through the warp in space very near the Sun. This measurement could only be made when the Sun is present. The beam of starlight would be deflected by the Sun because starlight contains energy, and energy is a form of mass, as Einstein discovered with his famous equation $e = mc^2$ (energy equals mass times the velocity of light squared). Thus, as the beam of starlight approaches the vicinity of the Sun, it will follow the path dictated to it by the curvature of space near the Sun—just as surely as the curved space tells the planets and comets exactly how they must move around the Sun. Einstein calculated that the precise deflection of the beam of starlight passing near the Sun would be 1.75 seconds of arc.

The suggested measurements were made by Sir Arthur Eddington on May 29, 1919. Einstein's New Law of Gravity was confirmed, within the limits of the precision of the experiment. Of course, there were critics who said that Eddington's measurements were not really exact enough to

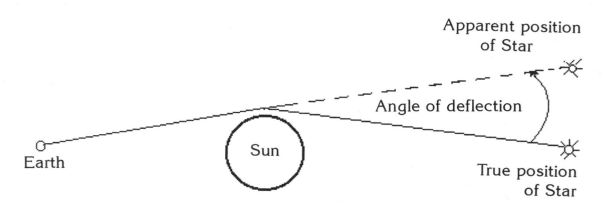

Fig. 5.2. The amount of deflection suffered by the beam of light is greatly exaggerated to indicate the apparent displacement of the star as it would be seen by an observer on Earth during a solar eclipse.

settle the matter. The deflection was, after all, very small and difficult to measure from the astronomers' photographic plates. Critics demanded further confirmation.

Fifty-six years after Eddington, and 20 years after Einstein's death, Edward Fomalont and Richard Sramek at the Radio Astronomy Observatory in West Virginia provided the needed confirmation. These two astronomers had the bright idea of using a beam of radio signals from a distant galaxy (3C273) to check the deflection of starlight near the Sun.

Radio signals are a form of light with much longer wavelengths and less energy than ordinary light. Very few stars in our galaxy send out radio signals, and those that do are not positioned in such a way as to allow the measurement of the deflection near the Sun. However, there are many distant galaxies that send out powerful radio signals. Some of these galaxies do line up with our Sun at certain times of the year.

The elegant part of the Fomalont and Sramek idea is that, because they used radio signals, they did not have to wait for a rare eclipse of the Sun. They could make their measurements in full daylight. A radio telescope is blind to visible light, thus it functions just as well during the day as in the night. Though Fomalont and Sramek had no need to wait for an eclipse, they did have to wait for the distant galaxy to come into a position in the sky directly in the line of sight with our Sun. When galaxy 3C273 and the Sun were in correct alignment, Fomalont and Sramek very precisely determined that the radio signal beam emanating from the distant galaxy was bent, when passing near our Sun, by *exactly* the amount called for by Einstein: 1.75 seconds of arc.

With this additional confirmation, perhaps now you can believe that space *is* curved by matter. However, our discussion of Einstein's New Law of Gravity is not finished. The new law says that not only will curved space bend starlight but it will also *slow down clocks*. The equations demand that time must be slowed down in curved space—the greater the curvature, the greater the slowing. If we could send an Earth clock to the Sun, we would find that it runs one hundred millionth of a second slow. The clock on the Sun runs slow because the Sun is more massive than Earth, which means that the space around the Sun is more curved than around Earth.

We cannot actually send a clock to the Sun, but we can observe atomic clocks on the Sun and compare them with identical atomic clocks on Earth. Atomic clocks are vibrating atoms that emit light with very precise wavelengths. Each type of atom has a unique wavelength, a "fingerprint" unique to the internal structure of the atom.

In 1962, J. W. Brault performed an atomic clock experiment to earn his Ph.D. at Princeton University. He analyzed the light coming directly from sodium atoms on the Sun and compared it with the light coming from sodium atoms in a laboratory on Earth. His results confirmed Einstein's prediction: The sodium atoms on the Sun vibrated more slowly than identical sodium atoms on Earth. It should be emphasized that we are talking about a trivial slowing of time when comparing the Sun and Earth. (It is important to understand this concept now because in chapters 7 and 8 we discuss space curvatures that are so enormous that they stop clocks altogether.)

Let's summarize what Einstein's New Law of Gravity has given us, in addition to upholding all the accomplishments of Newton:

1. Resolution of the 43 seconds of arc mystery of Mercury's orbit.

2. Prediction of bending of light rays by gravity.

3. Prediction of the retardation of time in gravitational fields.

Einstein's law, however, contains much more new information about the universe. For example, it predicts gravitational waves that can travel with the speed of light and can bring us news about catastrophic events throughout the universe. The New Law of Gravity says that a star moving gracefully around the galaxy curves the space it is in at any one moment, and that space reacts back on the star and, in a sense, "tells" the star exactly where to go.

If a star should explode, what happens to the space around it? What happens to the air if a firecracker should explode? Sound waves are generated in the air that spread the news of the explosion in all directions. An exploding star undoubtedly makes a lot of noise, but the sound cannot travel away from the star (sound waves cannot travel in empty space). However, the space around the star *is disturbed* and ripples (spreads out) in all directions. These ripples are gravitational waves and they move with the speed of light. Like light, *gravitational waves* travel forever unless their energy is absorbed by matter in their path. The energy of gravitational waves, however, is not easily absorbed. A gravitational wave can pass through the entire Earth with little loss of energy—even though the amount of energy carried by the wave is exceedingly small to begin with. What does it take to "see" gravitational waves?

In 1960 at the University of Maryland, Professor Joseph Weber used two solid cylinders of aluminum, five feet long and three feet in diameter, to try to detect gravitational waves. These cylinders (three and one-half tons each) were suspended from steel wires strung between two blocks of iron and enclosed in separate vacuum chambers—separated by about 1,000 kilometers. One cylinder was placed at the University of Maryland, the other at Argonne National Laboratory, near Chicago, Illinois. Weber called the cylinders "coincidence gravitational radiation antennae." The New Law of Gravity says that if a gravitational wave should pass through the aluminum cylinders, the cylinders would vibrate in a curious way. Professor Weber would not be able to see the cylinders move, but he would be able to detect atomic motion electrically using sensitive devices that respond to the oscillations of the entire aluminum cylinder.

However, there is an inherent difficulty: The atoms of the aluminum cylinder are always vibrating because atoms only "sit still" at a temperature of absolute zero (-273°C, which cannot be attained, even theoretically, in a laboratory). An aluminum cylinder, or any collection of atoms, could arrive at absolute zero temperature only by giving up 100 percent of its heat energy. To accomplish this, one would have to isolate the cylinder from the rest of the universe. Otherwise, it would absorb some heat energy from any object that the cylinder could "see"—if it had eyes (e.g., any object surrounding the cylinder that is not at the absolute zero temperature)!

Thus, a collection of atoms can never "sit still." Electrical sensors record these thermal vibrations as "noise." Sensors also pick up vibrations caused by lightning, passing vehicles, and earthquakes. The solution to recognizing a gravitational wave is to use two cylinders. Isolate the cylinders as much as possible (e.g., wire suspension). Separate the cylinders (e.g., 1,000 kilometers apart), and watch for coincidental signals. If both cylinders simultaneously record a sudden, sharp vibration, one can assume that it was caused by the arrival of a gravitational wave. It would be exceedingly unlikely that two receptors, 1,000 kilometers apart, would simultaneously register sharp disturbances from two different sources. The assumption that the disturbance was a gravitational wave becomes all the more credible if it can be shown that the signal was not due to an earthquake, or any other extraneous source.

In 1969, Professor Weber reported that his gravitational wave detectors had recorded bursts of gravitational radiation. However, repeated attempts by many scientists to duplicate Weber's results have been unsuccessful. Before a scientific result is accepted by the scientific community, the experiment and its result must be verified by repetition. The failure to duplicate Weber's detection of gravitational waves indicates a need for better-designed devices to detect gravitational waves. More sensitive, laser-based gravitational wave detectors are currently being built by a team of scientists under the supervision of Robbi Vogt at the Massachusetts Institute of Technology and at Caltech.

Catastrophic events, which could generate gravitational waves, have been observed through a telescope in the central regions of many galaxies. New telescopes sensitive to infrared light have recently been put into orbit around Earth to look for unusual events or strange objects in our galaxy. Astronomers are especially curious about what is going on at the very center of the Milky Way galaxy. The heart of our galaxy is 28,000 light-years distant from Earth and is shrouded by dust particles that cause us much difficulty in observing what is happening at its center. Curiously, we can easily see the turmoil (rapidly, chaotically moving stars) occurring at the center of distant galaxies (if a galaxy is oriented so that we see its disc face-on).

In 1943, Carl Seyfert discovered several galaxies whose central regions are in violent turmoil. It was obvious to Seyfert that something strange was stirring the very heart of these galaxies. Since Seyfert's original discovery, astronomers have observed many more galaxies with violent cores (called Seyfert Galaxies). At the center of each of these galaxies may sit a massive black hole. (We will discover the source of black holes in chapter 8.)

Tranquillity does not seem to be an attribute of our universe. The calm, quiet sky we observe with our naked eye is not the whole truth of the state of the universe. In the next chapter we will learn about a unique event that occurred in our past that by sheer magnitude defies comparison with anything that has ever happened to an individual star or galaxy. We will see how Einstein's relativity equations lead us to knowledge of the universe that defies even the wildest imagination. The key that unlocked this awesome view was Einstein's discovery that his equations would not allow the option of a calm, unchanging universe.

Chapter 5, Lesson Plan # 1

The Problem of a Scientific Discrepancy

TEACHING MODEL
Advanced Organizer

OBJECTIVES
1. The students will discover that Newton's Law of Universal Gravitation, as applied to the orbits of planets around a star, was flawed.

2. The students will propose a plan and possible solution to the scientific discrepancy over Mercury's orbit.

3. The students will examine the truths of the universe revealed by Albert Einstein's General Relativity.

4. The students will formulate an opinion of Albert Einstein's General Relativity and write an essay explaining and supporting their opinion.

VOCABULARY
1. *Gravity*—The effect of space curving around all objects within it. The larger the object, the greater the curvature of space and the greater the gravity.

2. *Degrees, minutes, and seconds of arc*—Units of measure by which astronomers measure angular distances in the sky. Think of the sky as a dome above us: There are exactly 180 degrees from horizon to horizon. They are not unlike the degrees, minutes, and seconds used to precisely measure angles in geometry. A portion of the sky equal to 1,800 seconds of arc will be equal to the diameter of the full Moon as seen from Earth.

MATERIALS
* Copy of "Student Handout—Graphic Organizer" for each student

* Copy of "Teacher Key—Graphic Organizer" for teacher reference

From *Gravity, the Glue of the Universe.* ©1997 Harry Gilbert and Diana Gilbert Smith. Teacher Ideas Press. (800) 237-6124.

PROCEDURE

Review of Prior Learning

Pose the following questions to the students:

* Who were the four scientists who have had the biggest roles in exploring gravity? (Aristotle, Galileo, Newton, and Einstein)

* Besides scientific laboratory experiments, what has been used by people like Max Born to study gravity? (mathematics)

* What is Albert Einstein's definition of gravity? (Gravity is an effect of space curving around all objects within it. The larger the object, the greater the curvature of space and the greater the gravity.)

Background

Albert Einstein's New Law of Gravity was published in 1915 as General Relativity. Today we are going to take a closer look at the consequences of Einstein's General Relativity and the public's reaction to it. At the end of this lesson you will be asked to give your opinion about these amazing ideas.

(Introduce the vocabulary words *degrees, minutes, seconds of arc.*)

Newton's Law of Gravity says that if there is just one planet orbiting a star such as our Sun, the path will be a perfect ellipse, and the planet will repeat the same path forever (as long as the masses of the star and of the planet retain their original values). If there are several planets orbiting the star, each planet will disturb the motion of the others in such a way as to induce a slow rotation of their orbits around the star (see fig. 5.1). Remember, the power of gravity belongs to all bodies. Thus, not only does the Sun attract the planets, but each planet attracts every other planet. The resultant forces between the planets continually disturb their orbits so that the paths traced out each year are slightly shifted from the previous year's paths.

The Problem

In 1840, astronomers noted just such a rotation in the orbit of the planet Mercury. Using Newton's mathematical equations, they slowly and carefully *calculated* the exact amount that Mercury's orbit should rotate in 100 Earth years. They came up with 531 seconds of arc every 100 years. Then they very carefully and precisely *measured* the actual 100-year rotation of Mercury's orbit. It was 574 seconds of arc, not 531 seconds of arc as previously calculated. Subtract 531 from 574 and you get 43. The scientists had a problem. How could they account for these 43 seconds?

Key Questions for Discussion

1. *Reflect on the discrepancy between the calculated rotation and the actual measured rotation in Mercury's orbit in 100 Earth years. Can you identify the problem?*

2. *Exactly how large is this discrepancy?* (574 − 531 = 43 seconds of arc per 100 years)

3. *If you were a scientist, would you consider 43 seconds out of 574 to be a problem? What would you do/say/think if you were one of these scientists? Would you say this amount is too small to worry about? Would you recalculate? Would you re-measure Mercury's orbit? Would you doubt Newton? Would you doubt your ability as a scientist? How important could 43 seconds of arc be anyway?*

One Possible Solution

In 1840, the astronomers were exceedingly unhappy with this 43-second discrepancy. They did come up with a possible solution. If there were another planet closer to the Sun than Mercury, this would explain the 43-second discrepancy. If Mercury had a close companion, its mass would disturb Mercury's orbit and account for the discrepancy. They were so confident that there *must* be another planet that they even named it—Vulcan. However, they never could find Vulcan with their telescopes.

What Would You Do?

1. Divide the students into teams of four or five students each. Have each team consider what they would do if they were the astronomers. Have the teams follow this procedure:

   a. Review the problem.

   b. Discuss all of the possible solutions.

   c. Develop a plan of action.

   d. Write out each step in your plan of action. Include as much information as possible about what you will do, how you will do it, and why (for each step). Also include your expected result.

2. Allow the teams time to develop and to write out their plans. Have each group share their ideas with the entire class.

3. Ask the question, *After all your hard, scientific work on this question, what would you think of someone who came along with an exact, provable answer?*

From *Gravity, the Glue of the Universe.* ©1997 Harry Gilbert and Diana Gilbert Smith. Teacher Ideas Press. (800) 237-6124.

The Story Continues

In 1915, Albert Einstein came along and gave the planet Vulcan a final and decent burial. His General Relativity very neatly accounted for Mercury's extra 43 seconds of arc.

Before I explain how Einstein did this, I need to tell you what he did *not* do. Albert Einstein did *not* set out to find the missing 43 seconds of arc, nor did he set out to find the missing planet Vulcan. Einstein definitely did not "fiddle" with Newton's mathematical equations looking for ways to stick in those extra seconds (some scientists did). This is not good science.

General Relativity was Einstein's attempt to expand his Special Relativity to include gravity. In writing General Relativity, Einstein was forced to develop a new definition of gravity. The new gravity included many of Newton's ideas, but it went beyond Newton's wildest imaginings. Six somewhat startling truths were revealed by Einstein's General Relativity.

(Pass out "Student Handout—Graphic Organizer," and set up a model organizer on a chart, chalkboard, or overhead projector. Use the "Teacher Key—Graphic Organizer" to present the material to the students. You may also wish to refer to the narrative text of chapter 5 for more background. Encourage the students to paraphrase ideas as they write and to ask questions as you go through the material.)

A Humble Hope

Albert Einstein hoped that the general public and the scientific community would accept his General Relativity, especially when they saw that he had found the answer to the missing 43 seconds of arc in Mercury's orbit. However, General Relativity was not accepted.

What do you think? Based on your knowledge of General Relativity, are you willing to give these new and amazing ideas a chance? Do you think this man who proposed these ideas is a "crazy crackpot"? Support your opinions with examples and the best evidence you can find.

Conclusion

For homework, have students think about General Relativity. Have them use their graphic organizers to recall what was discussed and to think further about General Relativity. Have each student write an essay to answer the questions in A Humble Hope, above.

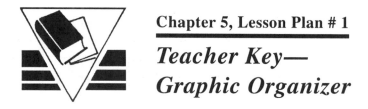

Chapter 5, Lesson Plan # 1

Teacher Key—
Graphic Organizer

Einstein's General Relativity Reveals Six Truths

I.   Gravitational fields bend light.

Explanation: As a beam of starlight approaches a massive object like the Sun, the starlight will follow the path dictated to it by the curvature of space near the Sun, just as surely as raindrops trace a path as they fall to Earth.

   A.   On May 29, 1919, Sir Arthur Eddington measured the locations of the stars seen during a solar eclipse and compared these positions to the locations measured at night.

   B.   In West Virginia in 1975, Edward Fomalont and Richard Sramek used radio signals (another type of light in the electromagnetic spectrum) from distant galaxies to measure how the gravity of the Sun bends light as the light travels past the Sun.

II.   Time slows down in a gravitational field.

Explanation: If we could transfer an Earth clock to the Sun, we would find that it runs one hundred millionth of a second slow. The clock on the Sun runs slow because the Sun is more massive than Earth, and the space around the Sun is more curved than the space around Earth.

   A.   In 1962, Dr. J. W. Brault performed an atomic clock experiment at Princeton University. He used light coming from the Sun to measure the vibration of sodium atoms on the Sun. Then he compared this to the speed of vibration of sodium atoms found on Earth. The sodium atoms on the Sun vibrated more slowly than the sodium atoms on Earth.

III.   The planet Vulcan does not need to exist to account for Mercury's 43-seconds-of-arc discrepancy.

Explanation: Einstein's equation for the orbits of the planets is not quite the same as Newton's. Einstein's equation says that the path of each planet around a star is an ellipse (as Newton had said), but also that the ellipse itself moves, regardless of the presence of other planets. The presence of other planets will add additional motion to the path of the orbit, but the orbit will rotate slightly every year even if it is by itself. Einstein plugged the numbers for Mercury into his new equation, and "out dropped" the missing 43 seconds of arc.

From *Gravity, the Glue of the Universe.* ©1997 Harry Gilbert and Diana Gilbert Smith. Teacher Ideas Press. (800) 237-6124.

IV. An exploding star sends gravitational waves pulsing through the universe at the speed of light.

Explanation: If massive objects distort the space around them, it is fairly easy to imagine that when a large object explodes in space, the space it was occupying feels a significant affect. Think about how a bomb exploding underwater in a lake would effect the water in the lake. Water waves would spread out from the center of the explosion in all directions, and the boundaries of the lake might not be enough to stop the waves. Now consider a very large star exploding in space. Gravitational waves would ripple out in all directions.

Particles that make up gravitational waves are called gravitons, which have zero mass. This enables them to travel at the speed of light. Like light, they will travel forever unless their journey is interrupted by something that absorbs them. The energy that gravitational waves release when they hit an object is so tiny that it is not easily measured. Gravitational waves pass through Earth all the time and we never notice it.

A. Professor Joseph Weber, at the University of Maryland, has tried unsuccessfully to detect gravitational waves hitting Earth (see p. 99 of the narrative).

B. Robbie Vogt at the Massachusetts Institute of Technology and at Caltech is building a more sensitive laser-based gravitational wave detector with which he hopes to detect gravitational waves, but he has not yet succeeded.

V. The universe must either be expanding or contracting; it cannot be static. The space between distant galaxies must be continuously increasing or decreasing.*

VI. There can be too much matter in one spot in the universe. If this occurs, the matter will collapse in on itself, forming a black hole.**

---

*This truth will be addressed in chapter 6, lesson plan #1.

**For more information about this truth see the narrative text of chapter 8.

Chapter 5, Lesson Plan # 1

Student Handout—
Graphic Organizer

Einstein's General Relativity Reveals Six Truths

I. _____

_____

Explanation: _____

_____

_____

_____

   A. _____

_____

   B. _____

_____

II. _____

_____

Explanation: _____

_____

_____

_____

_____

A. _____

_____

III. _____

_____

Explanation: _____

_____

_____

_____

IV. _____

_____

Explanation: _____

_____

A. _____

_____

B. _____

_____

V. _____

_____

VI. _____

_____

An Enigma

"Numbers are the language of nature."

—Pythagoras (550 B.C.)

". . . an enigma presents itself, which in all ages has agitated inquiring minds: how can it be that mathematics, being after all a product of human thought which is independent of experience, is so admirably appropriate to the objects of reality?"

—Albert Einstein (1922)

It is utterly amazing that certain equations of mathematics can tell us how the universe works. Mathematics is a product of the human mind and completely disconnected from everything we see, feel, or experience in the world. Instinctively, scientists over the centuries have suspected that the key to knowledge of our universe lies in the logical structure of mathematics. Pythagoras the Greek was so enthralled with the relationships and manipulations of numbers, he positively worshipped them. Albert Einstein did not worship mathematics, but he often wondered at the curious ability of some mathematical equations to describe the universe.

Real progress in science has always come from the ability of geniuses like Newton and Einstein to state a few simple postulates and then derive, mathematically, representations of the physical world. A postulate is, after all, a statement that one assumes to be true without proof. Not all postulates lead to correct representation of the natural laws of the universe. For example, Euclid's postulate that parallel lines remain parallel upon infinite extension is true only in a universe completely empty of matter.

It was Riemann who first suggested that Euclid's postulate might not apply to the real world. Riemann used mathematics to suggest that space might be curved in such a way as to force parallel lines to eventually cross each other. However, Riemann never lived to prove this. He died of tuberculosis in 1866, at the age of 40, while working on the problems of gravity, magnetism, and the geometry of space.

Einstein, who had a veritable mania for reading the works of great scientists, saw the important implications of Riemann's unfinished work. Forty-nine years after Riemann's death, fascinated by the idea that space might be curved, Einstein wondered what might cause the curvature of space. The fantastic idea occurred to Einstein that the curvature of space might be due entirely to the presence of matter—only empty space, free of all matter, would be flat. Einstein formulated the fundamental postulate for General Relativity—now simply stated as:

> Matter curves space. The geometry of space is determined only by the presence of matter.

This postulate and Einstein's Equivalence Principle (there is no way to distinguish between a gravitational force and the force inside accelerating objects) are the entire basis for General Relativity. The precise mathematical relationship between matter and space is what the General Relativity equations are all about.

In 1917, just two years after the publication of General Relativity, Einstein found that his equations *demanded* a universe that expanded or contracted. There was no "static" solution. Einstein was terribly upset with this result because it ran contrary to all the scientific observations and understanding of the universe. The dilemma Einstein faced—Astronomers told him: The universe that we can see all around us in the sky is essentially the same today as it was in antiquity, when Pharaohs looked up at the stars. The universe is unchanging, to the best of our knowledge. We have no reason to believe otherwise. The General Relativity equations told him: The universe *must* be either expanding or contracting there can be no permanent unchanging, static condition.

It follows from the equations that even if the universe were forced to be static, it would be in a terribly precarious situation. One could liken it to a tightrope walker trying to spend his entire life balanced on the rope. He could maintain balance only if he were completely motionless. The slightest movement would throw him off the rope. How long could he maintain this balance? A static universe would be in this situation, according to Einstein's equation. The equation says that the slightest movement in the universe by *any object* would set it off balance and start it in motion, either expanding or contracting. A static universe would not be stable for even a moment.

What would you have done if you were faced with this dichotomy? Would you tell the astronomers and all the scientific world they were mistaken, or

would you alter your equations? Einstein did the *human* thing—he altered his equations. He added a term to *force* his equation to call for a static universe. (In engineering schools this is called a "goose factor.")

Twelve years later, in 1929, the astronomer Edwin P. Hubble examined the light from distant galaxies gathered by a 100-inch telescope on Mt. Wilson, California, and announced: "The universe is expanding!" (Hubble 1929) Einstein's equation was indeed correct, and the added term (the goose factor) could be discarded. The relativity equation knew more about the universe than the astronomers. Einstein castigated himself ("The biggest blunder of my life") for tampering with his equation in 1917.

Don't blame the astronomers, for they had not truly misinformed Einstein. As far as they could see, in 1917, the universe was unchanging. They did not yet have a 100-inch telescope in operation. By a curious coincidence, the 100-inch glass mirror (used by Hubble to detect the expansion) was completed in 1917, the same year Einstein was "twisting" his equation to allow for a static universe.

The astronomers had seen fuzzy patches of light in the sky—some were clearly visible without a telescope—but they did not know the nature of these fuzzy patches, or where they were in relation to the stars. The fuzzy patches were later positively identified as galaxies, swarming with billions of stars—galaxies that were many light-years distant from the group of stars comprising our galaxy. What Hubble had seen in 1929 was a remarkable recession of these distant galaxies. They were all "running away" from us; and the farther out they were, the faster they were moving.

Why are all the galaxies receding from our galaxy? Are we somehow at the "center" of the universe? No. It is just that the expansion of the universe affects each galaxy equally. Imagine that Earth's surface is one solid landmass. Then imagine that all the people are equally distant from one another. Next, imagine that Earth started to expand: All the people standing near you would begin moving away from you, and the people that were originally quite distant from you would be moving away at a faster pace than those closer to you. If you asked any person at all what he or she was observing as Earth started to expand, each would give you the same report: Everyone is moving away from me.

The recession of the galaxies that Edwin Hubble observed in his telescope can be pictured in much the same way: Every galaxy will see their distant neighboring galaxies receding from them. The more distant the galaxy, the faster it will be moving. Which galaxy is at the center of the universe? This question, is not valid because there is no center, any more than there is a center to the surface of any sphere. There is no privileged position. If you are still in doubt, use a marker to draw spots on a balloon and watch what happens as you inflate it.

The galaxies are receding from one another because the volume of space between them is continuously increasing. This is not to say that the universe is expanding *into* space, because the universe is not expanding *into* anything. Actually, there is a continuously increasing "amount" of space between the galaxies as the universe expands (amount is in quotes because it is useless to speak of a "quantity" of space).

Soon after Edwin Hubble announced the recession of the galaxies, it became apparent to the astronomers that, in the distant past, the galaxies must have been much closer together. If we had a movie film of the receding galaxies, and ran the film backward, what would we see? Would they all come together into one gigantic mass? If so, all of the matter in the entire universe must have at some time in the distant past been in one place.

Today, most scientists agree that if you push time back far enough, you will come upon the primeval universe with near-infinite density and near-infinite temperature. The primeval universe contained all the matter that is present in our universe today—with this difference: The space available for the matter to "swim" was rather limited. It would be as though someone had removed more than 99.99999 percent of the space that exists in the universe today! You would not recognize any normal form of matter as we know it (water, rocks, air)—the tremendous gravitational field will have crushed everything into unimaginable densities and temperatures. The

atoms will have literally crumbled into their constituent parts (protons, neutrons, electrons). Together with the crumbled atoms will be the three "messengers of the universe"— photons, neutrinos, and gravitons, all of which travel at the speed of light.

Photons are the elementary particles that make up all electromagnetic radiation (see table 2.2, p. 38). Electromagnetic radiation is better known to us as (listed in order of lowest energy to highest energy):

* *Radio waves*, which send the music from a radio station to your radio.

* *Microwaves*, which heat the food in your microwave oven (actually heat the water in the food).

* *Infrared light*, which is emitted by all warm objects (our bodies, our homes), but it cannot be seen. Our eyes were not designed to respond to the low-energy photons of infrared light. We do know when strong infrared light is shining on our bodies because we feel this light as heat.

* *Visible light*, which we can see because our eyes were designed to respond to photons that have a little more energy than infrared light photons.

* *X-rays*, which have enough energy to penetrate your skin but not your bones.

It was Albert Einstein (in 1905) who made the momentous discovery that *all* electromagnetic radiation (from radio waves to X-rays) must be made up of individual photons.

Neutrinos are the elementary particles that come "flying" out of certain atoms that disintegrate spontaneously (radium, uranium, plutonium, and carbon-14), and out of all nuclear power plant reactors. If you live near a nuclear electric power plant, you are being penetrated by neutrinos continuously. Neutrinos cannot possibly hurt you because these fast-moving particles travel through your atoms without actually touching anything. Countless neutrinos can travel through the entire Earth without disturbing a single atom in their 12,700-kilometer path.

You can know that something is present in your environment only if you somehow interact with it. You might see, hear, smell, or touch an object. In each instance you would be interacting with the object, chemically or physically.

If you see it—photons, which are particles of pure energy and zero mass, have traveled from the object to your eye, passed through the lens of your eye, and caused a chemical reaction in your retina, which sent electrical signals to your brain through the optic nerve.

If you hear it—sound waves from the object have moved through the air, entered your ear, and set up a vibration in your inner ear, which sent electrical signals to your brain.

If you smell it—individual chemical molecules have left the object, traveled through the air, entered your nose, and stimulated nerves lining your nostrils, which sent electrical signals to your brain.

If you touch it—multitudes of atoms on the surface of the object have pressed against the atoms in your skin, which pressed against nerves under your skin, which sent electrical signals to your brain.

How can we detect neutrinos? How can scientists be sure they even exist? The problem with neutrino detection: They do not react with, vibrate, sensitize, or disturb much of anything. They will very occasionally react with the central core of hydrogen atoms (protons). Scientists have calculated that there is one chance in a nonillion (1 followed by 30 zeros) of a single neutrino reacting with an individual hydrogen atom!

These odds did not deter F. Reines and C. L. Cowen (in 1955) from designing an experiment to physically detect neutrinos. At the Savanna River Nuclear Energy Plant in Georgia, Reines and Cowen placed a generous supply of hydrogen atoms (i.e., a large container of water, or H_2O) directly in front of a plutonium-producing nuclear reactor, a powerful source of neutrinos. In 1956, they announced their results: positive identification of the neutrino. Scientists believe that the hot

primeval universe contained a multitude of neutrinos. These primeval neutrinos were generated by the spontaneous decay of neutrons during the first three minutes of the Big Bang.

Gravitons are the particles associated with gravitational waves. As the primeval universe expanded, there probably were gravitons and gravitational waves generated by all of the turmoil. Strong gravitational waves are produced by matter in rapid, chaotic motion. The Big Bang was the largest explosion in the history of the universe.

Photons, neutrinos, and gravitons, the three "messengers of the universe," are out there in space right now delivering the message of what happened when the universe started its expansion (now commonly called the Big Bang). However, to "read" their messages, you must first be able to detect these fast-moving particles.

It was worth a Nobel Prize (in 1978) to two young scientists who, in 1964, accidentally intercepted a startling "message" carried by a stream of photons. Arno Penzias and Robert Wilson detected the photons with a rather primitive radio telescope. These strange radio photons had been entering the telescope continuously, day and night. They were everywhere in the sky. No matter which direction Penzias and Wilson pointed their radio telescope, the photons kept on arriving with the same intensity. After the scientists decoded their instrument readings and did some calculating, the incredible message the photons carried was revealed:

Our temperature now is 2.7 degrees above absolute zero. We have been traveling through space for about 15 billion years. We have come directly from the primeval explosion. We were born in the space explosion— but we were not free to travel until our temperature had dropped to 3,000 degrees. At that point the electrons released us and the universe lit up with a stupendous flash.

Neutrinos and gravitons have been spreading through space ever since the Big Bang. They are at present just as cold as the Penzias and Wilson photons. This poses a problem: We do not now have the technical equipment or technology to detect cold, primeval neutrinos and gravitons, let alone to "read" any messages they might carry.

If you had been present when the primeval universe exploded, what would you have seen? To see this explosion, you would have had to be present *inside* of it because there was no outside (matter and radiation have always filled the entire space of the universe, just as they do today—the only difference being that the universe was very much smaller when it was young). You would have been immersed in a sea of radiation much hotter than 10 billion degrees, expanding explosively in all directions, then rapidly cooling down to a few billion degrees. Exactly 34 minutes and 40 seconds after the Big Bang, the temperature of the universe had cooled to 300 million degrees (scientists can precisely calculate the time it took the universe to cool down to a specific temperature).

All of the matter in the early universe consisted essentially of hydrogen and helium, the two smallest, lowest-weight atoms. It was much too hot for heavier atoms, such as carbon or iron, to exist. They would have been split to pieces by fast-moving, high-energy particles. Even the hydrogen and helium atoms were not completely whole because it was too hot for their electrons to stay with them (every normal hydrogen atom has one electron, and every normal helium atom has two electrons). We must allow the universe to expand and cool for about 300,000 years to attain a temperature low enough (3,000 degrees) to allow the electrons to properly join up with the hydrogen and helium atoms.

The wait is well worth it, because something quite spectacular happens at this moment of "joining up"—the universe suddenly lights up—billions of photons are set free from their electrons, free for the first time to travel through the expanding space of the universe. We recognize these photons today as the Penzias-Wilson photons. They are now only 2.7 degrees above absolute zero. You do not realize it, but you are bumping into these photons continuously. They are every-

where. The Penzias-Wilson photons can even be picked up on a television screen: A television tuned to an unoccupied channel fills the picture tube with white specks, called snow. About 1 out of every 100 of these specks is generated by a 2.7-degree (above absolute zero), 15-billion-year-old photon hitting the antenna of the television.

When the universe was 300,000 years old, it entered into a quiet time of consolidation. Gravity quietly pulled hydrogen and helium atoms into clusters. Within each cluster (protogalaxy), gravity orchestrated the formation of dense concentrations of hydrogen and helium gas (protostars). The pace of change begins to accelerate as the protogalaxies give birth to the first generation of stars.

Stars are born in the sense that an entirely new object is formed out of a collection of swirling atoms. Stars live a life of their own. They travel around their galaxies spreading photons of light everywhere. As stars grow old, some will violently explode, scattering chemical elements throughout the space around them, planting the seeds of planets that will orbit the next generation of stars.

Astronomers can determine the brightness, color, surface temperature, size, mass, and chemical composition of a star. In analyzing the light from stars, astronomers find that there are young stars, middle-aged stars, old stars, dying stars, and dead stars. The youngest stars are the small, hot, blue ones; the oldest stars are red and very large. All dead stars are either white or black and are very, very small. Surprisingly, like people, stars can be overweight—and they, too, can suffer the consequences.

In the next chapter we will learn about the life cycle of stars: birth, growth (providing for the next generation), and death—a pattern that repeats itself in many guises in our universe. We will learn how the chemical elements required for the formation of human beings and all living creatures are manufactured by stars in their death-throes, and how these precious chemicals are delivered to the birth cradles of stars like our Sun.

Einstein's Dilemma

TEACHING MODEL
Synectics

OBJECTIVES
1. The students will develop an understanding of the universe by relating it to familiar objects.

2. The students will formulate analogies to describe our expanding universe.

3. The students will use the Synectics model (see Joyce and Weil's *Models of Teaching*, 3d ed.) to create a personal model of the universe.

VOCABULARY
1. *Analogy*—A comparison of the characteristics of two different things.

MATERIALS
* Blank paper for each student to take notes

* Blackboard, overhead projector, or chart paper and writing instrument for the teacher

* Copy of "Sample Synectics Progression" for teacher reference

PROCEDURE

Part 1—A Dilemma (and a Surprise Revelation)
In 1917, just two years after the publication of General Relativity, it was found that the Einstein equations *demanded* a universe that expanded or contracted. There was no "static" solution. Einstein was terribly upset with this result because it ran contrary to all the observations and understanding that science had of the universe.

Here was the dilemma Einstein faced. Astronomers told him: The universe that we can see all around us in the sky is essentially the same today as it was in antiquity, when the Pharaohs looked up at the stars. The universe is unchanging, to the best of our knowledge. We have no reason to believe otherwise. The mathematical calculations in the General Relativity equations told him: The universe *must* be either expanding or contracting. There can be no permanent, unchanging, static condition.

(Before introducing the next set of questions, have the students set up for "Think-Pair-Share." When you get to "share," ask selected students to share their partner's opinion rather than their own.)

What would you have done if you were faced with this conflict between your mathematical calculations and what everyone else had believed for thousands of years? Would you tell astronomers and all the scientific world that they were mistaken? Or would you alter your equations?

Einstein knew how human knowledge of the universe has gradually increased throughout the ages. On the one hand, it might not be so unreasonable for us to be forced once again to re-examine our notion of a static, unchanging universe. On the other hand, Einstein remembered too clearly how much criticism he had encountered when he first challenged the notions of Galileo and Newton.

This time Einstein was not up to a battle. He did the *human* thing. He altered his equations. He added a term to *force* his equations to call for a static universe. This way he did not have to sell the public or other scientists on his *new* ideas.

Twelve years later, in 1929, Edwin P. Hubble, a famous astronomer, examined the light from distant galaxies gathered by a new 100-inch telescope on Mt. Wilson, California, and announced: The universe is expanding!

Einstein's mathematical equation was correct without the added factor! The relativity equations knew more about the universe than the astronomers. Einstein was quite upset with himself for doubting his mathematical calculations.

Our task in this lesson is to see if we can take all of this information and find a way to describe the expanding universe so that everyone can understand it and believe it is possible.

From *Gravity, the Glue of the Universe.* ©1997 Harry Gilbert and Diana Gilbert Smith. Teacher Ideas Press. (800) 237-6124.

Part 2—A New Solution*

1. Have students compile a list of facts that we know about our universe. The longer this list of known facts is, the better.

2. Ask the students to list direct analogies between the universe and objects. (The universe is like a _____.) Select one of the analogies to explore further.

3. Have the students describe the analogue as completely as they can. (How does it move? What does it do?)

4. Have the students imagine being the analogue (object from step 2). How does it *feel* to be the object? What do things look like from the "eyes" of the object?

5. From the words and phrases listed in steps 3 and 4, have the students pick out "compressed conflicts," words that seem to argue with each other (e.g., empty/crowded; hot/cold). Select the example with the truest ring of conflict.

6. Have the students generate another list of direct analogies that can be used to describe the chosen compressed conflict.

7. Have the students pick one of these analogies to explore further. Have them describe the key features of the chosen analogue.

8. Have the students take this final analogue and list the characteristics that it has in common with our universe.

9. Have the students use the final analogue (or any other analogue from step 6 or pieces from the entire eight-step sequence) to generate a description of our *expanding* universe. The final product should be in written form, but it may include a visual or three-dimensional element.

FOLLOW-UP

Have the students share and discuss their projects with the entire class.

---

*Note: As you guide the students through the following nine steps, keep a record of *all* student answers on a chart, overhead transparency, or chalkboard. Accept all student answers. Have the students keep a written record of the class discussion as well as a record of their own ideas as the lesson proceeds. We recommend that you use the Think-Pair-Share model at each step to encourage divergent thinking and risk taking. Refer to "Sample Synectics Progression" for clarification of the type of responses to anticipate. Most responses should consist of single words or short phrases.

Chapter 6, Lesson Plan # 2

Sample Synectics Progression

STEP 1—FACTS ABOUT THE UNIVERSE

lots of stars	empty space
many galaxies	bright spots
dark	gravity
expanding	enormous

STEP 2—DIRECT ANALOGIES BETWEEN THE UNIVERSE AND OBJECTS

Dalmatian (light and dark spots)	human knowledge
	ocean
balloon	hot-air balloon
computer (complex)	

STEP 3—SELECT ONE OBJECT AND DESCRIBE IT COMPLETELY

Ocean

deep, dark, light patches, many fish, expands and contracts (flooding), salt, sand, hot spots, cold spots, seaweed, changing colors (blue, green, red, brown)

STEP 4—HOW DOES IT FEEL TO BE AN OCEAN?

cold, hot, claustrophobic, empty, crowded, busy, angry, calm

STEP 5—IDENTIFY COMPRESSED CONFLICT LISTED IN STEPS 3 AND 4

empty—crowded	angry—calm
hot—cold	claustrophobic—empty

STEP 6—PICK ONE COMPRESSED CONFLICT AND GENERATE A NEW SET OF ANALOGIES BASED ON THE COMPRESSED CONFLICT

Empty-Crowded

restaurant, subway car, shopping mall, auditorium, highway, stomach, flower bud, airport

From *Gravity, the Glue of the Universe.* ©1997 Harry Gilbert and Diana Gilbert Smith. Teacher Ideas Press. (800) 237-6124.

STEP 7—PICK ONE ANALOGY AND DESCRIBE ITS KEY FEATURES

Subway Car

cold, vacant seats
used to be few cars per train
now longer and longer trains
crowded, squished passengers
hot, explosive tempers of passengers
no one talking, yet noisy

STEP 8—LIST THE CHARACTERISTICS OF YOUR ANALOGUE SIDE BY SIDE WITH CORRESPONDING CHARACTERISTICS OF OUR UNIVERSE.

Subway Car	Universe
cold, desolate, vacant seats	cold, desolate, vacant spaces
longer and longer trains (with more cars) to accommodate ever-increasing population	universe is expanding; mathematical calculations say it must
crowded, squished passengers with explosive tempers	some spots in universe are very crowded, squished molecules, hot, which explode—Red Giant Stars

STEP 9—PICK AN ANALOGY FROM STEP 6 AND USE THIS FINAL ANALOGY TO GENERATE A DESCRIPTION OF THE UNIVERSE

The universe is like a subway car, sometimes empty and sometimes crowded. In the wee hours of the morning, a subway car is empty. All we see are cold, desolate, vacant seats. Most of the universe is just like this—cold, desolate, vacant spaces. In the city, subway trains pull ever-increasing numbers of subway cars to accommodate the ever-increasing population. The number of subway cars is expanding to meet a need. So our universe is expanding because Einstein's General Relativity demands that it must. As the day progresses, the subway car becomes increasingly crowded. At rush hour, people are packed into the subway car so tightly that the car seems to explode open at each station. Similarly, red giant stars explode when they fill with too many elements.

Chapter 6, Lesson Plan # 2

Building Blocks of the Universe

TEACHING MODEL
BSCS Style Laboratory Work (Investigate a Problem)

OBJECTIVES
1. The students will use a spectroscope to inspect and analyze light emitted by selected elements.

2. The students will record color patterns (emission spectra) for each element studied.

3. The students will distinguish the variations in each element's unique emission spectrum.

4. The students will name and define the three principal parts of an atom: electron, proton, and neutron.

5. The students will name and define two elusive particles emitted by an atom: photon and neutrino.

VOCABULARY
1. *Atom*—The smallest part of an element capable of existing alone. The smallest particle you can chop something into.

2. *Elements*—The specific *kinds* of atoms (the names of atoms).

3. *Molecule*—Two or more atoms bound together.

4. *Nucleus*—The central core of all atoms.

5. *Proton*—A particle with a positive electrical charge, found in the center of an atom (nucleus). The number of protons in each particular kind of atom (element) is fixed and does not change. An element's atomic number is a statement of how many protons a particular element has.

6. *Neutron*—A particle with no electrical charge, found at the center of all atoms (except hydrogen). The number of neutrons inside the nucleus of any particular atom is variable. For example: Carbon atoms may contain six, seven, or eight neutrons. However, every carbon atom in the universe contains six protons. Neutrons act as buffers or insulators, preventing the protons from repelling one another. Because hydrogen has only one proton, there is no need for any neutrons.

7. *Electrons*—Particles with a negative electrical charge, found orbiting the nucleus of an atom. If we think of the atom as being like a hard-boiled egg, the electrons are living on the shell. It is important to understand that an atom's electrons "swim" around on the shell, and they may be anywhere on the shell at any given instant. Elements with large numbers of electrons have multiple shells (like layers of an onion). Each shell has a set number of electrons on it. In a stable atom, the number of electrons equals the number of protons. If an atom is agitated, it may lose electrons.

8. *Photon*—An elementary particle emitted by an electron. All light, visible and nonvisible, is comprised of photons. All electromagnetic radiation (particles that make up the electromagnetic spectrum) is made of photons.

9. *Neutrino*—An elementary particle that comes "flying" out of the atom's nucleus when a radioactive atom " bursts." Not all atoms burst and give off neutrinos. Certain elements are unstable. They are prone to decompose spontaneously (e.g., radium, uranium, and plutonium—these unstable atoms are called radioactive elements).

MATERIALS

* Piece of twine, to model the electromagnetic spectrum

* Onion, to model electron layers

* Hard-boiled egg, to model an atom

* Neon gas discharge tube

* Hydrogen gas discharge tube

* Argon gas discharge tube

* Krypton gas discharge tube

* Power supply unit for gas discharge tubes

* Spectroscope for each student (Note: Gas discharge tubes, power supply unit, and spectroscopes are available from Edmund Scientific; see references.)

* Blank drawing paper for each student to draw element "fingerprints" (emission spectra)

* Colored pencils for each student

* Periodic Table of the Elements

* Copy of "Teacher Fact Sheet—Chemical Elements of the Human Body," for teacher reference

PROCEDURE

Part 1—Background*

Today we are going to investigate the building blocks of the universe. Let's begin with a definition. *What is an atom?* An atom is the smallest particle you can chop something into. For example, let's look at a pencil. I start by cutting it in half, and then I continue to cut each piece in half. As I do this, what happens to the pieces? (They get smaller and smaller.) First, I have smaller and smaller pieces of a complete pencil. Then I have pieces of wood and pieces of graphite. Then I have cellulose molecules (which make up wood) and graphite molecules. Finally, if I continue chopping the cellulose, I will end up with a pile of carbon atoms, a pile of oxygen atoms, and a pile of hydrogen atoms. The graphite molecules break down into carbon atoms. These four piles are the original building blocks of a pencil. Notice that we end up with twice as many carbon atoms as other atoms. *(The teacher may wish to diagram this sequence on the chalkboard for student reference.)*

*Note: Have the students take notes while you read this background material.

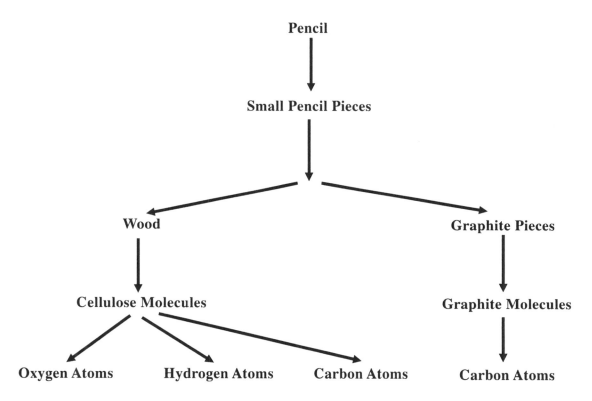

Fig. 6.1. Breaking down a pencil.

I can do the same thing with a grain of salt. I chop that grain of salt into smaller and smaller pieces until what I have is a pile of sodium chloride molecules. Then if I break one of the molecules apart, what I have is one sodium atom and one chlorine atom—the building blocks of a grain of salt. We know these are the building blocks because scientists have performed this experiment many times in the past.

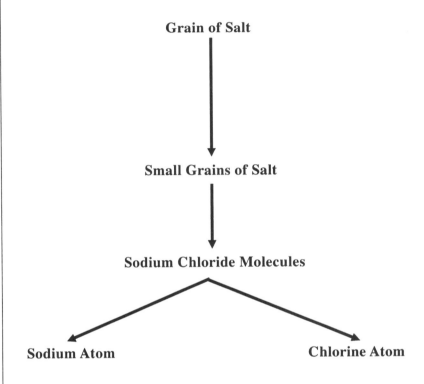

Grain of Salt

Small Grains of Salt

Sodium Chloride Molecules

Sodium Atom   **Chlorine Atom**

Fig. 6.2. Breaking down a grain of salt.

A set of Lego building blocks comes with white blocks, red blocks, blue blocks, yellow blocks, black blocks, and so on. Each colored block is a different size and shape and because of this, each piece fits into a given project in just the correct spot. Using different combinations of colored blocks, I can build almost anything. Think of atoms as being the Legos of the universe.

Scientists have discovered 94 types (colored blocks) of atoms, which comprise everything in our universe when combined in various ways. *(Show the class a Periodic Table of the Elements.)* In fact, scientists have determined that exactly 93 of these 94 elements occur naturally on Earth. One element, Technetium

(#43), is not present naturally on Earth. All 94 elements (types of atoms) are found scattered throughout our universe. Technetium is an unstable element that experiences radioactive decay. It has a half-life that is short enough that if any were present on Earth $4\frac{1}{2}$ billion years ago, it would be all gone by today.

You may have noticed that I have used another word for atom. Who can tell me what word I have used in place of atom? (element) Scientists call these 94 types of atoms, elements. In this case the word *atom* and the word *element* mean the same thing. Each element has its own name, and each element has been given a special number, its atomic number. To understand why each type of atom has been assigned an atomic number, we must take a closer look at an atom.

Part 2—Vocabulary and Fundamental Concepts

1. Pass out a copy of "Student Handout—Dissecting Atoms" to each student.

2. Read the handout together and discuss the concepts as you proceed. Be prepared to show examples of a hard-boiled egg and an onion at the appropriate points in the reading. Also, you may wish to demonstrate a prism splitting a beam of light with a piece of twine as described in the reading. Finally, be prepared to refer to the "Teacher Fact Sheet—Chemical Elements of the Human Body" at the appropriate time.

3. After the reading, restate the key question for investigation: *How do we know that the 93 elements that we have identified on Earth are also found scattered throughout the universe?* Tell the students that they will be doing an experiment where they will view and record the "fingerprints" of several elements.

Part 3—Investigation of Element Fingerprints

1. Give each student a sheet of drawing paper, colored pencils, and a spectroscope.

2. Explain to the students that they will be examining the light emitted by four gas discharge tubes. Each of these tubes contains only one pure element. Each tube is designed so that when the bulb is turned on, the element in the tube becomes very hot or excited. If we look at the light it gives off through a spectroscope, we will be able to see that element's unique "fingerprint," which is its emission spectrum.

From *Gravity, the Glue of the Universe*. ©1997 Harry Gilbert and Diana Gilbert Smith. Teacher Ideas Press. (800) 237-6124.

3. Have the students begin by looking at a beam of sunlight through their spectroscopes. (Do NOT point the spectroscope directly at the sun!) They should see a fingerprint that contains all the colors of the color wheel in order: red, orange, yellow, green, blue, indigo, and violet. Have the students draw the "fingerprint" of sunlight.

4. Put the first gas discharge tube into the power supply unit and have the students view the light emitted with their spectroscopes. The students will probably need assistance at first with how to look through a spectroscope. The spectroscope must be held one to two inches away from the eye. Do not look through the slit at the far end; instead focus the eye into the darkness at the front end inside the tube. The color pattern will appear suspended in the darkness there. Have the students draw the "fingerprint" and label it with the name of the element. Then proceed with the next discharge tube.

   Note: The gas discharge tubes get extremely hot after they have been on for a while. Use caution when removing each one to replace it with another tube!

5. At the end of the lesson, collect the "fingerprint" illustrations. The gas discharge tubes come with a brochure that explains the color bands emitted by each tube. Use this as a guide for marking the student illustrations. You will be able to quickly tell when you look at the students' illustrations if they have used the spectroscope correctly.

FOLLOW UP

1. Have the students write an essay answering the key question from the lesson: *How do we know that the 93 elements that we have identified on Earth are also found throughout the universe?*

2. Have the students use the Synectics Model steps to create their own analogy/model of an atom.

3. Have the students use the method used in chapter 2, lesson #1, "What Is Space?" (the Classroom Meeting or small group discussion model) to create a verbal and visual model of the atom.

Chapter 6, Lesson Plan # 2

Student Handout— *Dissecting Atoms*

Let's take a closer look at an individual atom. Can anyone name the three parts of an atom? (electron, proton, neutron) Traditionally, scientists and teachers have used a "solar system" model to illustrate the parts of an atom. They say the atom has a central core (the nucleus) that we can think of as a planet (Earth). Two types of particles, the neutrons and the protons, live inside this central core (the nucleus). Then this model of an atom describes the third part of an atom (the electron) as orbiting the central core in much the same way that the Moon orbits Earth. The two good things about this model are that everyone knows how and can understand how the Moon orbits Earth. Also, we know that the Moon circles Earth at a great distance. The electrons, too, orbit the central core (nucleus) at a great distance away, relative to their tiny size.

The more scientists learn about atoms and the tiny particles that make them up, the more they realize how insufficient the traditional model truly is. Today, we are going to compare an atom to an egg. This model, too, will be imperfect. I will point out some places where I think it gives a more accurate picture of what we know about atoms. After we discuss the egg model, I will ask you to think about ideas you can come up with for ways to model an atom. Maybe you will be able to come up with an analogy better than the egg.

The proton is a tiny particle found in the center of the atom. This center is called the nucleus. Think of an atom as being a hard-boiled egg. The proton would be the yoke of the egg. The proton has a positive electrical charge.

Different types of atoms have different numbers of protons. Hydrogen, for example, has only 1 proton, and oxygen has 8. Lead has 82 protons. Can you imagine an egg having 82 yolks? It is the different numbers of protons that make one type of atom different from another. The number of protons an atom has never changes, except in some unstable radioactive atoms such as radium and plutonium. The atomic number of an element is the number of protons inside the atom's nucleus.

What do you think happens inside the nucleus of an atom that has more than one proton? The positively charged protons repel one another. This would be a significant problem for the atom if it weren't for another particle that makes its home inside the nucleus—the neutron.

The neutron is a tiny particle the same size and weight as the proton, but it has no electrical charge. The neutrons act as insulators between protons. They keep the protons from getting too close together and repelling one another. There are only just enough neutrons present in a nucleus as are absolutely necessary to keep the protons from repelling one another. Naturally, an atom with more protons (such as lead) will have many more neutrons than an atom with fewer protons (such as oxygen).

The very smallest element, hydrogen, has only one proton. Can you guess how many neutrons hydrogen has? (zero) Because hydrogen has only one proton, there is no need for any neutrons. This makes hydrogen unique. It is the only element in the universe that has no neutrons inside its nucleus.

Let's go back to our egg analogy. We said that the proton was like—what part of the egg? (yolk) What part of the egg do you think is like the neutron? (the white part) Scientists believe that neutrons are distinct particles. Therefore, in our model, the egg white is representative of a cluster of neutrons, not a single neutron. So, if we are imagining a small atom like hydrogen with only one proton, it will have no white part. On the other hand, if we are imagining a large atom such as lead, with 82 protons, there will be quite a bit of white material in the nucleus. How many neutrons do you think would be needed to keep 82 protons from repelling each other? (lead has 125 neutrons)

There are two more atomic particles that are not covered by the traditional "solar system" model of an atom—the neutrino and the photon. Both of these particles are by-products of atomic disintegration. I will once again be using my own analogies to try to give an accurate picture of these elusive and amazing particles.

Our study of the atom continues with an almost unbelievable particle, the neutrino. The neutrino is not present in the nucleus of any atom, but it will come "flying out" of the nucleus of certain atoms when they "burst."

Now, you may wonder how, when an atom "bursts," something that does not exist inside that atom can suddenly come "flying" out of it. You already know of an example of how this can happen. What insect is it that goes through this type of magical transformation as it grows? (a caterpillar growing into a butterfly) Think about it. Doesn't a caterpillar go into a cocoon as a caterpillar and emerge, as the cocoon breaks, as a butterfly? Where does the butterfly come from? The butterfly was not in the cocoon with the caterpillar, yet it emerges from the cocoon as it bursts open. Similarly, the neutrino is not present in the nucleus of the atom, yet it emerges as the atom bursts. If this type of mystery intrigues you, you can go on to study nuclear chemistry and nuclear physics when you go to college.

The third basic part of the atom is the electron. Electrons are tiny particles that orbit the nucleus of an atom. These particles have a negative electrical charge. They are of much lighter weight than protons. (The weight of 1,800 electrons equals the weight of 1 proton.) Using our egg analogy, the electrons are living on the shell. It is important to understand that an atom's electrons are continuously in motion on the shell, and they may be anywhere on the shell at any given instant. Hydrogen, a small atom, has one electron "swimming" on its eggshell. Lead, a large atom, has 82 electrons. All of these electrons could not possibly be "swimming" on one shell. Large atoms have multiple shells (like layers of an onion) on which the electrons can "swim." Each shell holds a preset number of electrons. The number of electrons in a normal atom equals the number of protons. If the atom is agitated, it may lose electrons momentarily. If this is not amazing enough, there are more startling facts to learn about electrons and atoms.

In a normal atom, the number of electrons exactly equals the number of protons. Why do you suppose this is true? Do you remember what I said about the electrical charges of the proton and the electron? Could that have something to do with it? (it does) The positive charges of the protons are attracted to the negative charges of the electrons. What else do we know about that attracts in this manner? (the north and south poles of a magnet) So we can say that it is actually the attraction between the protons and electrons that holds the atom together as a single, complete unit. It follows logically that the natural tendency would be for an atom to have an equal number of protons and electrons.

Think back for a moment to the traditional atomic model I mentioned earlier. In that model, what is between the atomic nucleus and the orbiting electrons? (space) How much space? (an amount comparable to the distance between Earth and the Moon) Can you identify a problem, then, with my egg analogy? (the shell of the egg is right next to the yolk) We will learn later that at a certain point in the life cycle of a star (a white dwarf), gravity actually crushes all the atoms in tightly, forcing them to be much like our egg.

Atoms contain quite a bit of empty space. If we want to create a truer model of an atom, we must imagine the shell being peeled away from the yoke of the hard-boiled egg. Hang this peeled egg magically in the air in the middle of the Astrodome. This is the nucleus of the atom, composed of protons and neutrons. Now imagine that the shell of the egg is reconstructed on the outside wall of the Astrodome. Remember that the shell is where the electrons swim. Remarkably, these mostly empty space atoms are very stable in spite of the very great distance between the negative electrons and the positive nucleus. Hydrogen atoms are so stable that they have been here for 15 billion years without decomposing.

From *Gravity, the Glue of the Universe*. ©1997 Harry Gilbert and Diana Gilbert Smith. Teacher Ideas Press. (800) 237-6124.

This brings us to the second atomic by-product, the photon. Recall the "Nature of Light" handout in chapter 3. Photons are elementary particles that make up all light, visible and nonvisible. This means that all electromagnetic radiation is made up of photons. A light beam is like a piece of twine. It looks solid, but it is really a bundle of different strands. When a beam of light goes through a prism, the prism breaks the light into the individual threads. The difference between a beam of light and a piece of string is that when a beam of light splits up, it breaks into pieces of all different lengths. (each different wavelength of light is a different energy) Gamma rays are very short, whereas AM radio waves are very long. These "strings of light" are made up of millions of tiny particles we call photons. If all light is made up of these tiny particles called photons, where do photons come from?

Most photons in our universe are emitted by excited electrons. The most common way to excite an electron is to heat it. When electrons become very hot they jump around. While they are jumping around, they continuously "sweat" photons. Unbelievably, electrons have an unlimited supply of photons that they can "sweat" when they are hot—unlike you—your sweat is just water, and you do not have an unlimited supply. You don't light up when you sweat, but an electron does.

There are 94 different types of atoms (elements) that occur naturally in our universe. Ninety-three of these are found naturally on Earth. These elements are the sole building blocks of everything in our universe from the farthest star to the pen or pencil you happen to be taking notes with—as well as yourself. Countless billions of each type of element are scattered throughout the universe. However, they are not distributed evenly. Remember, most of the universe is empty space. If we look only at the occupied space of the universe, most of that contains only the two simplest types of atoms, hydrogen and helium. Only about 1 percent of the mass of our entire universe contains the other 92 types of elements. How many of these elements are found inside the human body? (24)

How do we know that the 93 elements that have been identified here on Earth are also found throughout the universe? We know that light is composed of photons. Photons are emitted by excited electrons, and electrons get excited when they become very hot. Scientists have discovered that as the electrons in each different element are heated, they give off a unique "fingerprint" of color. From Earth we are able to examine the light (photons) arriving from all over the universe. This analysis reveals that these 94 elements are truly out there. Today we will be doing an experiment where you will get to view and record the "fingerprints" of several elements.

Chapter 6, Lesson Plan # 2

Teacher Fact Sheet—
Chemical Elements of the Human Body

The human body contains 24 elements:

1. Ninety-nine percent of the human body is made up of the following elements:

hydrogen	calcium
nitrogen	phosphorus
carbon	iron
oxygen	sulfur

2. One percent of the human body is made up of the following elements:

silicon	chlorine
copper	nickel
fluorine	potassium
zinc	tin
magnesium	chromium
selenium	cobalt
sodium	vanadium
iodine	molybdenum

Birth, Death, and Transfiguration

"Gravitation is both the midwife and the undertaker of the universe."

—Kip Thorne (1961)

Are the stars alive, in that we speak of their birth, death, and transfiguration? No, they are not alive in the sense that you and I are. A star is born when its hydrogen atoms become hot enough to light up. It grows old and becomes "fat" with helium. It dies when its nuclear "heart" stops (it dies all the sooner if it was very large at birth). At death, a star is transfigured from a hot ball of gas into:

1. A solid super-dense sphere called a *white dwarf star*, or

2. A solid compact object (much denser and smaller than a white dwarf) sending out beacons of light and radio waves, called a *neutron star*, or

3. An invisible object (smaller than a neutron star) with exceedingly low surface temperature and near-infinite density, called a *black hole*.

Ultimately, a star's fate depends only upon how much "overweight" it is at the time of its death. Gravity plays the decisive role, from the star's spectacular beginning to its end—which can be even more spectacular.

The universe is literally stuffed with stars. Each galaxy contains billions of stars, and there may be as many galaxies in the universe as there are stars in a single galaxy. These stars were not all born at the same time. The first stars to appear in the universe were formed from the gravitational collapse of clouds of hydrogen during the first billion years of the expansion of the universe following the Big Bang. We are now in the 15 billionth year of the expansion. New stars have been forming continuously ever since the early days.

Gravity orchestrates the formation of all stars by converting a cloud of hydrogen atoms into a brilliant white-hot ball of gas. First, the hydrogen atoms in the cloud must be brought close together. Because matter bends space and space tells matter where to go, the bent space around the hydrogen atoms effectively pulls them together and, as the cloud shrinks, energy is released in much the same way that a falling rock on Earth releases energy as it smashes into the ground. This energy heats up the cloud.

As the contraction slowly continues (over a period of about 500,000 years), the surface temperature of the ball of hydrogen atoms will rise to about 5,000 degrees. The star now becomes easily visible, just as any other object at 5,000 degrees

130

would be visible—pouring out copious quantities of photons in all directions. The rapidly agitated atoms at the center push back on the overlying layers and control the contraction. The heat energy from the interior supports the outer portions of the star, preventing them from falling into the central region as they would otherwise do within an hour or two. Gravity becomes exactly counter-balanced, leaving a stable, hot ball of glowing hydrogen gas called a protostar.

How long can this delicate balance last? If nothing else happened to the interior, the new star would slowly radiate away its heat. The core of the star would slowly cool down as its heat energy was passed along to the cooler outer layers (hot objects must give up their heat to nearby cooler objects). Now the balance would be lost and collapse of the star would start up again. This time it would be a disaster—the heat from the interior would be insufficient to counter-balance the gravity of the heavy outer layers. A catastrophic collapse would severely compact the atoms in the core. The protostar now faces a critical mass situation (fig. 7.2, p. 136). If its mass is below the critical value of 8×10^{28} kilograms (8 followed by 28 zeros), it will be still-born. The gravitationally generated heat from collapsing outer layers will be insufficient to "light up" its nuclear furnace in its core. Astronomers suspect our planet Jupiter may be just such a still-born star.

Fortunately, something else does occur in the interior of stars weighing above the critical mass needed for ignition. The collapsing outer layers are massive enough to heat up the core to 10 million degrees. This temperature is just hot enough to start fusing hydrogen into helium. The heat from this nuclear fusion balances the crush of gravity. At this instant, the star is ready to start a long, stable "life" spreading its photons all over the universe and, incidentally, providing generous quantities of energy to any nearby water-covered rocky planet (like Earth). Gravity is responsible for every star in the sky, including one particular second-generation star situated 93 million miles (eight light minutes) from Earth—our Sun. That particular cloud of hydrogen lit up about $4\frac{1}{2}$ billion years ago.

Unlike our Sun, first-generation stars led a rather lonely existence. Their only possible companions were neighboring "twin" stars. All stars in the early universe were born in pristine birth cradles with no trace of dust anywhere. This dust is composed of the chemical elements needed to make rocky planets and comets. Second- and third-generation stars such as our Sun, with its entourage of rocky planets and comets, were all born in dusty cradles. Where the chemical dust was made and how it infiltrates second-generation star cradles will become clear as soon as we examine how all stars grow old and die.

Death must come to each star when it has consumed all of its atomic fuel. It is as though a child at birth were given a fixed lifetime quantity of food. The child could consume the food slowly and live a long time, but when all the food had been eaten, there would be no source of additional nutriment. So it is with the stars. A lifetime supply of hydrogen was "given" to every star in the universe when it first fragmented away from its "parent" cloud of hydrogen. The fragments, protostars, were not all of equal size. Stars in the universe range in mass from 4 percent of the mass of our Sun to more than 100 times the mass of our Sun. The massive "fat" stars burn up their hydrogen much faster than the "lean" stars because their tremendous weight drives up the temperature in their cores, and the high temperature speeds up the rate of conversion of hydrogen into helium.

Table 7.1, page 132, shows the duration of various stages in the life cycle of stars as a function of their mass. Note the remarkably short life span of a star five times more massive than our Sun.

Table 7.1
Time Line for Birth, Life, and Death of Stars

Event	Duration		
	Mass: 0.8 sun	1.0 sun	5.0 suns
BIRTH From contraction of Protostar to start-up of nuclear furnace	500,000 to 1,000,000 years		
LIFE Hydrogen burning phase Red giant phase	20 billion years 3.0 billion years	10 billion years 1.0 billion years	80 million years 20 million years

DEATH
All fuel used up, nuclear furnace shut down
  Cools down as white
    dwarf
  Explodes as supernova
	5.0 billion years
	
	_____
		5.0 billion years
		
		_____
			_____
			
			Seconds

A star the size of our Sun will quietly consume the hydrogen in its central region over a period of several billion years. In due course, however, trouble arises because stars do not have a proper waste "disposal" system. The helium waste product accumulates at the central region (the core) of the star. Eventually, the entire core of the star is depleted of hydrogen. The core is now essentially pure helium. The hydrogen burning must shift away from the core to a thin shell of hydrogen surrounding the core.

This change in the location of the star's source of energy has disastrous consequences for both the star and its planets. Its multibillion-year calm existence as a uniformly bright object comes to an end. The presence of a shell of burning hydrogen closer to the outer layer of gas again upsets the balance between the contraction caused by gravity and the expansion caused by the outflow of heat from the central region. The star is now fated to swell prodigiously as the shell of burning hydrogen creeps outward. All the while, gravity is contracting and heating its central core of "waste" helium. The swelling may continue until the star is 100 times as large as it was during its quiet years.

Imagine the consequences for planets dependent on this star for a steady source of heat. When the ill-fated time arrives for our Sun to swell, it will envelop and vaporize the inner planets, Mercury and Venus. Earth will be located only a few million miles from the surface of the swollen Sun! The intense heat will quickly boil all the water in the oceans, lakes, and rivers. Then there will be a tremendous "meltdown" of the surface soil—the rocks on Earth will last about as long as an ice cream cone in a Turkish bathhouse. This disaster will not happen anytime soon. Our Sun has sufficient hydrogen to maintain its present size for about 5 billion years (according to the best calculations).

Astronomers call these dying swollen stars red giants. On any clear winter night (in the Northern Hemisphere), without the aid of a telescope, you can easily see a red giant star in the constellation Orion. To the naked eye, the star looks like any other, except for a faint reddish coloration.

It is gravity, again, that controls the onset of the next phase of the star's existence. In this critical phase, the red giant star will manufacture the chemical elements that make up more than 90 percent of the composition of the bodies of human beings. The remaining 10 percent is hydrogen, all of which was made during the Big Bang (see appendix F). The manufacturing of the crucial chemical elements begins when the gravity-driven contraction of the helium core drives the temperature of the helium up to 100 million degrees. At this temperature, helium atoms fuse together to form carbon atoms—the most precious atoms in the universe. Without carbon there would be no life as we know it. The helium-to-carbon reaction generates large quantities of heat (nuclear fusion). This heat is sorely needed to restore the balance against gravitational contraction of the star. After most of the helium has been converted to carbon, contraction of the star will begin again. Gravity will drive the temperature of the core up to 500 million degrees, just hot enough to convert carbon into oxygen, along with creating a generous supply of heat. This fusion process repeats itself (making heavier and heavier atoms) until iron atoms are synthesized at 3 billion degrees.

With the arrival of iron on the scene, the red giant has reached its Waterloo. The star cannot ignite the iron because iron is the ultimate "dead" matter in the universe. Iron atoms cannot participate in any nuclear reactions that will generate heat. Iron fusion reactions always absorb heat. The star can ill afford to supply heat energy to its iron atoms. The star has been depending on the atoms in its core to generate the needed energy to support its tremendous weight; now it suddenly finds that its source of energy is gone.

What happens next to the red giant star depends upon its mass. If it has about the same mass as our Sun at the moment of its nuclear reactor shutdown, it will gravitationally collapse down to a sphere about 1/100th of its original size (or 1/10,000th of its red giant size). In a matter of moments, the tenuous red giant will have been converted into a super-compact, white-hot sphere, called a white dwarf. There are thousands of white dwarfs in our galaxy. These dense, shrunken stars will slowly, over a period of thousands of millions of years, cool down to the point where no visible light will radiate out into space. Now they are black dwarfs. Eventually, they will approach the absolute zero temperature—the coldest temperature in the universe.

Luckily for human beings, quite a different fate awaits stars more massive than our Sun when they reach their "iron Waterloo." But there is still a problem. Many of the chemical elements of which our bodies are composed (carbon, nitrogen, oxygen, calcium, phosphorus, sulfur, and iron), plus the elements that compose Earth (silicon, aluminum, magnesium), lie locked in the central portions of red giant stars. How are these precious atoms going to escape from the star? How do they get to where they are needed?

Red giant stars—greater than 1.4 times more massive than our Sun—can spontaneously explode when they arrive at their "iron Waterloo," scattering their chemicals all over space. Astronomers have photographed them exploding and have noted the sudden appearance of an exceedingly bright star in a position of the sky where the previous night there was a very faint star (or no star at all). The new star (called a supernova) may remain visible to the naked eye for many months. The power and magnitude of supernovas are truly frightening. The exploding star can instantly generate more light than 1 billion stars put together. A supernova may generate as much energy in a few weeks as our Sun will radiate in 1 billion years. The aftermath of a supernova that occurred in our galaxy in the year 1054 (the Crab Nebula) is still visible in the night sky through a four-inch-diameter telescope.

What we see with the telescope is a cloud of dust—chemical elements that had been locked inside the star—now scattered over 8.5 trillion miles from the original explosion. We see a vivid picture of how one exploding star delivers the chemical elements to the next generation of stars. (Our Sun is a second- or third-generation star.) New stars are being born every day in our galaxy. In the sword of the constellation Orion there exists a star cradle—a huge cloud of warm hydrogen gas and chemical dust that is a prolific source of new stars.

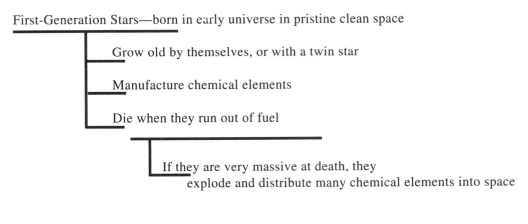

First-Generation Stars—born in early universe in pristine clean space

Grow old by themselves, or with a twin star

Manufacture chemical elements

Die when they run out of fuel

If they are very massive at death, they explode and distribute many chemical elements into space

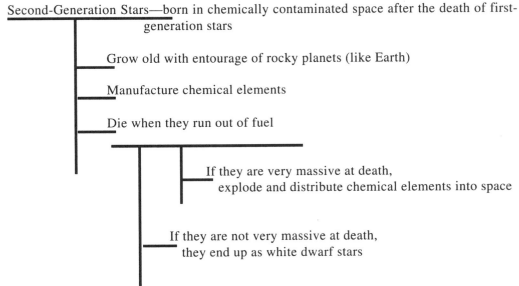

Second-Generation Stars—born in chemically contaminated space after the death of first-generation stars

Grow old with entourage of rocky planets (like Earth)

Manufacture chemical elements

Die when they run out of fuel

If they are very massive at death, explode and distribute chemical elements into space

If they are not very massive at death, they end up as white dwarf stars

Fig. 7.1. Genealogy of star systems containing rocky planets.

Figure 7.1 shows the "genealogy" of star systems that contain rocky planets, such as our solar system.

We should thank the supernova explosions for more than simply delivering the rock-forming and life-forming (see appendix F) chemical elements to the second-generation stars. Every atom of gold and silver that exists in the universe today was formed during the first few moments of supernova explosions, and these explosions are rather rare events in our universe—there have only been eight recorded supernova explosions in our galaxy in the past 2,000 years. Only in the tremendous turmoil and heat of a supernova can elements heavier than iron—like silver and gold—be synthesized. Red giants synthesize large quantities of iron during their last years—how many years they stay in the red giant phase, depends on their mass (see table 7.1, p. 132).

Does that mean that eight stars have been entirely removed from our galaxy by these explosions? Is there nothing left after a supernova? As the outer layers of the star scatter into space, gravity again comes to the fore: The extraordinarily high temperatures of the star's core generate neutrinos, which carry away energy—gravity then forces the core to plunge headlong into a catastrophic collapse.

The fate of the collapsing core depends critically on its mass. If the core is 1.4 to 2 times the mass of the Sun, the plunge to the center has sufficient gravitational force to act as an atom compactor, whereby the electron clouds surrounding each atom are pushed into the nuclear protons, converting them into neutrons. The dying star comes to rest as a strange, extraordinarily dense, compact spinning ball of pure neutrons—called a neutron star. This matter is so dense that one teaspoon of it weighs 50 billion tons. The diameter of the ball will be about 20 kilometers ($12\frac{1}{2}$ miles). Imagine a quantity of matter equal to 1.5 times our Sun (3×10^{30} kilograms, or 495,000 Earths) compressed into a space 20 kilometers in diameter. In 1969, a neutron star was accidentally discovered at the center of the Crab Nebula. Curiously, it was found only because it was projecting a powerful radio signal—not the expected signal—but a signal *blinking* at the incredible rate of 33 times per second—somewhat like a lighthouse beaming light in continuous revolution but millions of times faster. The location of the source of the signal was the clue to its identification with a neutron star. Coming from the center of the remains of a supernova—the Crab Nebula—meant the source had to be the "corpse" of a dead star. It was soon realized that its mass and speed of rotation matched the expected characteristics of a neutron star. These strange stars were originally called pulsars before anyone knew they were composed of pure neutrons.

The fast spinning was not surprising to the astronomers because as a star shrinks in size, it must increase its rate of rotation. The appearance of radio beams did astonish everyone, and scientists are still searching for a plausible explanation. Since the initial discovery in 1969, many more neutron stars have been detected. There may be several hundred million of them in our galaxy. All have the characteristic radio beacons. All are spinning rapidly (up to hundreds of revolutions per second), and all are slowing down gradually. Ultimately, each will stop spinning, will stop sending out radiation, and will cool down to near absolute zero temperature.

Einstein's equations dictate quite a different fate for dying stars if the mass of their core is greater than about two times the mass of our Sun. For these heavy stars, there is absolutely no way to prevent gravity from pushing the core past the neutron stage all the way into an infinitesimally small spot at their center. At this spot, called a *singularity*, "all the laws of nature break down." (Wheeler 1996)

The genesis of objects with singularities at their centers, now called black holes, goes back to 1916. A few months after Albert Einstein published his General Relativity equations, a German astronomer, Karl Schwarzschild, discovered an act solution to the equations. In mathematical language, this solution to the relativity equations describes the structure of space outside a perfectly spherical, collapsed star. Nobody realized the potent content of Schwarzschild's exact solution until 1939, when J. Robert Oppenheimer and H. Snyder (Oppenheimer's student at the University of California, Berkeley) took a closer look at Schwarzschild's work. Oppenheimer and Snyder found that a dying star (a star that has used up all of its nuclear fuel and contains a residual core mass greater than about two times the mass of our Sun) must rapidly—in less than one second—collapse *through* its gravitational radius, a strange invisible trapdoor-like boundary, leaving an unimaginable object.

The critical masses controlling the life cycle of all stars are shown in figure 7.2, page 136.

In summary, gravity dictates the fate of all stars at the moment they have consumed all of their fuel:

1. Sun-sized stars become white dwarfs.

2. Stars with residual cores 1.4 to 2 times more massive than our Sun become neutron stars.

3. Stars with residual cores more than 2 times more massive than our Sun collapse into singularities generating black holes.

In the next chapter, we will discover the consequences for a star that collapses through its gravitational radius.

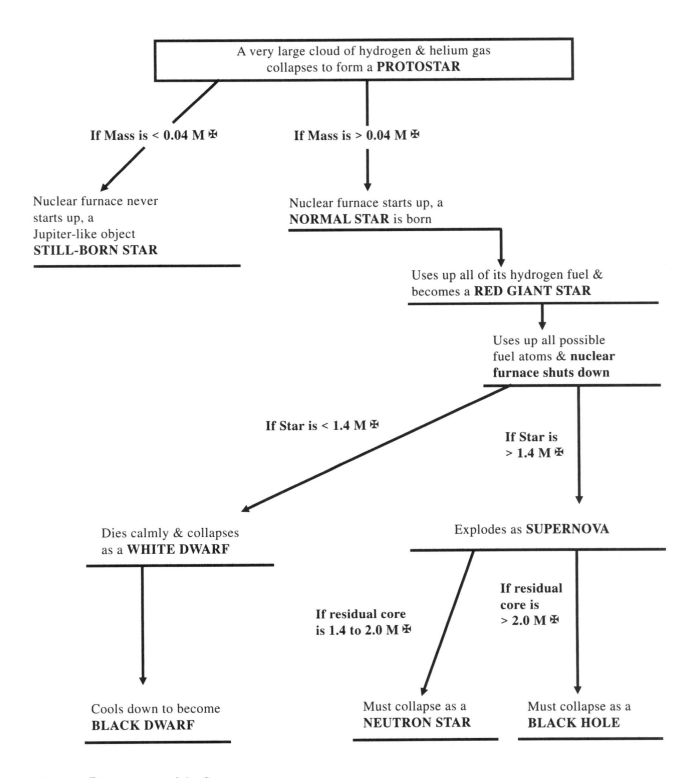

Note: M ✠ is the mass of the Sun.

Fig. 7.2. Critical masses in the life cycles of stars.

Chapter 7, Lesson Plan # 1

The Life Cycle of a Star

TEACHING MODEL
Teacher-Enacted Role-Play

OBJECTIVES
1. The students will recite in proper sequence the phases in the life cycle of a star.

2. The students will paraphrase the distinguishing features of each phase in the life cycle of a star.

VOCABULARY*
1. *Protostar*—A cloud of hydrogen and helium gas at least 0.04 times the mass of our Sun. Protostars do not produce any of their own light.

2. *Star*—A tightly packed ball of mostly hydrogen gas and some helium gas with a nuclear furnace that produces a huge amount of heat and light.

3. *Still-born star*—A sphere of collapsing hydrogen whose interior is not quite hot enough to start a nuclear reaction.

4. *Red giant*—A star that has burned all of its hydrogen into helium and is now burning the helium to produce carbon and other elements.

5. *White dwarf*—The leftover iron core of a star. The star's nuclear furnace is now shut down, but the iron core continues to glow and emit light as the star slowly cools.

6. *Black dwarf*—A white dwarf star that is cold and dark.

7. *Supernova*—An exploding star.

---

*Note: Do not give the students the definitions of these words before the role-play demonstration. This set of definitions is to be used for review and testing only. More complete definitions of all of these words are given in the script of the role-play for this lesson.

8. *Neutron star*—A very small, hot, spinning ball of neutrons that was once a star. As it spins, it appears to pulse radio waves on and off with extreme regularity. When they were first discovered, they were sometimes called pulsars.

9. *Black hole*—A star that has imploded, or collapsed in upon itself.

10. *Singularity*—A pinpoint of space that contains all the mass of a collapsed star—a region of space wherein scientists have no idea what is happening.

MATERIALS

* Copy of "Student Handout—Star Vocabulary" for each student

* Copy of "Student Handout—The Life Cycle of a Star" (blank) for each student

* Copy of "Teacher Key—The Life Cycle of a Star"

* Copy of "Role-Play Script—The Life Cycle of a Star" for teacher and performer reference

* Costumes and props for the dramatic enactment (see the script for suggestions)

PROCEDURE

Introduction to the Role-Play

Are stars alive in that we can speak of their birth, growth, and death? No, stars are not alive in the sense that you and I are alive. Stars are born in the sense that an entirely new, different object is formed out of a collection of swirling atoms. A star is born when its hydrogen atoms become hot enough to "ignite." A star dies when its nuclear heart (the nuclear furnace inside the star) stops functioning.

Today I am going to enact for you the life cycle of a star. If you watch my presentation closely, you will find the true answer to our opening question. I do not want you to take notes during my presentation. We will go over the information for notes at a later time. For now, I want you to just watch and listen. I will give you some key words you can listen for. See how many of these words you can hear in my story. *(Pass out a copy of "Student Handout— Star Vocabulary" to each student. Do not include any definitions of the words at this time.)*

Role-Play—The Life Cycle of a Star

Perform the role-play. For those teachers who are not comfortable performing in front of the class, there are several options. You can give this script to an older student (not in your class), and ask that student to come to your class as a guest performer. You can ask one of your highly creative and outgoing students to perform the story. You can form a committee of selected students to practice and perform the play for the class as extra credit. You can divide your class into groups and have the class do the role-play. You can have a group of selected students create a puppet show from the script, where the puppets are the star phases. The variations are endless. Feel free to try several different options until you find one that works for you and for your students.

Role-Play Follow-Up

1. Ask the students the following question: How many of you heard all of the vocabulary words as they were used in the presentation? Tell the students that they will now get a chance to take notes about the ideas presented in the presentation. Pass out a copy of "Student Handout—The Life Cycle of a Star" (blank) to each student.

2. Draw a chart on the chalkboard or overhead projector that shows the nine phases in the life cycle of a star (refer to "Teacher Key—The Life Cycle of a Star"). Have each student copy the chart.

3. After the students have completed step 2, review the words on the star vocabulary sheet. Have the students fill in definitions for each word. You may wish to refer to the narrative text as well as to the script of the role-play demonstration and to the vocabulary section of the lesson plan for elaboration of definitions. Encourage the students to ask clarifying questions.

4. Conduct the following Review of What Was Learned. As you ask the review questions, have the students add brief notes about the various phases in the life cycle of a star to their life cycle charts.

From *Gravity, the Glue of the Universe*. ©1997 Harry Gilbert and Diana Gilbert Smith. Teacher Ideas Press. (800) 237-6124.

Key Questions for Review of What Was Learned

1. *What are the nine different names scientists give to stars as the stars progress through their life cycles?* (protostar, star, still-born star, red giant, white dwarf, black dwarf, supernova, black hole, neutron star)

2. *What factors determine which path a star will take as it comes to the various crossroads in its life cycle?* (When a protostar separates from the parent cloud of hydrogen, it is at its first crossroad. It will either become a still-born star or a regular star, depending on its mass. When a star becomes a red giant, it is at its second crossroad; the deciding factor is the star's original size when its nuclear furnace first ignited. When a star has exploded into a supernova and is at its third crossroad, the deciding factor is the size of the core that remains after the explosion.)

3. *Which have the longest lives, stars that are small at birth or stars that are large at birth?* (Smaller stars live longer. The larger a star is at birth, the faster it will burn through its fuel. Also, larger stars tend to come to more violent deaths.)

Assessment

Provide the students with another blank chart of the life cycle of a star and have them complete the chart as a quiz.

From *Gravity, the Glue of the Universe.* ©1997 Harry Gilbert and Diana Gilbert Smith. Teacher Ideas Press. (800) 237-6124.

Chapter 7, Lesson Plan # 1

Student Handout— Star Vocabulary

Vocabulary List—Listen for these words in the role-play:

1. protostar

2. star

3. still-born star

4. red giant

5. white dwarf

6. black dwarf

7. supernova

8. neutron star

9. black hole

10. singularity

From *Gravity, the Glue of the Universe.* ©1997 Harry Gilbert and Diana Gilbert Smith. Teacher Ideas Press. (800) 237-6124.

Chapter 7, Lesson Plan # 1

Teacher Key—
The Life Cycle of a Star

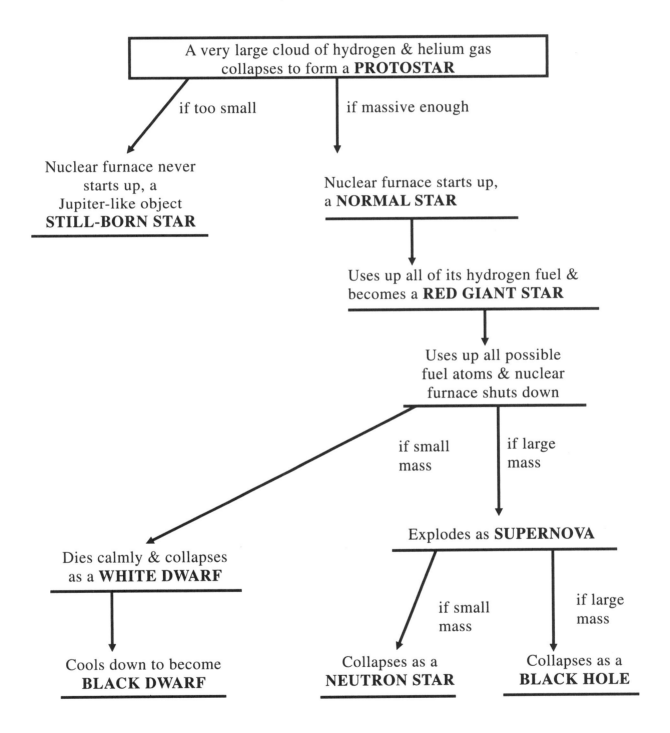

A very large cloud of hydrogen & helium gas collapses to form a **PROTOSTAR**

if too small

if massive enough

Nuclear furnace never starts up, a Jupiter-like object **STILL-BORN STAR**

Nuclear furnace starts up, a **NORMAL STAR**

Uses up all of its hydrogen fuel & becomes a **RED GIANT STAR**

Uses up all possible fuel atoms & nuclear furnace shuts down

if small mass

if large mass

Dies calmly & collapses as a **WHITE DWARF**

Explodes as **SUPERNOVA**

if small mass

if large mass

Cools down to become **BLACK DWARF**

Collapses as a **NEUTRON STAR**

Collapses as a **BLACK HOLE**

Chapter 7, Lesson Plan # 1

Student Handout—
The Life Cycle of a Star

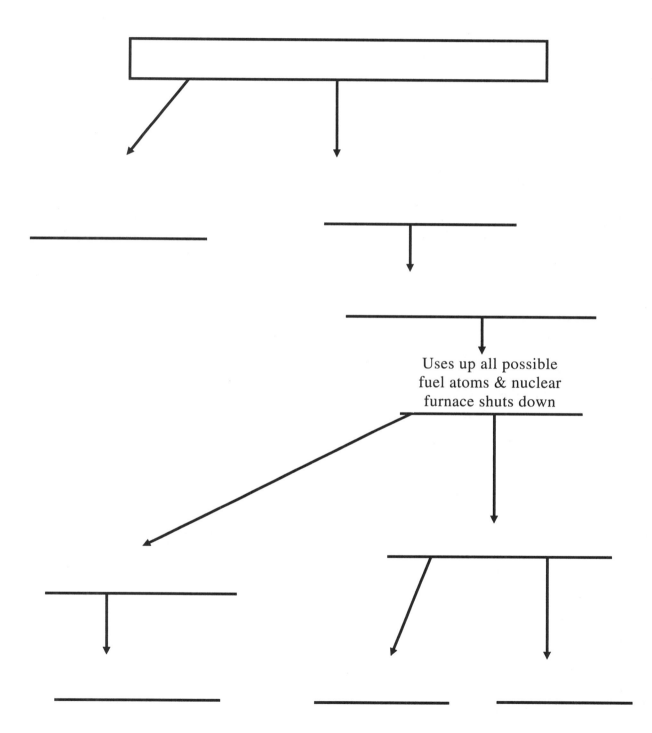

Uses up all possible
fuel atoms & nuclear
furnace shuts down

Chapter 7, Lesson Plan # 1

Role-Play Script— The Life Cycle of a Star

APPROXIMATE PERFORMANCE TIME
20 to 30 minutes.

PROPS AND COSTUME IDEAS
The most important factors for consideration in costume selection are color and ease of transition. A layered outfit is suggested, so that all you need to do is pull off layers as you go. All manner of hats, scarves, gloves, sweaters, and jackets (in different colors) are helpful. The base layer should be black (e.g., black slacks and a black turtleneck or T-shirt) because interstellar space is black, and all stars end up black in the end. A large, red umbrella on the front table works well for the red giant phase as well as providing a backstage area for costume changes. A lit sparkler works well for the supernova phase. If you use a sparkler, be sure to have on hand matches and a jar of water to put the sparkler in to extinguish. Explain to student holding sparkler to hold it pointed away, at arm's length from their body, as well as away from other students. Only the teacher should light the sparkler.

THE SCRIPT

Phase 1—The Protostar
(Costume colors: Yellow, red, and green over a black base.)

I am a protostar. I am a cloud of swirling hydrogen and helium gases. I am a dark spot in the midst of light colors. The dark is from all of the swirling dust. I am not producing any light of my own. I glow slightly because nearby stars heat up the outer layer of my dust.

I am in the process of collapsing into smaller and smaller space. Gravity is pulling my dust and gases in tighter and tighter. Imagine collapsing a jet plane until it is as small as a grain of salt. I shrink from 1 trillion miles in circumference down to just 50 million miles in circumference. It gets hotter and hotter inside of me as all of my matter is crunched down into a smaller and smaller space.

I live like this for about 500,000 years.

To become a real star, gravity must make me hot enough as I shrink to ignite a nuclear furnace in my core. If I am not a large enough cloud of gas and dust to begin with, I will never become hot enough, and I will end up much like Jupiter, a still-born star.

But I am a lucky protostar. I have become hot enough. My nuclear furnace has ignited, converting hydrogen atoms into helium atoms.

Phase 2—The Star
(Costume colors: Yellow and blue over a black base.)

I am a star. I am very bright and very hot. I have a nuclear furnace in my core that is fusing hydrogen atoms together to make helium atoms. This is what generates my heat and my light. The outward pressure of the fusion energy is perfectly balanced by the constant inward pressure of gravity. This perfect balance makes me very stable. My color depends on the temperature of my furnace. If I am red, my furnace is cool, as far as nuclear furnaces go. If I am blue, my nuclear furnace is extremely hot! Yellow and white are hotter than red but cooler than blue, and white is hotter than yellow.

How long I will live in this stage of my life depends entirely on how big I am when my furnace ignites. If I am the size of your Sun, I will be a star for 10 billion years. If I am $\frac{1}{2}$ the size of your Sun, I will be a star for 100 billion years. If I am 3 times the size of your Sun, I will live only 250 million years. In other words, don't feel sad if you are the smallest one in your class. If you were a star, you would know that the smallest stars live the longest lives! Smaller stars burn at a lower temperature than the big stars; hence, they consume their fuel much more slowly.

Phase 3—The Red Giant
(Costume color: Red.)

I am a red giant now. I am a much older star, perhaps 100 billion years old. As I have aged, I have burned all of my hydrogen into helium. When I first ran out of hydrogen to burn, my nuclear furnace stopped burning. Then gravity acted quickly and squeezed in on my core of helium, making it much smaller and hotter again, until finally the helium became hot enough to ignite the furnace once again. Now the helium is burning and forming carbon. The heat from this new fire makes my outer core burn, and I begin to expand. When your star, the Sun, becomes a red giant, it will swallow Mercury and

Venus. The surface of Earth will become so hot that the oceans will boil away and the rocks making up the crust of Earth will melt. My diameter has increased 100 times, and I am 1,000 times brighter than I was in my younger days.

My insides are filling up with all of the new elements I am making in my nuclear furnace. In fact, I am making elements #3 through #26. Element #26 is iron. I cannot get the iron to heat up enough to make element #27. I will live like this for millions of years. What happens next depends upon how big I was when I first became a star. If I have about the same amount of mass as your Sun, I will become a white dwarf.

Phase 4—The White Dwarf
(Costume color: White.)

I am a white dwarf. I am nothing but a hot ball with an iron core. Iron is unusual in that in a nuclear furnace, it will not give off heat; it only absorbs heat. As my core fills with iron, my furnace cools down and shuts off. Now I am in trouble because gravity pushes in from my outer edges, and I collapse down to a sphere 1/100th of my original size (or 1/10,000th of my red giant size). In a matter of moments, I am transformed from a red giant into a super-compact, white-hot sphere about the size of your planet Earth. Gravity's hold on me is extremely strong now. If you weigh 100 pounds on Earth, you would weigh 100 million pounds on a white dwarf like me. In other words, you'd be squashed as flat as a pancake!

I continue like this, an extremely hot, glowing ball with an iron core, for billions of years as I slowly cool down. Eventually I will become one of the coldest things in the universe—approaching a temperature of absolute zero.

Phase 5—The Black Dwarf
(Costume color: Black.)

Now I am a black dwarf. I am actually a cold, dark white dwarf. My temperature is extremely cold. It approaches absolute zero. I am a bit like a solid iron planet traveling through the galaxy. I still have the pleasure of the company of those planets that orbited me when I was a star (that is, except for those planets I swallowed when I was a red giant). Of course there is no life on any of these planets, because I am no longer giving off any light and warmth to support life. But gravity insists that they orbit me forever. I have the same amount of gravity that I had in my younger days. I have lost size, not mass. I will be like this forever. I am truly a dead star.

Phase 6—The Supernova

(Costume colors: Black with sparkles.)

Remember that, back in the good old days when I was a red giant, I mentioned that what I became next depended upon my original size as a star? Well, let's go back to that point and take a look at the second possibility. If I began my nuclear furnace as a star with a mass at least 1.4 times larger than your Sun, then when I have produced all of the iron I possibly can, my furnace again shuts off, and I begin to cool. But this time I have so much mass, and it collapses so fast, that I explode *catastrophically*! I am now a supernova. *(Light sparkler here.)*

The initial explosion lasts only a few seconds. During this explosion, every element beyond iron in the Periodic Table (#27 through #94) is made in just a few seconds! Wow!

The explosion blows away a good portion of my mass. In fact, it blows the surrounding dust and gas and other particles trillions of miles out into space! This is how all of the elements that I made in my nuclear furnace earlier in my life (and the new ones that were formed during the few seconds it took me to explode) get scattered around the universe.

The power and magnitude of my explosion are truly frightening. I generate more light than 1 billion stars. I might generate as much energy in a few weeks as your Sun will generate in 1 billion years! The visible light from my explosion may last up to 6 months. This is because all of the matter in and around me has become so hot.

All gold, silver, and rare metals you find on your planet Earth were made during a supernova explosion.

How often do supernovas occur? Scientists estimate that in other galaxies they may occur two or three times every 100 years. In our galaxy there have been eight recorded supernovas in the past 2,000 years. That comes out to about one every 150 years. If, after my supernova phase, I have enough mass left to equal more than two times the current mass of your Sun, then I become a black hole.

Phase 7—The Black Hole

(Costume color: Black.)

Immediately following the catastrophic explosion that marked the beginning of my supernova stage, gravity grabbed my remaining mass and pushed it down into a tiny pinpoint called a singularity. I am now a black hole.

I am the greatest mystery in the universe! I am completely invisible. I am as black as empty space. I am undetectable. You will never see me, even if you were to shine the most powerful light in the universe on me.

I have an insatiable appetite! If you come close to me, I will pull you into my singularity, the pinpoint at my center that holds all of my mass. You will like it there because at my singularity you do not have to follow any of the rules of the universe—because they all break down there! The one thing you will not like is that once I have you, you will not be strong enough to escape!

Phase 8—The Neutron Star
(Costume colors: White over a black base.)

If the matter left after my supernova explosion is not more than two times the mass of the Sun, I collapse into a neutron star.

I am a very small, hot ball of neutrons. I am spinning extremely quickly. All of my matter has been squeezed down into an area 10 miles in diameter. If you were to weigh one teaspoon of my matter, it would weigh 50 billion tons. I have tremendous surface gravity. I give off tremendous heat. I am spinning tremendously fast (about 33 revolutions per second).

I am sending out radio and light waves in beams. From where you are they appear to pulse or blink. I am not actually blinking on and off. It is my spinning beams, like a lighthouse, that cause me to appear to blink. I will continue to send out these radio and light beams as I spin until I have completely cooled down, and then I become a cold, black ball of neutrons.

This is the end of the story of the life cycle of a star.

CHAPTER

8 The Point of No Return

"The undiscover'd country from whose bourn
no traveler returns . . ."

—William Shakespeare (1600)

A black hole is truly an unimaginable conception. Most amazing is that Einstein's New Law of Gravity equations predicted, in 1915, the existence of black holes. Scientists believe that black holes have actually been identified in our galaxy and at the heart of distant galaxies.

Twenty-four years after Einstein's original publication, J. Robert Oppenheimer found General Relativity demanded the existence of black holes. The theory states that when massive stars burn up the last of their fuel, gravitational instability will relentlessly push the star into a catastrophic collapse—beyond the white dwarf size, beyond the neutron star size, and transform it into a singularity of near-infinite density, a region where the laws of nature break down.

Imagine that NASA has launched a space probe equipped with television cameras to a distant star (with a mass three times that of our Sun) in its death throes. The star has converted most of its interior atoms into iron and is about to explode as a supernova. The space probe arrives just in time to watch the star explode and to observe the gravitational collapse of the core that will immediately follow if the mass remaining after the explosion is at least twice the mass of our Sun (assume that the probe will be unaffected by the supernova explosion). The probe sees the collapsing core of the exploded star as a brilliantly white object rapidly shrinking in size and fading into a dull red sphere. Unaccountably, the shrinking stops and the probe views it as if in the freeze-frame mode on a VCR (videocassette recorder).

General Relativity says that nobody can ever see the formation of a black hole. Anyone watching the catastrophic collapse of a star will always see it "freeze frame" at the moment it is about to become a black hole—though the star continues gravitationally collapsing and transforming into a black hole. To learn more about black holes, we must turn to the General Relativity equations.

Einstein's New Law of Gravity tells us that the space occupied by a dead star whose mass is three times the mass of our Sun will measure 35.4 miles (57 kilometers) in circumference after its catastrophic collapse (the freeway that circles Washington, DC, has a larger circumference). The mass of the core is equal to three times that of our Sun. Our Sun has a mass equal to 330,000 Earths (3 x 330,000 = 990,000 Earths). We know that the mass of Earth is contained inside a space whose circumference is 25,000 miles (40,000 kilometers). In other words, the mass of 990,000 Earths will collapse into a point that scientists call a singularity, a region of space with near-infinite curvature (which means we have no idea what is happening there). We do know that the entire mass of the collapsed star resides at this singularity. Here time does not only slow down, *it comes to an end!* But according to Einstein, time is inexorably linked to space—thus, at the singularity not only time but also space ceases to exist. (Thorne 1994) Is this scenario possible? Relativity teaches that this is not only possible, but unavoidable.

We are left with a curious object containing a vast amount of crushed matter. Professor Wheeler coined the term *black hole* in 1967 in a lecture at the American Association for the Advancement of Science. It is a hole in the sense that whatever falls onto it, falls into it, and will keep on falling straight toward the center (the singularity), like falling into quicksand (the quicksand being gravitation). It is black because the gravitational field surrounding a black hole is so strong that neither light nor heat has sufficient energy to escape. A space probe could not possibly see an isolated black hole because none of its sensing devices would pick up a signal (we can, however, detect black holes that are not isolated). Just prior to the star's headlong collapse, it existed as a bright, hot sphere; seconds later it was transformed into what must be the most unimaginable object in the universe:

* Its boundary is colder than anything in the universe.

* It is blacker than anything imaginable—it neither radiates nor reflects light.

* Its entire mass is concentrated in the singularity at its center.

We can easily see objects every day that transmit no light of their own, by simply shining a light on them. A black hole is truly black—it absorbs every photon of light that crosses its boundary. In the utter blackness of space, such an object will remain invisible to an observer. You can see a piece of black coal because the coal reflects some of the light back to your eyes. The intense gravitational field surrounding a black hole will "swallow" any light shined directly on its forbidden boundary.

A black hole cannot be touched or sensed in any way. A black hole's boundary is as intangible and invisible as the imaginary plate glass door that a mime establishes onstage. Unlike the mime's door, however, this boundary of a black hole (a bourn surrounding the dead star) is very real. Its position in space can be very accurately calculated. The temperature of the boundary is close to the lowest possible attainable temperature in the universe (absolute zero), yet the many tons of matter that collapsed to generate this surface were millions of degrees hot.

The most incredible attribute of the boundary of a black hole is its ability to make time stand still (strong gravity slows down clocks—see chapter 5). If you could observe a clock approaching a black hole, you would be astonished to witness time being stretched out. As the clock moved closer and closer to the forbidden boundary, the passage of time, as recorded by the clock, would appear to come to a halt (that is, if you could *see* the clock). If you traveled with the clock to the boundary, but were very careful *not to cross over it*, time would stop, for both you and the clock! If the clock were illuminated by the most powerful light one could imagine, you still would not be able to see it. The light reflected back from the clock to your eyes would spend so much of its energy trying to escape from the gravitational field of the black hole that your eyes would tell you there is nothing before you but total and complete darkness. A sort of "cosmic censorship" forbids anyone from seeing this strange boundary. One could see the clock only if one waited an infinite time for the infinitely redshifted photons to reach your eyes.

This boundary, the black hole's "surface," is known variously as:

1. *The Gravitational Radius:* Einstein's relativity says that every object has a definite size—a gravitational radius—below which it must be crushed in order to force all of its atoms into a singularity of near-infinite density at its center. The gravitational field surrounding the crushed object is so powerful that nothing could ever escape. The gravitational radius of Earth is 0.9 centimeters (0.35 inch), which means, if you could crush

Earth down to a ball measuring less than 0.9 centimeters radius, Earth would immediately turn into a black hole. (See appendix G for details on how to calculate the gravitational radius of any object, including yourself.)

2. *The Event Horizon:* Any event that happens at or below this "surface" can never be known to anyone outside the black hole. No signal of any kind can possibly reach an observer on the outside.

3. *The Point of No Return:* Anyone passing through this boundary—it is very easy to move through it—can never return—even if all the energy of the universe were available.

Call it what you will, the boundary of a black hole is a place to avoid if, like Hamlet, you lack the resolve to visit an "undiscovered country from whose bourn no traveler returns." Once you pass through the gravitational radius of a dead star, you have forever cut yourself off from the rest of the universe. If the black hole is very large, you may not be instantly killed, but you would be gradually crushed by gravity as you continue your journey, like Alice in Wonderland, down, down, down to the curious singularity where time itself comes to an end. Once begun, there is no way of reversing this fall. How long it takes you to reach the singularity depends on the mass of the black hole. If you are lucky enough to fall into a very old black hole that has already sucked in great quantities of matter from its surroundings (making it billions of times more massive than the original star), your fall will last a few hours. However, I doubt that you will be able to do much sightseeing on this trip. During your entire fall, gravity will be pulling on your head and your feet while pressing your body flat as a pancake. If you are unlucky enough to fall through the boundary of a "fresh" star corpse, you will have little time to think about anything. Here, your free-fall time from the point of no return to the singularity has been calculated to be 0.000006 second. (Shipman 1976)

Consider what might have happened to the twin in chapter 3 who went on a 14-year space trip

if his rocket ship had encountered and fallen into a black hole. It would have been a sad ending. He would have been swallowed and destroyed by the black hole, without so much as a by-your-leave. The most sophisticated radar equipment would have been useless to the pilot of the rocket ship. The radar signal would have disappeared into the black hole instead of bounding directly back. The pilot would have felt the tug of the strong gravity near the boundary but by the time he sensed the danger, the rocket ship would have crossed the point of no return. Future space travelers will have to accept disclaimers stating: "The management of this rocket ship cannot be responsible for the loss of life of those aboard due to being swallowed by a black hole."

Nobody knows how many dead stars entombed in black holes are lurking out there in space, but "no one who accepts General Relativity has found any way to escape the prediction that black holes must exist in our galaxy." (Misner, Thorne, and Wheeler 1973) Professor Wheeler estimates that there may be as many as 10 million black holes in our galaxy.

Does this pose a danger to us on Earth? Earth itself is a spaceship of sorts, guided by the Sun. Earth is carrying us around the Sun along a path determined by the curvature of space in the vicinity of the Sun. Note, however, that the Sun is not standing still—it is sailing through space at 136.4 miles (229 kilometers) per second. The Sun has already made 22½ trips around the disc of our galaxy during the 4.5 billion years that have elapsed since its hydrogen atoms ignited. This means that Earth has so far traveled around the galaxy 22½ times without disappearing into a black hole.

What might happen on our next trip around the galaxy? An Earth encounter with a black hole is rather unlikely, according to calculations made by astrophysicists at the California Institute of Technology. They estimate that the nearest black hole in our galaxy is about 15 light-years away from Earth, leaving our path in the galaxy quite clear and free from these catastrophically collapsed stars. There is somewhat disconcerting news, however, for the future: Scientists estimate that new black holes are forming in our galaxy at the rate of about one every five years. Millions of years from now, our path may not be as clear as it is today.

The skeptic might insist that, though General Relativity *demands* the existence of black holes, their true existence is purely speculation. It is not an easy matter to find a black hole. After all, the only way to detect an isolated black hole would be to probe its gravitational field—that is, by tracking a moving object's changing path as it approaches a black hole. However, this presumes that one already knows the location of the black hole. Thus, it is quite hopeless to search for isolated black holes.

What about a black hole that is not isolated? If one star of a pair of stars (and there are many so-called twin stars, or double stars—two stars orbiting a common center) were to die and collapse into its gravitational radius, we would have a good chance of finding the collapsed star. We could find it by the light (X-rays) it would generate as it quietly consumed its companion star. The black hole would pull gas away from its companion star, and this gas would form a disc surrounding the black hole. The gas would be pulled closer and closer to the boundary of the black hole, become exceedingly hot and wildly chaotic: Swarming gas atoms would be emitting sporadic bursts of powerful X-rays.

When looking for black holes, astronomers search the sky for mysterious X-rays coming from a pair of stars in which one of the pair is seen in ordinary light and the other is seen only by its sporadic emission of X-rays. This is a plausible way to look for a black hole, except in one detail: X-rays cannot easily penetrate the ozone layer at the top of our atmosphere (see table 2.2, p. 38). To see X-rays from outer space, we must send an X-ray telescope up in a satellite orbiting high above our atmosphere.

In 1970, a joint NASA/Italian rocket put an X-ray telescope into orbit. In 1973, R. Giacconi announced that the first black hole had been detected! It was named Cygnus X-1, after the constellation Cygnus, the Northern Cross, where it was found. Its companion star is 12 times more massive than our Sun and can easily be observed by a moderately powerful telescope. Cygnus X-1 is estimated to be about six times more massive than the Sun, yet it emits no visible light. It does emit sporadic bursts of powerful X-rays. All known properties of Cygnus X-1 fit the predicted properties of a black hole orbiting close to a "live" star.

The search for black holes was now on in earnest. In 1975 at Princeton University, John N. Bahcall detected bursts of X-rays coming from a black hole in our galaxy with a mass of 1,000 suns! In 1994, the new, improved Hubble Space Telescope found a black hole at the center of a distant galaxy (called M87) that has a mass of approximately 2 to 3 billion suns—a mass equivalent to about 3 percent of the mass of all stars in our galaxy! Russian scientists are looking for black holes with their *Kosmos 428* satellite. The Netherlands, with their ANS satellite, is currently looking for bursts of X-rays that could be coming from black holes "eating" companion stars.

If large black holes that have a mass of 3 billion suns exist, what is the *least* amount of matter that a black hole could contain? Answering this question took the brilliant, young British physicist Stephen Hawking down a path to a startling paradox. It was in 1970 that Hawking speculated about the possible existence of black holes no larger than a single atom. Hawking picked up a suggestion by Professor Charles Misner concerning the turmoil that might have existed shortly after the Big Bang explosion. In this turmoil, Hawking deduced, there might have been many highly compressed regions of space—compressed enough, in fact, to form miniature black holes. Hawking calculated that these primordial black holes might be no larger than a proton (an atom of hydrogen without its electron). Each of these miniature black holes would contain about 2 trillion pounds of matter (this is the equivalent of about 23 trainloads of coal—if each train reached from New York to San Francisco).

It would require fantastic quantities of energy to compress 2 trillion pounds of matter into the space occupied by an atomic particle. However, there was an overabundance of energy at the time of the Big Bang. The greatest explosion in the history of the universe had just occurred.

During the Big Bang every ounce of matter-energy that is present in every star (living or dead) in every galaxy in the universe today burst out of a condition of near-infinite density and near-infinite temperature. It was in this chaos, Hawking suggested, that countless miniature black holes could easily have formed.

If such things had originated at the birth of the universe, where would they be now? They might be orbiting our Sun. A miniature black hole would be just like a dead-star black hole in that it would have the ability to pull in anything that fell through its event horizon, including another black hole—two black holes can merge into one.

Hawking's paradox had its origin in the curious mathematical calculation that indicated to him that when two black holes merge, the resulting new event horizon has a *greater* area than the sum of the horizons around the original two black holes. He knew very well that if you combine two spheres into one, the resulting new sphere has an area that is *less* than the sum of the areas of the original two spheres. Hawking wondered why the merged black holes should be *larger* than the combined area of the original two black holes. He wondered whether this enlargement of the event horizon might be related to an increase in disorder. He knew that the disorder of the atoms and molecules in any object is related to its temperature.

In 1972, Jacob D. Beckenstein of Princeton University made a quite serious suggestion that black holes ought to have a measurable temperature. Beckenstein said that a black hole should radiate photons just like any other object that is warmer than its surroundings, which means that it should give off light and heat—which means that something is escaping from a black hole, from which *nothing* is supposed to be able to escape.

Put yourself in Stephen Hawking's place: You respect Beckenstein, so you must take his reasoning seriously. Yet, you know very well that black holes cannot radiate photons or anything else, because nothing can escape the event horizon. Here is your choice: You can decide to struggle with this paradox, or give up on the whole business of science altogether—which you may be sorely tempted to do because your doctors have told you that you have an incurable progressive disease (Lou Gehrig's disease). It is the year 1973. You are already confined to a wheelchair. What would you do? Hawking decided that he did not need the rest of his body to do physics—his brain was still working—so he continued to do theoretical physics.

Hawking struggled with the black hole paradox for two years. Then a solution occurred to him: Maybe forbidden particles could escape from black holes the very same way that forbidden particles escape from the center of an atom—even though they lack the energy to escape. The mechanism used by the particles to get out of the atom originates from quantum mechanics and is well known to physicists. Hawking showed how forbidden particles could use the quantum mechanism to escape from a black hole. He discovered that the number of particles capable of escaping depends only on the mass of the black hole—the more massive the hole, the more difficult it is for a particle to escape. The rate at which particles escape is a measure of the temperature of the black hole. Massive black holes, such as those from dead stars, have exceedingly low surface temperatures. Low-mass black holes, such as Hawking's miniature black holes, are exceedingly hot. The surface temperature depends solely upon the total amount of matter within the event horizon.

The calculated temperature of the surface of a typical dead-star black hole is indeed low, so low, in fact, that this object must be the coldest thing in the universe. Its temperature is only a fraction of a degree above absolute zero ($-273°C$). One of Hawking's miniature black holes contains only a fraction of the mass of a dead-star black hole. The miniature black hole's surface temperature must be about 120 billion degrees, hotter than the interior of the hottest stars in the universe. The heat pouring out from a single atomic-sized black hole is equivalent to the continuous release of energy from six nuclear power plants. As this tremendous outpouring of energy continues, the mass of the miniature black hole steadily decreases and the temperature steadily increases. In the end, there must be a powerful explosion. Hawking calculated that this explosion could equal the violence of 10 million hydrogen bombs! Not just miniature black holes, but all black holes will eventually explode. However, dead-star black holes contain so much mass, they will not arrive at their explosion point until thousands of billions of years from now.

No one has yet detected one of Hawking's miniature black holes. Hawking believes we should be looking for exploding atomic-sized black holes. A black hole exploding in empty space would not be easy to detect from Earth. There would be no bright flash of visible light. Just prior to the explosion, the miniature black hole will be 100,000 trillion degrees hot. Instead of ordinary light, very high-energy photons (gamma rays) will be released in abundance. Land-based optical telescopes would be useless because gamma rays, like X-rays, cannot penetrate the ozone in our atmosphere (see table 2.2, p. 38). To detect the existence of Hawking's black holes one needs gamma ray-sensitive telescopes above the atmosphere. We now do have such a telescope in orbit. NASA's Compton Gamma Ray Observatory can easily detect gamma rays in outer space.

What if one of these atomic-sized black holes exploded near the surface of Earth? The extent of the devastation would depend upon just how close to the ground the explosion occurred (recall what happened to Hiroshima when *one* "small" atom bomb exploded about $\frac{1}{2}$ mile above that city). If the black hole exploded several miles above the ground in an uninhabited area, the result might look something like Tunguska: On June 30, 1908, at Tunguska in the Yenisei Valley in Siberia, there was a tremendous explosion. The curious thing about this explosion was that nobody knew what had exploded. Trees were blasted to the ground and the forest erupted into flames. Luckily, the Yenisei Valley was very sparsely inhabited. Many months passed before an investigative team arrived at the site. At first they thought a meteorite had impacted the forest, but no crater and no meteorite fragments were found. Later calculations revealed that the force of the explosion must have been equal to 50 million tons of TNT. (A large meteorite striking Earth could easily cause an explosion equaling 10,000 million hydrogen bombs. Just such a meteorite is speculated to have wiped out the dinosaurs.) Some astronomers now speculate that a fragment of Encke's Comet struck Tunguska. However, if you like wild speculation, consider that it could have been a Hawking atomic-sized black hole that exploded high over Tunguska.

We may never know what destroyed Tunguska, but scientists now think they know what may destroy our universe. In the next chapter we will examine the fate of the universe, as dictated by Albert Einstein's New Law of Gravity.

Chapter 8, Lesson Plan # 1

A Mysterious Encounter

TEACHING MODEL
Inquiry Training

OBJECTIVES

1. The students will observe/imagine a puzzling scientific situation.

2. The students will ask questions to verify the facts about the puzzling scientific situation.

3. The students will design test questions, test hypotheses, and test experiments to gather more data and further their understanding.

4. The students will examine their data and formulate a conclusion about the puzzling scientific situation.

5. The students will evaluate their discovery process.

VOCABULARY*

1. *Gravitational radius*—Einstein's relativity says that every object has a size, a gravitational radius, below which it must be crushed to force all of its atoms into a singularity of infinite density at its center. The gravitational field surrounding the crushed object is so powerful that nothing can ever leave the object. The gravitational radius of Earth is 0.9 centimeters (0.35 inch), which means that if you could crush Earth down to a ball measuring less than 0.9 centimeters radius, Earth would immediately turn into a black hole.

2. *Event horizon*—Any event that happens at or below the "surface" of the black hole (the gravitational radius) can never be known to anyone outside the black hole. No signal of any kind could reach an observer on the outside. The event horizon expands as the mass of a black hole grows.

---

*Note: Do not give these vocabulary words to the students before the lesson. Use them only in part 5, when you reveal the truth about black holes, and to review what was learned as a conclusion to the lesson. These three vocabulary terms are different names for the same phenomenon—the black hole's "surface," or boundary.

3. *The point of no return*—Anyone or anything passing this boundary (the gravitational radius) on the way into a black hole can never get back out, even using all the energy in the universe. It is very easy to pass through this boundary.

MATERIALS

* Copy of "Student Handout—Planning and Data Collection" for each student

* Copy of "Teacher Fact Sheet—Black Holes" (to be used by the teacher)

PROCEDURE

Introduction

Today you are going to experience a truly puzzling scientific event. It will be your job to gather facts about the event, to verify that what you saw is what actually happened, to design tests to gather more information about the event, and to come to a scientific conclusion about the puzzling event.

I am going to give you some guidelines and some clues to help you in your task. *(Pass out "Student Handout—Planning and Data Collection." The guidelines for how to proceed are noted at the top of the handout. Have a student read the rules to the class.)*

Everyone must follow these steps as we proceed. Are there any questions at this time about the steps?

You will be working in a group (or with a partner). You will have the greatest success if you encourage everyone in your group to talk and to share ideas. Do not let any one person do all of the thinking and all of the talking. This handout is designed to help keep you focused on the task at hand. Follow it carefully. If I respond that a question cannot be answered, stop and examine the question. Did you ask a "yes-or-no" question? How can you reword your question? It is possible that I could not answer it because I do not know the answer. Do not let this stop you. Find a different question to ask that may get an answer. You may present to me a situation of your creation and questions about the situation if it is related to obtaining information about this puzzling event. Finally, take another look at rule 8 on your handout: Do not focus on *naming* the event. Focus on learning as much as you can about the events and the objects involved.

(Divide the students into groups of at least two students each. Have them fill out the top part of the handout.)

Part 1—Presentation of the Puzzling Event

Imagine that you are a scientist working for NASA. You and your team have traveled for many years to reach a red giant star that you expect will soon go into a supernova explosion. You are using newly developed technology that will protect your ship from being destroyed in the explosion. If you succeed, you will be the first humans to witness and study a supernova explosion as it happens. Not only will you be famous but also rich when you return to Earth. The pictures you take of the explosion will sell for large amounts of money.

You arrive at the star, and you can see that it is definitely on the verge of exploding. The star has converted most of its interior atoms into iron. Gravity is preparing to close in on the star. You expect that, as it does, the star will heat up and explode in a brilliant burst of light. Your team readies its cameras and other scientific equipment.

Just as you predicted, the supernova explosion occurs, and you manage to take some pictures. Then something unexpected happens. From the window of your spaceship you see a very bright object at the center of the explosion rapidly shrinking in size. Before you get a chance to shout, "Hey, look at that thing in the middle!" the object suddenly reddens and the shrinking apparently stops. As you watch, the light coming from the reddish object is slowly getting dimmer. (This reminds you of turning off a light with a dimmer switch.) For quite some time before the light goes out completely, the reddish object at the center of the explosion seems to hang frozen in space. (It looks as though you had been watching a movie and someone paused the videotape.)

Part 2—Verify the Facts

1. Your job, as a team, is to ask me "yes-or-no" questions about this puzzling event. In this first round, try to focus your questions on the task of clarifying what you have just witnessed. *Plan* your questions. Keep track of all questions, including questions from other teams, and questions that I cannot answer. This will help you develop other questions and also develop a plan for further investigation at the end of the lesson. *(Allow the students time to plan their questions.)*

2. *Take clarifying questions from the groups. Do not answer any questions that are not in a "yes-or-no" format. Use "Teacher Fact Sheet—Black Holes" for reference. You can also use information taken directly from the narrative text. Do not hesitate to say that you cannot answer a particular question.*

From *Gravity, the Glue of the Universe.* ©1997 Harry Gilbert and Diana Gilbert Smith. Teacher Ideas Press. (800) 237-6124.

If the students jump ahead into asking questions that change variables or propose new conditions, encourage them to hold these questions until everyone is clear about what they have just witnessed. Remind the students that they need to ask questions about

- *the objects involved,*

- *the events involved,*

- *the conditions of the events, and*

- *the properties of the objects.*

Part 3—Testing Ideas

1. We should pause in our questioning here to regroup and plan some different types of questions. Go back to your planning sheets. Look at the answers you received. What conclusions, if any, can you draw at this time? What types of information do you need before proceeding? What strategies would help your team gather more data about this puzzling event? Once you decide on a plan, formulate "yes-or-no" questions. For example, if your team wants to launch a space probe to investigate, describe your probe and its functions to me as completely as you can. Then ask me "yes-or-no" questions about what happens during the probe's launch and exploration. To receive accurate information, make your questions as specific as possible. Keep track of all questions. *(Allow the students time to plan strategies and questions.)*

2. *Take clarifying questions from the groups. Remind the students that they should be keeping track of the answers not only to their own team's questions, but also to questions from other teams.*

Part 4—Conclusions and Explanations

Now it is time for you and your team to take a closer look at the information you have gathered. What conclusions can you draw about what is going on outside your spaceship? What evidence did you gather to support your conclusions? Write down your conclusions. *(Allow the groups time to examine their data and to reach conclusions. Encourage the students to be open to alternative viewpoints. When all of the groups have reached conclusions and have written down their ideas, have the groups share ideas with the entire class.)*

Part 5—The Truth About Black Holes

Now I am going to share with you the truth about what you saw from your spaceship window. You may have already correctly deduced some of the facts that I am about to reveal. Other facts are so utterly amazing that you may not believe me, but they are true. *(Share the information about black holes from the Vocabulary section and "Teacher Fact Sheet—Black Holes." As you do so, address the conclusions drawn by each group. Praise those groups that were able to reach sound conclusions and ferret out good details and facts about black holes. Help those groups that became sidetracked understand where they went awry: Which questions led them down the wrong path? Where and why did they hit dead ends? You may wish to give the students copies of "Teacher Fact Sheet—Black Holes" at the end of the lesson.)*

Part 6—The Final Step

Take a final look at "Student Handout—Planning and Data Collection." As a group, answer the four questions in Part 4—Evaluation of Mission. *(Allow the groups time to answer the questions. Discuss the answers as a class. These four questions are the key questions of the lesson. The students' answers will reveal if they gained some understanding of the scientific inquiry process through the activity in this lesson. You may wish to encourage your top students to pursue further research on black holes. Also, you may wish to share information on miniature black holes from the narrative text.)*

Review of What Was Learned

1. How big is a black hole? *(A black hole formed from a star whose mass was three times the mass of our Sun will measure 35.4 miles, or 57 kilometers, in circumference.)*

2. Describe the role of gravity in forming and sustaining a black hole. *(It is gravity that crushes the core of the star until it is smaller than its gravitational radius. At this point the dead star has a tremendous amount of gravity for an object its size. Remember, it still has most of its original mass, minus the mass that blew away during the supernova explosion.)*

3. Identify the surface temperature of a black hole. *(Its boundary is the coldest possible temperature in the universe, approaching absolute zero.)*

4. Describe the characteristics of the event horizon of a black hole. *(A black hole's surface is as intangible and invisible as the imaginary plate glass door that a mime establishes on a stage. Yet, unlike the mime's door, this surface is very real. The event horizon lets all objects slip through effortlessly. Nothing can escape, including light, radio waves, heat, and sound. Anything that happens at or below this boundary cannot be observed by someone outside the boundary. The event horizon expands as the black hole absorbs more mass.)*

5. What is the relationship between time and a black hole? *(Time stands still at the surface of a black hole because strong gravity makes clocks run more slowly. If you could observe a clock approaching a black hole, you would be astonished to see time being stretched out. As the clock moves closer and closer to the forbidden boundary, the passage of time, as recorded by the clock, would appear to you to go more and more slowly until it comes to a stop—that is, if you could see the clock.)*

6. Define the event horizon, gravitational radius, and the point of no return. (See Vocabulary.)

7. Explain how we can locate black holes next to companion stars. *(The black hole will pull gas away from its companion star. This gas will form a disc surrounding the black hole. As the gas comes closer and closer to the point of no return, it will become exceedingly hot and emit sporadic bursts of powerful X-rays. All you have to do is to look for mysterious X-rays coming from a pair of stars where one of the pair is seen in ordinary light and the other is seen only by sporadic bursts of X-rays.)*

Assessment/Homework

* Use the questions in Review of What Was Learned as a quiz.

* Collect and evaluate "Student Handout—Planning and Data Collection."

Chapter 8, Lesson Plan # 1

Teacher Fact Sheet— Black Holes

Note: Refer to the narrative text for elaboration of all the following facts.

1. The star that exploded had a mass three times the mass of our Sun (or the mass of 990,000 Earths).

    Note: These are *not the minimum* requirements for the formation of a black hole. These data apply to the specific event in this lesson.

2. The circumference of the event horizon of this black hole is 35.4 miles.

3. The temperature at the event horizon is the coldest possible temperature in the universe, approaching absolute zero.

4. A space probe could not see the black hole because none of its sensing devices would pick up a signal.

5. You cannot see the black hole by shining a light on it, even an extremely bright light, because the object will absorb every photon of light that hits it. Some of the light shined toward the black hole may scatter about as it comes close to it. This light is not visible because there is nothing there for the light to reflect on. The object will swallow all light that crosses the event horizon.

6. A clock placed at the event horizon would stop (the clock could not be seen).

7. Any object that crosses the event horizon can never return.

8. The event horizon will expand outward if the black hole absorbs extra mass.

9. A person would be crushed to zero volume at the heart (singularity) of a black hole.

10. The pilot of a spaceship entering a black hole would have no indication on the instrument panel that the ship was crossing the event horizon.

11. An observer watching a probe or spaceship approach a black hole will see an illusion. Although the probe crosses the event horizon and continues its journey into the black hole, the observer will see the probe or spaceship "freeze" in space the moment it reaches the event horizon. To the observer the image will gradually fade out like an old picture.

12. Black holes have been located by finding stars that are slowly being consumed by companion black holes. These black holes were once companion stars. The black holes will be emitting sporadic bursts of X-rays.

13. Between the singularity at the heart of a black hole and the event horizon there is nothing except empty space.

14. Gravity around black holes is stronger than anywhere else in the universe.

15. A black hole will form from any object that is crushed down to its gravitational radius.

16. Gravity will crush a dead star into a black hole if it is at least two times more massive than our Sun (our Sun will never become a black hole).

17. At the very center of the black hole (the singularity), all of the known rules of the universe break down and no longer exist.

18. (Note: This fact involves quantum mechanics and may be too complex for an introductory lesson on black holes.) It may *not* be entirely true that *nothing* ever comes back out of a black hole. Recently, "Hawking Radiation" has been proposed. These are subatomic particles that can, using a quantum mechanism, escape from a black hole, even though, paradoxically, they do not have enough energy to escape.

Chapter 8, Lesson Plan # 1

Student Handout— Planning and Data Collection

Date: _____

Team Members:

_____

_____

_____

_____

RULES

1. All questions must be "yes-or-no" questions.

2. Follow all steps on this planning sheet (do not skip steps).

3. Decide as a group what questions you would like to ask and write them down.

4. Record the answers to your questions.

5. Record answers and important facts gathered by listening to other groups' questions.

6. Form and record your conclusions based on the answers to your questions.

7. Keep track of unanswered questions.

8. Do not focus on naming the event. Focus on learning as much as you can about the event and the objects involved.

PART 1—DATA GATHERING—VERIFICATION

Verify the facts you already "know" (are you certain that what you witnessed is what actually happened?). Identify all objects involved. Be certain you know exactly what happened, and when it happened. Be sure that you are clear (and in agreement with your group members) about the events.

"Yes-or-No" Questions We Will Ask:

Questions About Events:

Questions About Objects:

Information from Other Groups' Questions:

Summaries and Conclusions:

PART 2—DATA GATHERING—EXPERIMENTATION

Develop experiments that might give you more information. Change selected conditions to see if you might get different results.

Experiments We'd Like to Try:

"Yes-or-No" Questions We Will Ask About Our Experiments:

Answers and Information from Other Groups' Questions and Experiments:

PART 3—FINAL EXPLANATIONS

Examine all data collected and formulate your conclusions about what has happened outside your spaceship. List all of the evidence that supports your conclusions. Be specific.

Conclusions: Evidence:

PART 4—EVALUATION OF MISSION

1. Which questions revealed the most information to your team?

2. Which questions were pivotal questions (questions whose answers forced a change in your thinking)?

3. Which questions were left unanswered?

4. How might you use the unanswered questions to further investigate this phenomenon?

CHAPTER

The Ultimate Fate

> "All [universes] arise from space, and into space, they return: space is indeed their beginning and their end."
>
> —The Chandogya Upanishad (800 B.C.)

> "Can we picture to ourselves a . . . universe which is finite, yet unbounded? The usual answer is 'no,' but that is not the right answer."
>
> —Albert Einstein (1921)

> "I'll take back the universe"—an apt paraphrase of General Relativity's prediction of the collapse of a finite, yet unbounded universe.
>
> —the Authors (1995)

Stars are born, grow old, and die in other words, they are mortal. That was the stark message of the preceding two chapters. The fate of each of the billions of stars in every galaxy is sealed: white dwarf, neutron star, or black hole—there are no other choices. Does this imply that the fate of the universe itself is sealed?

It is said that in ancient times in Greece, the people would climb Mt. Parnassus to ask the Oracle difficult questions. If the Oracle were still there, we might ask: What is the ultimate fate of our universe? Will every star grow cold as the galaxies expand away from each other *forever*? Will the expansion of the universe inexorably slow until it stops, and then reverse, leaving the universe to collapse upon itself? Cannot the very same gravity that caused the stars to light up, that caused the synthesis of the carbon atoms that made our life possible, cause the universe to be reborn in another expansion? The answer to each question: Look to Einstein's General Relativity, and then examine the curvature of your space.

With bated breath we turn to Einstein's equations. In precise mathematical terms they tell us: The ultimate fate of your universe depends upon whether it contains sufficient mass-energy to curve up the geometry of space into closure. Simply stated, if the average density of matter in the universe is *below* the critical value, which calculates out to about three atoms per cubic meter of

166

space, the universe is open (infinite). In an open universe, the infinite number of galaxies will continue to move away from each other forever.

The picture is quite different if the average density of matter is *above* the critical value. If you could uniformly spread out all the atoms in all the stars in all the galaxies throughout all of space and find that you had more than three atoms per cubic meter of space, then the universe must be closed (finite). Einstein's equations dictate that a closed universe can expand only up to a fixed maximum value.

The total quantity of matter (and nothing else) uniquely specifies the maximum volume attainable by our expanding universe. Why? Because Einstein's Relativity is based on the postulate that the curvature of space is determined only by matter. It follows that the curvature of the universe must be shaped by the quantity of matter in the universe and by nothing else. If you find yourself asking what determined how much matter there would be in the universe, the answer is: You are asking an impossible question, scientifically! Science cannot explain *why* the universe is the way it is.

Scientists can discover the laws of nature ("nothing can travel faster than light," or "matter curves space"), but science cannot explain why photons travel at exactly 186,000 miles per second and not some other speed. Scientists cannot explain why there is just so much matter in the universe and not 1,000 times more or 1,000 times less. Scientists do know that all of the mass-energy in the universe today was present in the universe when space and time began about 15 billion years ago and will be present in the universe until space and time come to an end.

The miracle of Einstein's equations is their ability to describe how the universe works. The equations tell us that the maximum radius of the universe is determined only by the quantity of matter floating in space. If the universe is finite, gravity will collapse it back to the same exceedingly dense state from which it emerged a split second after time-zero (15 billion years ago). It is not known what happened at time-zero because, as Professor Misner puts it, "There is a curtain drawn over space-time at a fraction of a second from time-zero." (Yourgrau 1977) A new Law of Gravity must be discovered before we can remove that curtain. We must wait for another Einstein to draw that curtain aside. (Penrose 1989)

If indeed the universe is fated to collapse, could it ever reappear again? The universe appeared once, so perhaps it could reappear again. The expand/collapse scenario attains only if the average density of the universe is sufficient to impose closure on space. How can we visualize closed space? To understand the shape of space, imagine a journey within it: Get into a spaceship and tell the pilot to travel straight ahead at 99.99999 percent of the speed of light. If the space in our universe is closed, at the end of our trip we will be right back where we started. Closure means that we are living in a galaxy that is, in a sense, floating on the surface of a sphere. This should be a comforting feeling for all of us. We have been living on the surface of a sphere (Earth) all of our lives! This may seem startling and incomprehensible, but where is it written that the space in which our galaxy exists *must* be open and infinite?

Return to the year 1492. A native of Cogoletto, Italy, is conversing with the Queen of Spain. They are discussing the merits of an old Greek idea that Earth might be spherical rather than flat. Because there are no records of the actual conversation, we can only imagine:

Isabella:

Everyone says Earth is flat. You have only to look around to see for yourself. Look out over the Mediterranean. It is as flat as the floor on which you are standing. If Earth were round as a ball, we should be able to see that it has a spherical shape. What a startling and incomprehensible idea, that Earth might be shaped like a ball!

Columbus:

Earth *appears* flat to us because we see only a small portion of it at one time. You must travel great distances to become aware of its spherical shape. Earth is indeed a much larger ball than you ever imagined! If you could travel in the same direction long enough, you would find yourself *back at your starting place.*

Isabella:

I have never heard anyone tell of having such an experience.

Columbus:

Must Earth be *flat* because nobody has yet ventured so far as to find that it indeed has a spherical shape?

Now let us come back to the present. Let us talk about the *space* in which our galaxy exists rather than the *surface* on which we exist. Must the space in which our galaxy exists be open and infinite merely because nobody has ventured far enough to prove it to be curved around on itself like the surface of a sphere? Einstein's gravity equations *allow* space to be closed—to be curved around on itself. Closed space is finite, yet unbounded space. It is not difficult to imagine a closed, finite, unbounded *surface*. We all take for granted that the surface of Earth is exactly that. Why could not our galaxy be, in a sense, floating on the surface of spherical space—and be constrained to move along such a surface?

There are no boundaries in a closed universe. There is no place to leave or enter. There is no center. There is no special position for any one galaxy. The view from one galaxy is much the same as the view from any other galaxy in the universe.

The Oracle on Mt. Parnassus gave us only two choices when he referred us to Einstein's equations:

1. If space is open, the universe will expand forever. Open space is *infinite* space. The galaxies will recede from each other until each is absolutely alone. Alone and cold—all of the stars in all of the galaxies will be dark and cold. There will be only one universe, without a "second chance."

2. If space is closed, the universe is riding on a round-trip ticket. The expansion of space will proceed until it reaches the maximum size allowed by General Relativity. At that instant, gravity will transform the expansion into a collapse. The universe must collapse to a singularity, just like the singularity at the center of every black hole. Here, as in all singularities, space and time are obliterated. What might happen after this is pure speculation.

Some scientists (Roger Penrose, for one) claim that we will have no real understanding of any beginning or end or rebirth of the universe until a new theory, which combines General Relativity with Quantum Theory, is developed. Penrose points out that the collapsed universe singularity will be totally chaotic, quite unlike the Big Bang singularity, which, he claims, was as opposite from chaotic as you can get. Other scientists (John A. Wheeler, for one) speculate that a new universe might emerge from the collapsed universe singularity, but it might not resemble our universe in any way.

If John Wheeler is right, the "reprocessed" universe may be even less like the universe we know than a redwood tree is like a dandelion. Our universe is absolutely unique. Never before was there a universe like ours, and never again will there be another one like it. Perhaps there will never again be stars of just the right temperatures and lifetimes to synthesize the chemical elements out of which we are made. There may be an infinite number of Big Bangs, but the chance of there being another universe exactly like ours is vanishingly small. Just as all identity of an object is lost as it falls through the event horizon of a black hole, so all identity of this universe would be lost as gravitation crushes it down to infinite density and infinite temperature. The reprocessing would be total and complete. No one knows *what* might emerge from another Big Bang.

Which is it, open space or closed space? Albert Einstein opted for closed space. He felt closed space was both necessary and appropriate. (See appendix H for details on why Einstein opted for a closed universe.) Some scientists agree with Einstein because closed space simplifies the mathematical analysis of an expanding universe. Others disagree with Einstein, citing current estimates that the average density of matter throughout space is insufficient for closure of the universe. Professors Misner, Thorne, and Wheeler call it "the mystery of the missing matter." They call it "the third cycle of doubt [of Einstein's Relativity] . . . with the final decision yet to come." They remind us that "the first and second doubts ended with dramatic vindication of Einstein." (Misner, Thorne, and Wheeler 1973)

The first doubt came in 1915 when astronomers told Einstein the universe is not expanding. This contention held until 1929, when the astronomer Edwin P. Hubble announced that the universe is expanding. The second doubt arose in 1940 when measurements of the distance of receding galaxies led to an impossibly short duration for the expansion of the universe. In 1958, an error was discovered in the distance measurements, and Einstein was again proven correct.

Will scientists find the "missing matter" and vindicate Einstein's belief in a closed universe? A trend, at least, is clear: Every year astronomers discover more matter in the universe. Calculations in 1979 indicated that there must be huge concentrations of unseen dark matter in some galaxies to account for the stability of the known paths of the stars. In 1980, scientists Margaret J. Geller and John P. Huchra, at the Harvard-Smithsonian Center for Astrophysics, announced that the density of the universe may be "only just short of the critical value needed to close the universe"—based on their measurements of the rate our galaxy is moving in relation to other galaxies in our cluster of galaxies. In 1989, Professor Lawrence Krauss of Case Western Reserve University said that there are powerful and persuasive theoretical arguments implying that the universe may contain perhaps 100 times as much matter as we can see.

We have seen how gravitation shows Earth its path around the Sun, and the Sun its path around the galaxy. Will gravity now show the universe its path to a new beginning? Some one of us, whose very atoms were forged in gravitationally collapsing stars, may find the answer. Then all of us will gain a better understanding of this strange and wonderful place in which we live. To paraphrase Rabbi Tarfon: *It is not up to us to finish this task, yet neither are we free to abandon the search.* (Pagels 1983)

Epilogue

Our story began with Aristotle's "Earth things" falling toward the center of Earth, trying to find their natural resting place. It ended with the possibility of all the galaxies with their suns and planets, white dwarf stars, neutron stars, and black holes gravitationally collapsing toward a singularity in a closed Einstein universe.

We have seen our notion of gravity evolve from

Aristotle's—
A natural attraction of Earth for all objects on Earth

to

Newton's—
A mysterious attraction of all objects in the universe to each other

to

Einstein's—
A curious interaction between space and an object situated in that space.

We followed Albert Einstein as he picked up the clue—the equivalence of inertial mass and gravitational mass—and developed his astonishing relativity equations that tell us how the universe works.

Again and again we found that gravitation is the "power behind the throne"—from the first lighting up of the stars to the possible final collapse of the entire universe, if there is sufficient mass to rein in the current expansion.

The curtain falls, but the drama has not ended. The ultimate fate of the universe—expand forever or collapse back to a singularity—is not yet resolved.

A Concluding Note to Teachers

In confronting the exact nature and identity of the universe, we find ourselves to be like Christopher Columbus. We are sitting on the edge of an ocean of space wondering what we might find when we venture out there.

The allure of this large unknown has drawn science fiction writers for hundreds of years. Today's students are well versed in modern-day stories about what might be found beyond the boundaries of our solar system. Yet it is vitally important to expose students to the mystery, wonder, and uncertainty of *science*.

As scientists and science teachers we have been drawn in by the exciting possibility of being the first person to solve a great mystery. So how do we best proceed with the task of instilling this wonder and hope in our students? We must build and enforce two levels of trust. First, our students must come to know and to trust the process of scientific inquiry. Then they must learn to trust themselves. They must trust all of the questions that come to their minds, and they must trust their own abilities to find answers where others have failed.

Each group of students is unique. As individuals they bring to a science class their own set of ideas, concepts, and values about the question-asking and answer-finding processes of science. In field testing, my students requested a two-day wrap-up session. During these classes I answered lingering questions. I suggest that you share chapter 9 of the text with the students. Use the conflicting ideas about a closed or an infinite universe to start a Classroom Meeting-type discussion. My students always seem most comfortable asking questions within the context of a discussion class.

Appendix I contains questions that my students raised throughout the unit. Some of these questions were easily answered, but others gave me an opportunity to encourage students to research current science magazines and books.

SUGGESTED FOLLOW-UP ACTIVITIES

The following four projects are each designed to provide an end-of-unit summary activity, one for each of the four unit goals:

1. Have students write an essay tracing the history of and changes in scientific thought that have led to our current understanding of gravity.

2. Have students write an essay explaining how popular attitudes toward science, scientists, and new ideas have affected the lives of scientists.

3. Have students write a report on the multitude and variety of scientific techniques used from Aristotle to Stephen Hawking. The focus of the report should be on explaining and evaluating the various methods of inquiry.

4. Have students write an essay exploring and evaluating the consequences for our society and culture if we accept Einstein's theories of Special and General Relativity.

Following is a list of suggested follow-up units in science, math, literature, writing, and history.

Science

* Magnets and magnetism

* Using a moving magnetic field to generate an electric current (alternators and generators)

* Electricity

* Newton's Laws of Motion and Law of Universal Gravitation

* Astronomy

* Space travel

* Light

* Sound

* The physics of radio and TV communication

* Chemistry—the nature of the elements

* Biology—conditions that support life

* Electromagnetic spectrum

* Electric fields

* Radio telescopes

Math

* Algebra (Newton's Laws can serve as an introduction)

* Statistics/Data analysis—how to collect a statistical sample and how to analyze and evaluate data gathered

Literature

* Read science fiction stories and evaluate their scientific content—what is scientifically impossible versus what is scientifically valid. (Note: For examples of this type of analysis see *The Physics of Star Trek* by Lawrence M. Krauss [New York: Basic Books, 1995].)

* Older science fiction stories (e.g., by Jules Verne) might be evaluated for ideas that later became scientifically valid.

Writing

* Write science fiction stories that contain unusual and creative ideas and solutions to problems.

* Write science fiction stories based on the startling scientific truths revealed by Einstein's General and Special Relativity.

History

* Research and write an early years biography of Albert Einstein.

* Research the lives of great mathematicians.

* Research the work and discoveries of great scientists (e.g., Michael Faraday, James Clerk Maxwell, Stephen Hawking).

* Investigate the variety of methods used historically for the telling of time and marking the passage of time.

* Research the beliefs of ancient peoples about our world and the universe (Chinese, Egyptian, Greek, Native American, Polynesian, Incan, Mayan, etc.).

* Explore the effect of world politics on scientific research (and vice versa).

* Consider scientific values: What moral obligations do scientists have toward society? What moral obligations do humans have towards preserving natural systems?

Newton Does a "Back of the Envelope" Check on His Postulates

Shortly after Newton derived his Law of Universal Gravitation, he thought of a way to check his postulates.

Newton basically said to himself, I cannot possibly measure the force of gravity acting between two masses in the laboratory. The force of attraction between ordinary objects that I could lift is much too weak to measure. I can, however, compare the way the Moon falls toward Earth with the way an apple falls to the ground. I do know the distance between Earth and the Moon (240,000 miles), and I know the distance between the apple and the *center* of Earth (4,000 miles). Thus, the Moon is about 60 times farther from the center of Earth than the apple. So, if the force of gravity between two masses truly is inversely proportional to the square of the distance between the two masses, the force pulling on the Moon is to the force pulling on the apple as 1^2 is to 60^2. Force is proportional to acceleration, so the *distance* the Moon falls in one second is to the *distance* the apple falls in its first second of free fall as 1 is to 3,600. I calculate how many feet the Moon must fall every second to stay in a circular orbit around Earth—otherwise it would fly off in a straight line—as follows:

According to Galileo, distance fallen per sec = $\frac{1}{2}$ acceleration x time of fall squared

The Moon's acceleration is centripetal; thus, $a = v^2/r$, where r is the Moon's radius of orbit

Therefore the Distance fallen by the Moon, $D = \frac{1}{2}(v^2/r)t^2$

We are interested in the fall during the first second, so t = 1. Thus, $D = \frac{1}{2}(v^2/r)$

But $v = 2\pi r/t$, where t is the orbit time

Therefore $D = \frac{1}{2}([2\pi r/t]^2/r)$

But I know that r = 240,000 miles = 1.267×10^9 ft

and t = 27.3 days = 2.36×10^6 sec

Therefore, Distance fallen by the Moon in one sec = 0.00449 ft

Therefore, the distance the apple falls in its first second of free fall must be 0.00449 times 3,600, or about 16 feet, which is the value I measure in the laboratory.

Conclusions: The force of gravity between two masses is inversely proportional to the square of the distance between the centers of the two masses. The Moon is falling every instant to stay in orbit around Earth.

If the force of gravity between two masses is inversely proportional to the square of the distance between the centers of the two masses,

the force pulling on the Moon is to the force pulling on the apple as 1^2 is to 60^2, or

$F_{(moon)}/F_{(apple)} = 1/3,600$; therefore,

(Distance moon falls in one second)/ (Distance apple falls in the first second) = 1/3,600, or

(0.00449)/(Distance apple falls in 1 second) = 1/3,600 = 0.00028, or

Distance apple falls in the first second of free fall to Earth = 0.00449/0.00028 = 16 feet.

ꞟow to Weigh Earth

You do not need a spring scale to weigh Earth using Newtonian gravity. What you do need is the following information:

1. The radius of Earth (the distance from the surface to the center), which is 6.38×10^8 cm.

2. The fact that Earth's gravity causes any falling object to accelerate at a constant rate, which is 980 cm/sec^2.

3. The value of the gravitational constant, G, in Newton's Law of Universal Gravitation: 6.67×10^{-8} cm^3 gm^{-1} sec^{-3} (in units of grams-centimeters-seconds).

4. The strange fact that the gravitational mass of any object is equal to its inertial mass.

The Law of Universal Gravitation says that the force needed to cause the 980 cm/sec^2 acceleration is $G((M_1 M_2)/d^2)$, where

G is the gravitational constant,

M_1 is the gravitational mass of the object falling,

M_2 is the mass of Earth,

d is the radius of Earth.

The force needed to accelerate M_1 (at 980 cm/sec^2, if it is on a smooth, flat surface) is the inertial mass of M_1 times 980, because force is, by Newton's definition, mass times acceleration. Because the inertial mass of M_1 is the same as its gravitational mass, it follows that M_1 times 980 must equal the force needed to accelerate M_1 during its fall to Earth. Thus:

$$(M_1)(980) = G((M_1 M_2)/d^2), \text{ or}$$

$$(M_1)(980) = 6.67 \times 10^{-8}((M_1 M_2)/(6.38 \times 10^8)^2).$$

Cancel M_1 from both sides and solve for M_2:

$$M_2 = [980(6.38 \times 10^8)^2]/6.67 \times 10^{-8}, \text{ or}$$

$$M_2 = 5.98 \times 10^{27} \text{ grams, which is the mass of Earth.}$$

Permittivity Defined

An electrical property of space that can be measured very precisely is its permittivity. Permittivity is a measure of the resistance any material shows to the formation of an electric field.

Space does show a measurable resistance to the presence of an electric field. A laboratory experiment that measures the ratio of charge to voltage of two electrified metal plates separated by a vacuum (space) is all you need to determine the permittivity of space.

The measured permittivity of space is 8.85419×10^{-12}, with $C^2/N\ m^2$ as the unit of measure (C is coulombs, a unit of electric charge equal to 1 ampere per second; N is newtons, a unit of force, the force required to accelerate 1 kg of mass 1 meter per sec^2 and m is meters).

If you place any nonconductor between the two electrified metal plates (glass, for example), you can measure the specific permittivity value of that material.

Thus, we can say that space is not "nothing," but is just as real as a piece of glass or any other material.

Experimental Proof of Special Relativity

Scientists all over the world now believe that Einstein's Special Relativity theory correctly represents the way the universe works. For more than 90 years, countless experiments have confirmed every prediction of the theory. Following are a few examples.

The Theory Predicts

The mass of any object must increase as the speed of the object increases.

The Proof

Every day, physicists working at Brookhaven Laboratory in New York, at the National Laboratory in Japan, at CERN in Switzerland, at Fermi Laboratory in Illinois, at BESR Laboratory in China, and at the UNK-I accelerator in Russia all take note of the fact that as accelerating atomic particles are pushed faster and faster, the experimenter must supply a greater amount of energy to obtain the next small increment in acceleration. Prior to Einstein, nobody anticipated this behavior of accelerating particles. Prior to Special Relativity, there was no explanation. Einstein's theory says that you must supply a greater amount of

energy to obtain the next increment in acceleration because the mass of the particle is increasing as the speed of the particle is increasing.

The Theory Predicts

The velocity of light in empty space is a universal speed limit.

The Proof

In every accelerator laboratory all over the world, no matter how much energy was supplied to a particle, the operators were not able to get the particle to travel at the speed of light. Remarkably, it is able to attain speeds of 99.99999 percent of the speed of light. Physicists are now convinced that not even all the energy in the universe would get their particles to travel at the speed of light.

The Theory Predicts

Time is dependent upon the state of motion of the clock. A moving clock will "tick" at a slower pace than an identical stationary clock. A "clock" is anything that notes the passage of time, from a biological process (the nine months it takes to make a human baby) to the lifetime of a radioactive particle.

The Proof

In 1966 in Geneva, Switzerland, an atomic particle called a muon, which has a short but well-measured lifetime, was put on a fast track in an atomic accelerator. The physicists found that muons moving at 99.7 percent of the speed of light lived 12 times longer than slow-moving muons.

The Theory Predicts

Energy equals mass times the velocity of light squared.

The Proof

Ask any operator of any nuclear power plant anywhere in the world if $e = mc^2$. They turn a portion of the mass of uranium atoms into pure energy every day—the amount of energy released from the uranium is exactly the quantity predicted by Einstein's equation.

The last word goes to Professor Will:

Special Relativity is now a totally accepted and integrated part of modern physics, a basic ingredient in our picture of atomic structure, the atomic nucleus, elementary particles, everything in the world of microscopy. Experimentally, there is simply no doubt about its validity; it has been checked and rechecked and confirmed time and time again.

—Clifford M. Will
Was Einstein Right?
(New York: Basic Books, 1986)

The Momentous 43 Seconds

Before Einstein was born, it was known that the perihelion (the point of closest approach of the orbit to the Sun) of the planet Mercury advanced an excess of 43 seconds of arc per 100 Earth years (calculated against the predictions of Newtonian gravity).

Einstein's gravity (General Relativity) says that the advance of the perihelion of any single planet orbiting any star is determined by the relationship $A = 24\pi^3(a^2/T^2c^2(1-e^2))$, where

A is the advance of the perihelion at the completion of each orbit, measured in radians,

a is the semi-major axis of the ellipse traced out by the orbit, measured in centimeters,

T is the time for the planet to complete one orbit, measured in seconds,

c is the velocity of light in space, measured in centimeters per second,

e is the eccentricity of the ellipse.

$24\pi^3$ is $(24)(3.14159)^3 = 744.15$,

a^2 is $(5.8 \times 10^{12})^2 = 33.64 \times 10^{24}$,

$T^2 = (7.6 \times 10^6)^2 = 57.76 \times 10^{12}$,

$c^2 = (2.998 \times 10^{10})^2 = 8.988 \times 10^{20}$,

$(1 - e^2) = 1 - 0.206^2 = 0.95756$,

Therefore, $A = (744.15)(6.767 \times 10^{-10}) = 5.035 \times 10^{-7}$ radian

To convert radians to seconds of arc, multiply by 206,265:

$A = (5.035 \times 10^{-7})(206,265) = 0.10385$ seconds of arc.

It takes Mercury 88 days to complete one orbit of the Sun, and we need the number of seconds of arc per 100 Earth years (i.e., in terms of 365-day years):

$A = (0.10385)(365/88)(100) = 43$ seconds of arc per 100 Earth years.

The Origin of the Chemical Elements Needed to Make a Human Being

Of the 93 different chemical elements found on Earth, 24 of them are required to put together your body. However, they are not needed in equal quantities.

* Ninety-nine percent of your body is made of just 8 elements:

   Hydrogen, Carbon, Nitrogen, Oxygen, Calcium, Phosphorus, Sulfur, and Iron

* One percent of your body is made of 16 elements:

   Silicon, Fluorine, Magnesium, Sodium, Chlorine, Potassium, Chromium, Vanadium, Copper, Zinc, Selenium, Iodine, Nickel, Tin, Cobalt, and Molybdenum

Ten percent of your body is hydrogen, all of which was made 15 billion years ago during the first three minutes after the Big Bang. The elements carbon through vanadium (in the "chronological" listing above) were made in first-generation red giant stars that subsequently exploded as supernovas. The elements copper through molybdenum were made about 5 billion years ago, *during* supernova explosions. Thus, there is not one atom in your body that is less than 5 billion years old!

Calculating the Gravitational Radius of Any Object

General Relativity says that every object in the universe has a calculable gravitational radius. This radius of the invisible boundary of a black hole is dependent only on the mass of the object that has collapsed.

The equation for calculating the radius is $r = (2G/c^2)(M)$, where

G is the universal gravitational constant, 6.67×10^{-11}, with $Nm^2 kg^{-2}$ as the unit of measure* (N is newtons, a unit of force defined as kilogram meter per second squared of force),

c is the velocity of light in space, 2.998×10^8 meters per second,

M is the mass of the collapsed object, measured in kilograms.

For example, if Earth could be subjected to the kind of pressures present at the core of a collapsing star, Earth, which has a mass of 5.96×10^{24} kilograms, would be instantly transformed into a black hole with a radius of:

$r = (2G/c^2)(5.96 \times 10^{24})$, or

$r = (1.484 \times 10^{-27})(5.96 \times 10^{24}) = 0.009$ meter (0.35 inch).

Calculate the gravitational radius of yourself by converting your weight to kilograms and solving the equation:

$r = (1.484 \times 10^{-27})(\text{your weight})$

---

*Note: The value of G given in the above equation is in kilograms and meters. In appendix B, the value of G is given in grams and centimeters.

Albert Einstein Opts for Closed Space

In his last published scientific paper, *The Meaning of Relativity*, 5th ed. (Princeton University Press, Princeton, New Jersey, 1974), Albert Einstein states his reasons for favoring a finite universe with closed space over an infinite, open-space universe. He sums up his argument with three conclusions:

1. From the standpoint of the theory of relativity, to postulate a closed universe is very much simpler than to postulate the corresponding boundary condition at infinity of the open universe.

2. The idea that Mach expressed, that inertia depends upon the mutual action of bodies, is contained, to a first approximation, in the equations of the theory of relativity; it follows from these equations that inertia depends, at least in part, upon mutual actions between masses. But this idea of Mach's corresponds only to a finite universe, bounded in space and not to an infinite universe. It is more satisfying to have the mechanical properties of space completely determined by matter, and this is the case only in a closed universe.

3. An infinite universe is possible only if the mean density of matter in the universe vanishes. Although such an assumption is logically possible, it is less probable than the assumption that there is a finite mean density of matter in the universe.

Professor Misner agrees with Einstein's rejection of an infinite-space universe and adds the following argument:

Only by combining the General Relativity field equations with Einstein's boundary condition of closed space, can one arrive at the value for the maximum diameter of the expanding universe that is uniquely determined by the amount of matter present. (Misner, Thorne, and Wheeler 1973)

Answers to Common Student Questions That Arose During Field Testing*

1. *How do we know how much the Earth weighs?*

   We can calculate the weight of Earth using two equations developed by Newton: his Law of Gravity equation

   $$F = G(M_1M_2/d^2)$$

   and his force equation

   Force = mass times acceleration

   The first equation requires the radius of Earth (d). The second equation requires the acceleration 32 feet per second per second, the rate of objects falling to Earth. (See appendix B for the exact details for using these equations.)

2. *How do we know how much the Sun weighs?*

   To weigh the Sun, there are three numbers you need to know:

   a. The time it takes any planet to orbit the Sun, T (in units of seconds).

   b. The semi-major axis of the orbit of that planet, a (in units of meters).**

   c. The constant in Newton's Law of Universal Gravitation, G (in units of Nm^2kg^{-2}).

   Then you do a calculation involving the relationship between the mass of the Sun (M); the planet's orbital time (T); the planet's semi-major axis (a); and Newton's constant (G):

   $$M = (2\pi/T)^2 (a^3)(1/G).$$ (The mass of the Sun is given in kilograms in the equation.)

3. *How do we know nothing can travel faster than 186,000 miles per second?*

   We know nothing can go faster than 186,000 miles per second because:

   a. We have never witnessed anything going that fast.

   b. We have tried very hard to get the smallest, lightest-weight things we know of (parts of atoms) to go that fast and have failed every time. If you cannot get a tiny mass to go that fast (using all the energy available to us), how could you get *any* mass to go that fast?

---

*Note: The questions are in the students' words, edited slightly for clarity. We have attempted to simplify the answers in a manner that will make them appropriate for the middle school student.

**Note: The teacher may wish to ask the students to look up the word *ellipse* in an encyclopedia to find out that "semi-major axis" means half of the major axis of the ellipse.

c. We are confident that Einstein was correct about this velocity because his theory has been proven right about everything else it predicted.

4. *How fast does Earth rotate?*

Earth rotates once every 24 hours. If you want to know how fast you are moving as you stand on Earth while it is rotating, you must first know *where* you are standing. If you are at the North or South Pole, you will be just *rotating* once every 24 hours—it would be like sitting on a piano stool and slowly rotating once around. If you are at the equator, you will be moving 1,000 miles per hour as Earth rotates. If you are somewhere between the North Pole and the equator, or between the South Pole and the equator, you will be moving somewhere between 0 and 1,000 miles per hour.

5. *How fast does Earth revolve around the Sun?*

Earth revolves around the Sun at 66,600 miles per hour.

6. *At what speed is the Sun moving around our galaxy?*

The Sun is moving at 561,000 miles per hour around the galaxy.

7. *How many trips has our Sun made around the galaxy since its birth?*

It takes the Sun 200 million years to make one trip around the galaxy. The Sun is $4\frac{1}{2}$ billion years old. Thus, the Sun has made $4\frac{1}{2}$ billion divided by 200 million, or $22\frac{1}{2}$ trips around the galaxy.

8. *What source of energy makes electromagnetic fields travel at the speed of light?*

Remember that an electromagnetic field is made up of millions of tiny particles called photons. These photons get the energy they need to be able to travel 186,000 miles per second from the same energy source that excited their "parent" electrons. Recall how an electron must get excited (hot) before it is able to "sweat" photons? We excite electrons in a variety of ways. Any object will give off visible light if it is stuffed full of excited electrons. For example, the wood burning in a fireplace is the source of energy for the photons of light hitting your eyes as you watch the fire flicker and glow. Photons have zero mass, making it possible to move at the speed of light using less energy than you need to pull your hand rapidly away from the flame and say "ouch."

9. *If I hit a magnet with a hammer, it will lose its magnetic field. Does the field travel at 186,000 miles per second?*

If you hit a magnet really hard, the magnetic field does not "fly away," it just disappears because the blow disorients all the molecular-sized "little magnets" (the atoms) inside the bar magnet. To shake loose a magnetic field from a bar magnet, you would have to *vibrate* the magnet exceedingly fast—at least 1 million times per second.

10. *What makes our body's biological systems slow down when we travel at the speed of light?*

Our body systems (metabolism and heartbeat) are clocks in the sense that they go at a regular pace. Now, Special Relativity says that *all* clocks must slow down when traveling fast. Thus, your body's systems must slow down. If you could travel at the speed of light, you would be in "suspended animation." This is just the way the universe works.

11. *Why does gravity pull harder on a heavy object than on a light object?*

The reason gravity pulls harder on heavy objects is that Newton's Law says the pull of gravity is proportional to the quantity of mass, so a larger mass gets more "pull."

12. *If gravity pulls harder on heavy objects than it does on light objects, how can a light object and a heavy object hit the ground at the same time?*

Gravity *must* pull harder on a heavy object to get it to accelerate *at the same rate* as the light object. If it pulled equally on both light and heavy objects, the light object would fall toward the ground faster and hit the ground before the heavy object.

13. *When a star explodes, does the gravity concentrate around the black hole, or does it stay the same as before the star exploded?*

After a star explodes, it loses some of its mass, so the gravity *afterward* is less than it was before the star blew up. However, the gravity that is left is still very strong. Although the black hole is very small, it is also very massive. When a large amount of gravity surrounds a small, massive object such as a black hole, the gravity that surrounds the black hole is very concentrated and very strong.

14. *If I could travel fast enough, could I reverse the growing cycle (or go back in time)?*

You would travel backward in time if you could travel *faster* than the speed of light. There is a limerick that goes:

> There once was a lady named Bright
> Who traveled much faster than light.
> She departed one day in a relative way
> And came home the previous night.
> (Gamow 1957)

15. *How many of the 94 elements are in the human body?*

There are 24 elements in the human body (see appendix F).

16. *Do electrons move at the speed of light?*

No, they cannot. They have mass, and objects with mass can never travel at the speed of light.

17. *If sound cannot travel through space, why do we use radio telescopes?*

Radio telescopes receive *radio* waves, not sound waves, from outer space. The radio telescope uses computers to *convert* the radio waves into visible light or numerical data.

18. *If my experiment has proved my hypothesis was wrong, has my experiment failed?*

No. An experiment only "fails" if it is performed sloppily. An experiment gives you "nature's answer" to the question you asked when you designed the experiment.

19. *Is our Sun a first-generation star?*

No. It cannot be a first-generation star. First-generation stars could not possibly have had rocky planets orbiting them. Rocks are made out of many different chemicals. None of these chemicals were present in the universe when the first-generation stars were born. Our Sun is a second- or third-generation star.

20. *How do scientists know that there are only 94 types of elements scattered throughout our entire universe if we have never been out there?*

We know that these elements are out there because we see their "fingerprints" (their spectra) in the light coming from stars in the galaxies. We know that there are *only* 94 elements present in the universe because we only "see" 94 elements in the stars. The higher-number elements that you see in the Periodic Table are only made in the laboratory. These elements self-destruct soon after they are made. The further along the line you go, the less stable they get. So, if they ever were in the universe at all, they would have all self-destructed by now.

21. *Is there or is there not such a thing as a simultaneous event?*

Yes, there is. All you need is one or more persons who are "standing still" watching the event. All the people sitting in a sports stadium will agree on the event being "simultaneous"—it is only when a person is

188 / Appendix I

moving relative to another person that they will not agree on what is simultaneous.

22. *How does Pluto's distance from the Sun affect Pluto's gravity?*

The force of gravity *between* two objects (the Sun and Pluto) decreases rapidly as you separate the two objects. Pluto is very far from the Sun; therefore, the pull of the Sun on Pluto is very weak. The gravity you would feel if you were standing on Pluto does not depend upon *where* Pluto is in relation to the Sun. Pluto's mass is small; therefore, its gravity is also small.

23. *If gravity pulls everything toward Earth, why does a helium balloon rise?*

When you release a helium-filled balloon in the air, it rises for the same reason that a piece of wood released at the bottom of a swimming pool rises. Wood is less dense than water (a cubic inch of wood weighs less than a cubic inch of water). Helium is less dense than air; therefore, helium floats on top of air. The "top of air" is the top of the atmosphere, about nine miles high. If helium balloons did not pop because of the changes in atmospheric pressure as they rise through the atmosphere, we could have many helium balloons floating at the top of our atmosphere that had been released on the ground.

24. *If I stood at the back end of a large boat moving smoothly through the water and suddenly jumped straight up, would I come down in the water?*

No. You would not get wet. Galileo was correct. If you jumped *straight* up, you would come down to the very same spot where you were originally standing.

Selected Bibliography

Listed here are books that may be helpful for teachers who wish to research topics covered in the text or lesson plans. The annotations indicate coverage particularly relevant to gravity.

Abbott, Edwin A. *Flatland: A Romance of Many Dimensions.* New York: Dover Publications, 1952.
  A delightful account of what it would be like to live in two-dimensional space.

Adair, Robert K. *The Great Design: Particles, Fields, and Creation.* New York: Oxford University Press, 1987.
  Special and General Relativity and cosmology are discussed in language suitable for the collegiate science major.

Born, Max. *Einstein's Theory of Relativity.* Rev. ed. New York: Dover Publications, 1965.
  Born (a close friend to Einstein) writes in a semi-popular style about electromagnetism and Special and General Relativity.

Davies, P. C. W. *Space and Time in the Modern Universe.* New York: Cambridge University Press, 1977.
  Davies covers the relativity revolution, the bending of space, and modern cosmology.

Einstein, Albert. *Relativity: The Special and the General Theory.* New York: Crown, 1952.
  In its 15th edition, this is Einstein's first attempt to tell the story of relativity to the general public.

Einstein, Albert, and Leopold Infeld. *The Evolution of Physics.* New York: Simon & Schuster, 1951.
  Einstein and Infeld go to great lengths to explain the concept of a field. Galilean Relativity and Special and General Relativity are all covered.

Feynman, Richard. *The Character of Physical Law.* Cambridge: MIT Press, 1965.
  A series of popular lectures given at Cornell University in 1964. Feynman discusses Newton's Law of Universal Gravitation as a perfect example of a law of nature—"[a] physical law, a rhythm and a pattern between the phenomena of nature," as Feynman puts it.

Hawking, Stephen W. *A Brief History of Time: From the Big Bang to Black Holes.* New York: Bantam, 1990.
  For a general audience, this book covers today's most important scientific ideas, provides background discussion and equations relating to the works of Galileo, Newton, and Einstein, and makes quantum mechanics, black holes, and much more very accessible.

Hoffmann, Banesh. *Relativity and Its Roots.* New York: W. H. Freeman, 1983.
    Hoffmann traces the history of General Relativity back to Pythagoras. Vocabulary is suitable for the collegiate science major.

Joyce, Bruce, and Marsha Weil. *Models of Teaching.* 3d ed. Englewood Cliffs, New Jersey: Prentice-Hall, 1986.
    An outstanding textbook for teachers. The ten lesson styles used in *Gravity, the Glue of the Universe* are derived from models thoroughly explained in this text.

Krauss, Lawrence M. *The Physics of Star Trek.* New York: Basic Books, 1995.
    Professor Krauss cleanly separates the science facts from the science fiction. What is possible and what is impossible in time travel are delineated within the constraints of Einstein's Special and General Relativity.

Lightman, Alan. *Ancient Light: Our Changing View of the Universe.* Cambridge: Harvard University Press, 1991.
    Lightman gives a thorough overview of modern cosmology.

Marschall, Laurence A. *The Supernova Story.* Princeton, New Jersey: Princeton University Press, 1994.
    Everything you might want to know about supernovas can be found here. A thorough, up-to-date presentation.

Misner, Charles W., Kip S. Thorne, and John A. Wheeler. *Gravitation.* San Francisco: W. H. Freeman, 1973.
    The definitive graduate-level textbook on Einstein's gravity. The chapters are divided into two levels: Track 1 and Track 2. The first track "assumes, as a prerequisite, only vector analysis and simple partial-differential equations." The second track is, according to the authors, largely "enrichment material" that assumes a good knowledge of differential forms and exterior calculus.

Penrose, Roger. *The Emperor's New Mind: Concerning Computers, Minds, and the Laws of Physics.* New York: Oxford University Press, 1989.
    A thorough discussion of Einstein's simultaneity, the Faraday-Maxwell fields, and modern cosmology.

Shipman, Harry L. *Black Holes, Quasars, the Universe.* Boston: Houghton Mifflin, 1976.
    Shipman does an excellent job of describing black holes for the "educated layman."

Thorne, Kip S. *Black Holes & Time Warps: Einstein's Outrageous Legacy.* New York: W. W. Norton, 1994.
    The best reference for research. Kip Thorne describes everything that black holes can do, and everything you can do with black holes. He even gives instructions on how to exchange one year of your time for several million years of Earth time! (See his section on the stretch-out of time by gravity, p. 100.)

Wald, Robert M. *Space, Time, and Gravity: The Theory of the Big Bang and Black Holes.* Chicago: University of Chicago Press, 1977.
    A series of college lectures on curved space, relativity, and the birth, growth, and death of stars.

Weinberger, Steven. *The First Three Minutes: A Modern View of the Origin of the Universe.* New York: Basic Books, 1988.

Basic cosmology, but mostly just the first few minutes when all the hydrogen and most of the helium in the universe were synthesized.

Wightman, William P. D. *The Growth of Scientific Ideas.* New Haven, Connecticut: Yale University Press, 1951.

A thorough history of science, covering Newton's discovery of the Law of Universal Gravitation in detail in the chapter "The Dawn of Universal Mechanics."

Will, Clifford M. *Was Einstein Right? Putting General Relativity to the Test.* New York: Basic Books, 1986.

Will describes in detail the experiments done to verify Einstein's General Relativity.

INTERNET RESOURCES

NASA. 1997. *Hubble Space Telescope Public Pictures.* Available: http://www.stsci.edu/EPA /OPO/ OPO/Pictures.html (Accessed March 15, 1997)

Select "HST's Greatest Hits 1990–1995 Picture Gallery" to get your choice of great color photos taken by the orbiting Hubble telescope. See a Supernova's newly forged atoms scattering into space (Supernova 1987A), a huge star cradle (the Orion Nebula), a ring around a suspected black hole, and many other wonders in the sky.

NASA. 1996. *Gamma Ray Astronomy.* Available: http://enemy.gsfc.nasa.gov/cossc/ce.html (Accessed March 15, 1997)

Select: "Gamma Ray Astronomy in the Compton Era" click on "Introduction" for basic information on gamma ray light photons and photos of gamma ray detectors—some of which are presently orbiting Earth and looking for Hawking's exploding black holes.

NASA Jet Propulsion Laboratory. 1995. *Galactic Time Scale.* Available: http://www.jpl.nasa.gov (Accessed March 15, 1997)

Select: "Image/Information archives," click on "Education Archives," then click on "galaxies.text" to get a lesson plan, "Galaxies and the Galactic Time Scale" suitable for middle school students, to help them grasp the enormity of the time spans involved in the life of a star.

PBS Station WGBH Boston. 1996. *Einstein Revealed.* Available: http://www2.pbs.org/wgbh/pages/ nova/einstein (Accessed March 15, 1997)

Click on "Relativity and the Cosmos" for an excellent essay by Professor Alan Lightman covering Einstein, Relativity, Black Holes, and the Big Bang. Click on "Time Travelers" for an example of the Twin Paradox. Click on "Teacher's Guide" for a lesson plan for students who have viewed the NOVA TV program "Einstein Revealed" (available on tape). Click on "Geniuses among Geniuses" for a comparison of the intellectual feats of Newton, Einstein, and Hawking.

References

Born, Max. *Einstein's Theory of Relativity.* Rev. ed. New York: Dover Publications, 1965.

de Santillana, Georgio. 1955. *The Crime of Galileo.* New York: Time Inc.

Edmund Scientific, 101 E. Gloucester Pike, Parrington, New Jersey 08007.

Einstein, Albert. 1934. *Essays on Science.* New York: Philosophical Library.

———. 1950. *Out of My Later Years.* New York: Philosophical Library.

———. 1974. *The Meaning of Relativity.* 5th ed. Princeton, New Jersey. Princeton University Press.

Eley, George Jr. 1987. Conversations with the author. University of Maryland. College Park, Maryland.

Gamow, George. 1957. *One, Two, Three . . . Infinity: Facts and Speculations of Science.* New York: The New American Library.

Glasstone, Samuel. 1965. *Sourcebook on the Space Sciences.* New York: D. Van Nostrand Company.

Hawking, Stephen W., and W. Israel, eds. 1987. *Three Hundred Years of Gravitation.* New York: Cambridge University Press.

Hubble, E. P. 1929. A Relation Between Distance and Radial Velocity Among Extragalactive Nebulae. Proc. Nat. Acad. Sc. 15:169–173.

Joyce, Bruce, and Marsha Weil. 1986. *Models of Teaching.* 3d ed. Englewood Cliffs, New Jersey: Prentice-Hall.

Knedler, John Warren Jr., ed. 1973. *Masterworks of Science.* Vol. 2. New York: McGraw-Hill.

Lorentz, H. A. et al. 1952. *The Principle of Relativity.* New York: Dover Publications.

Lyman, Frank Jr. 1987. Conversations with the author. University of Maryland. College Park, Maryland.

McKeon, Richard, ed. 1966. *Basic Works of Aristotle.* New York: Random House.

Misner, C. W. 1977. Conversations with the author. South Bristol, Maine.

Misner, C. W., Kip S. Thorne, and John A. Wheeler. 1973. *Gravitation.* San Francisco: W. H. Freeman.

Oppenheimer, Robert J. 1964. *The Flying Trapeze: Three Crises for Physicists.* London: Oxford University Press.

Pagels, Heinz R. 1983. *The Cosmic Code: Quantum Physics as the Language of Nature.* New York: Bantam Books.

Penrose, Roger. 1989. *The Emperor's New Mind.* New York: Oxford University Press.

Schilpp, Paul A. 1949. *Albert Einstein: Philosopher—Scientist.* Evanston, Illinois: The Library of Living Philosophers.

Shipman, Harry L. 1976. *Black Holes, Quasars, the Universe.* Boston: Houghton Mifflin.

Thorne, Kip S. 1994. *Black Holes and Time Warps: Einstein's Outrageous Legacy.* New York: W. W. Norton.

Westfall, R. S. 1980. *Never at Rest: A Biography of Isaac Newton.* New York: Cambridge University Press.

Wheeler, John A. 1996. *At Home in the Universe.* Woodbury, New York: American Institute of Physics.

Wightman, William P. D. 1953. *The Growth of Scientific Ideas.* New Haven, Connecticut: Yale University Press.

Williams, L. Pearce. 1968. *Relativity Theory: Its Origins and Impact on Modern Thought.* New York: John Wiley.

Yourgrau, W. 1977. *Cosmology, History, and Theology.* New York: Plenum Press.

Index

Abbott, Edwin A.
  Flatland, 33
  quotation by, 33
Absolute zero temperature, 99, 112, 113, 133, 135,
    146, 150, 153, 159, 161
Acceleration
  definition of, 24
  and mass, 73, 89, 186-87
  and motion, 2, 50
  and rate of speed, 15, 17
Accelerator laboratories
  worldwide, 62, 69, 179
Accuracy, 52, 54
Age
  of human body, 182
  of Sun, 186
Air resistance, 17
Air space, 34
Alexander the Great, 1
Algebra, 174
Alpha Centauri A, 56
Alternators, 174
Aluminum, 133
American Association for the Advancement of
    Science, 150
AM radio
  "interference" on, 37
  waves, 128
Analogy, 114, 118
Andromeda Galaxy, 34, 47, 48
ANS satellite (Netherlands), 152
Apollo moon rocket, 43
Argonne National Laboratory, 99
Aristotle, xi, xiii, xiv, 13, 23, 26, 35, 44, 48, 173
  in "Play About Gravity," 77, 81, 82, 83, 84, 85,
    86, 87, 89, 90, 92, 93
  quotation by, 1
  on space, 33, 34, 42
  teachings on gravity by, 1, 5, 6, 7, 8, 10, 12, 63,
    102, 171
Aristotle's Assistant (Paul)
  in "Play About Gravity," 81, 82, 84, 91

Astronaut (Sally Jones)
  in "Play About Gravity," 81, 87, 89, 92, 93
Astronomers, 97, 98, 132, 135
  definition of, 39
  on expanding universe, 169
  Milky Way investigations by, 100
  numbers used by, 51
  units of measurements used by, 96, 101
Astronomy, 174
Astrophysicists, 151
Atomic clocks, 48, 64, 98, 105
Atomic numbers, 125
Atoms, 37, 56, 123. *See also* Electrons; Neutrons;
    Photons
  description of, 121
  parts of, 34, 49, 111, 119, 125, 127
  space within, 34, 42
  and speed of light, 49
Attribute, 24
Automobiles, xiii

Bahcall, John N., 152
Balance scales, 78
Bar magnets, 35
  magnetic field around, 36 (fig.2.1)
  shaking magnetic field loose from, 186
Beckenstein, Jacob D., 153
BESR Laboratory, China, 179
Big Bang, xii, 112, 113, 130, 152, 169, 182. *See also*
    Universe
Biology, 174
Black dwarfs, 133, 136 (fig.7.2), 140, 141, 142, 146
  definition of, 137
Black holes, xii, 100, 106, 130, 135, 136 (fig.7.2),
    140, 141, 142, 147-48, 159, 166, 171
  companion, 162
  dead star, 153, 154
  definition of, 138
  description of, 150
  event horizon of, 169
  and General Relativity, 151, 152

Black holes (*continued*)
  gravity concentrated around, 187
  miniature, 153, 154, 159
  predictions of, 149
  radius of invisible boundaries of, 183
  singularities at center of, 168
Born, Max, 102
  coin experiment of, 72, 73, 75, 87, 88, 89, 90, 92
  in "Play About Gravity," 81, 87, 88, 89
Brault, J. W., 98, 105
Brookhaven Laboratory, New York, 179
Bruno, Giordano, 97
Bulk, 5

Calcium, 129, 133, 182
California Institute of Technology, 99, 106, 151
Carbon atoms, 119, 129, 133, 166, 182
Carbon-14, 111
Case Western Reserve University, 169
Cavendish, Lord Henry, 4, 26, 28
Central Elementary School, Simsbury, CT, xiii
CERN, Switzerland, 179
Chandogya Upanishad
  quotation from, 166
Characters
  in "Play About Gravity," xiv, 81
Chemical elements
  inside human bodies, 113, 128, 129, 133, 182, 187
Chemistry, 174
China
  acceleration experiments in, 62, 69
Chinese people
  beliefs about world and universe by, 174
Chlorine atom, 122, 129, 182
Chromium, 129, 182
Clocks. *See also* Time
  and black holes, 150, 160, 161
  and gravitational fields, 105
  and gravity, xii
  moving, xii, 179
  and relativity, 48, 49, 50, 62-66, 69, 179, 186
  stationary, xii, 179
Closed universe, 167, 168, 169, 171, 173, 184
Cobalt, 129, 182
Coincidence gravitational radiation antennae, 99
Collapsed stars, 152
Columbus, Christopher, 168, 173
Comets, 4, 28, 34, 131
  definition of, 24
  Encke's, 154
  and gravity, 73
Common sense, 1, 5, 63, 83
  versus science, 2, 6, 7, 8, 48
Companion black holes, 162
Companion stars, 160, 162
Compton Gamma Ray Observatory (NASA), 154
Concept Attainment Cards, 24, 25

Conclusions
  and evidence, 158, 165
Constellations. *See also* Stars
  Cygnus, the Northern Cross, 152
  Orion, 132, 133
Copernicus, 74, 90
Copper, 129, 182
Cowen, C. L., 112
Crab Nebula, 133, 135
Crime of Galileo, The (de Santillana), 2
Cueing devices, 25
Cuisenaire rods, 52
Curvature of space, 42, 75-76, 93, 94, 97, 109, 110, 151, 166
Cygnus, the Northern Cross, 152
Cygnus X-1, 152

Data gathering, 164
Dead star black holes, 153, 154
Dead stars
  gravitational radius of, 151
  and gravity, 162
Decelerating rate of speed, 15
Degrees, 96, 101
de Santillana, Georgio, 2, 18
Descartes, René, 35, 42
Dialogue Concerning Two New Sciences (Galileo), 44
Dinosaurs, 154
Direct Instruction Lesson, 24
Distance
  and gravity, 74
  of space, 34
  and time, 16, 17, 19-20, 59, 111, 175, 176
Double (or twin) stars, 152
Dying stars, 135
Dynamical Theory of the Electromagnetic Field, A (Maxwell), 35

Earth, xiii, 23, 34, 93, 100, 146, 151, 167-68
  Aristotle's teachings about, 8
  elements found on, 122, 124, 128
  gravitational radius of, 155
  mass of, 73, 76, 89, 149, 183
  motion of, 26, 27, 28, 44
  Newton's gravity law and weighing of, 177
  north/south axis of, 4 (fig.1.1)
  orbit of the Moon around, 125, 175, 176
  path around the Sun by, 75, 169
  rotation speed of, 186
  weight of, 4, 94, 185
"Earth things," 5, 8, 82, 171
Eddington, Sir Arthur, 97, 98, 105
Edmund Scientific, 120
Egyptians
  beliefs about world and universe by, 174

Einstein, Albert, xi, xii, xiv, 29, 34, 68, 102, 171
  closed space ideas of, 169, 184
  education of, 43
  electromagnetic radiation discovered by, 111
  energy and mass equation by, 97
  experimental proof of Special Relativity Theory
     of, 179
  on Faraday-Maxwell discoveries, 37
  General Relativity Theory of, xiii, xiv, 1, 4, 29,
     35, 50, 72, 74, 75, 96, 101, 102, 104,
     105-6, 114-15, 118, 135, 166, 167, 174
  graphic organizer on Special Relativity Theory
     of, 69
  Meaning of Relativity, The, 184
  New Law of Gravity by, xv, 50, 73, 74, 77, 92, 94,
     96, 97, 98, 99, 102, 149, 151, 152, 154,
     155, 181
  origins of relativity theory of, 2, 3, 8, 45
  in "Play About Gravity," 77, 81, 89
  Principle of Equivalence by, 50, 75, 90, 91, 92,
     110, 171
  "Problem of Space Ether and the Field in
     Physics," 35
  quotations by, 43, 45, 72, 95, 109, 166
  and relative motion, 44
  relativity field equations of, 75, 93, 100, 171
  Special Relativity Theory of, xiii, 45, 46, 48,
     49, 50, 59, 61, 62-66, 67, 74, 104,
     173, 174, 186
Einstein's Assistant (Hansjorg)
  in "Play About Gravity," 81, 82, 91
Electrical permittivity, xiii, 34, 178
Electric charges
  and stresses, 36
Electric fields, xi, 35, 36 (fig.2.2), 74, 93, 174, 178
Electricity, 36, 60, 174
  and Special Theory of Relativity, 46
Electromagnetic experiments, 59, 60, 68
Electromagnetic fields, xi, 36, 43
  generating of, 30 (Tab.2.3)
  laboratory setup to loosen, 37 (fig.2.3)
  photons in, 59
  in space, 36-37
Electromagnetic radiation, 111, 128
Electromagnetic spectrum, 38 (Tab.2.2), 53, 56, 105,
     120, 174
Electromagnetic waves, 45
Electromagnetism, 60
Electrons
  in composition of atoms, 34, 49, 111, 119,
     125, 127
  definition of, 120
  experiments on fast-moving, 67, 69
  and mass, 187
  photons emitted by, 53, 56, 128, 186
Elements, 119, 120, 123
  atomic numbers of, 125
  on Earth, 128

  inside human body, 128, 129, 133, 182, 187
  nature of, 174
  and red giants, 146
Eley, George, Jr., xiii
Emission spectra, 119, 123
Emperor's New Mind, The (Penrose), 47
Empire State Building, 34, 42
Empty space
  speed of light in, 56
Encke's Comet, 154
Energy
  Einstein's equation on mass and, 97
  and Special Relativity Theory, 180
Equations, 58, 59
  to describe universe, 109, 110, 114-15, 118, 166,
     167, 168
  and dying stars, 135
  Newton's force, 185
  Newton's Law of Gravity, 185
  for orbits of planets, 96, 105, 181
  relativity field, 75, 93, 100, 171
Euclid, 35, 42, 93, 109
Event horizon, 151, 153, 155
  of black hole, 160, 161, 162, 169
Evidence
  and conclusions, 158, 165
Experimentation, xi
Experiments. *See also* Hypotheses
  in "Aristotle's Ideas About Gravity," 6
  atomic clock, 105
  and data gathering, 164
  for Einstein's Special Theory of Relativity, 46
  electromagnetic, 59, 60, 68
  of Galileo, 2, 44-45
  in "Galileo Asks Nature a Question," 13-17
  and hypotheses, 187
  inertial, 73
  mathematical, 58, 61, 64, 66, 69
  mechanical, 52, 55, 59, 60, 61, 68
  physical, 58, 61, 62, 67, 69
  by scientists, 1, 7, 8, 15, 82, 83
  to "see" gravitational waves, 99
  simultaneity, 62-63, 71
  thought, 47, 58, 61, 63, 64-65, 69, 75
Exploding stars, 99, 106
Exponents, 96

Facts
  verifying of, 157, 164
Falling bodies (or objects), 80
  acceleration of, 2, 3, 18, 19, 186-87
  Aristotle on, 1, 82, 83
  Einstein on, 2
  Galileo on, 1, 14-16, 83, 84
Faraday, Michael, xi, xiv, 35, 36, 37, 43,
     74, 174
Fermi Laboratory, Illinois, 179

"Fingerprints"
  of elements, 123-24, 128
Flatland (Abbott), 33
Fluorine, 129, 182
FM radios
  "interference" on, 37
Fomalont, Edward, 98, 105
Free fall, 2, 14, 175
  definition of, 11
  experiments on, 11, 14-17, 18-19

Galaxies, xii, 171
  "fingerprints" of elements throughout, 187
  Milky Way, xi, 100
  neutron stars in, 135
  radio signals from, 98
  receding of, 110, 111
  Seyfert, 100
  speed of our Sun within, 186
  stars in, 130
  supernovas in, 147
Galaxy 3C273, 98
Galileo, Galilei, 5, 7, 12, 13, 23, 26, 62, 68, 102, 188
  death of, 27
  Dialogue Concerning Two New Sciences, 44
  experiment on falling bodies by, 1, 2, 9, 14-16, 83, 175
  in "Play About Gravity," 77, 81, 82, 83, 84, 85, 86, 87, 88, 89, 92, 94
  principle of relativity of, 44, 46, 55, 59
  Two New Sciences, The, 2, 18
  and uniform motion, 44
Galileo's Assistant (Anthony)
  in "Play About Gravity," 81, 82, 91
Gamma-ray sensitive telescopes, 154
Gamma rays, 38, 128, 154. *See also* Photons
Garnow, George, 187
Geller, Margaret J., 169
General Relativity Theory (Einstein), xiii, 1, 4, 29, 50, 75, 96, 101, 135, 166, 167, 173, 174.
    See also Principle of Equivalence; Special Relativity Theory
  and black holes, 149, 151, 152
  clues for, 72
  and expansion of universe, 114-15, 118
  fundamental postulate for, 110
  and gravitational radius calculation, 155, 183
  and perihelion of planet Mercury, 104, 181
  published paper on, 35, 74, 102
  six truths revealed by, 105-6
Generators, 174
Geometry
  of space, 35, 42, 75-76, 93, 94, 97, 109, 110, 151, 166
Giacconi, R., 152
Gilbert, William, 36
Glasstone, Samuel, 33

Gold, 134
Gravitational collapse, 149
Gravitational field, xi, 35, 74, 111, 152, 155
  around black holes, 150
  bending of light by, 105
  strength of, 75
Gravitational force, 92, 110, 135
Gravitational mass, xii, 72, 73, 77, 78, 80, 89, 171, 177
Gravitational radiation, 99
Gravitational radius, xiii, 150-51, 152, 155, 159, 160, 162
  calculation of, 183
Gravitational waves, xii, 98, 99, 106, 112
Gravitons, 106, 111, 112, 113
  zero rest mass of, 50
Gravity, xi, xiii
  Aristotle's teachings on, 1, 5, 6, 7, 8, 10, 12, 102, 171
  bending of light rays by, 97, 98
  and black holes, 159, 187
  and clocks, xii
  definition of, 101
  and distance, 74
  Einstein's views of, 2, 29, 50, 73, 74-76, 80, 92, 94, 96, 97, 98, 102, 171, 173
  Galileo's definition and ideas on, 11, 14, 18-19, 84, 102, 171
  and mass, 73, 85, 175, 176, 186-87
  Newton's definition and ideas on, 3, 4, 23, 26, 72, 74, 85, 102, 171, 175-76, 181, 186
  Play about, 78, 79, 81-94
  Riemann's work on, 109
  and space, 34, 93, 94
  and stars, 130, 131, 132, 133, 134, 135, 144-45, 146, 147, 157, 162
  and time, 150, 160
Greeks
  beliefs about world and universe by, 174

Halley, Edmund, 4, 28
Harvard-Smithsonian Center for Astrophysics, 169
Hawking, Stephen W., xiii, xiv, 3, 28, 173, 152, 153, 154, 174
Hawking Radiation, 162
Helium atoms, 113, 128, 188
  in stars, 131, 132, 133, 145
Hertz, Heinrich, 36, 37
Hiroshima, 154
History, xiii
  suggested follow-up units in, 174
Hitler, Adolf, 97
Hubble, Edwin P., 110, 111, 115, 169
Hubble space telescope, 73, 87, 152
Huchra, John P., 169
Human beings
  need for preserving natural systems by, 174

Human bodies
    chemical elements within, 113, 128, 129, 133, 182, 187
    speed and biological systems within, 186
Hydrogen atoms, 127, 128, 129, 182
    in early universe, 113, 131
    single proton in, 119, 125, 126
    in stars, 130, 131, 132, 145
Hypotheses, 31
    attributes of, 25, 26
    definition of, 23
    and experiments, 187
    rules for writing of, 30
    testing of, 155

Ideas
    testing of, 158
Illinois
    acceleration experiments in, 62, 69
Incans
    beliefs about world and universe by, 174
Inertia, 73, 86
Inertial experiments, 73
Inertial mass, xii, 72, 74, 77, 78, 80, 87, 89, 171, 177
Infinite, 59
    definition of, 24
Infra-red light, 34, 38, 111
    telescopes sensitive to, 99-100
Interior decorator
    definition of, 39
Iodine, 129, 182
Iron, 129, 133, 146, 182
Isabella, queen of Spain, 167, 168

Japan
    acceleration experiments in, 62, 69
Joyce, Bruce, 24, 114
Judge (John Upright)
    in "Play About Gravity," 81, 82, 83, 84, 85, 88, 89, 90, 94
Jupiter, 23, 145

Kosmos 428 satellite (Russian), 152
Knedler, John Warren, Jr., 2, 3, 18, 19
Krauss, Professor Lawrence M., 169, 174

Lakes
    effect of gravity on tides in, 4, 28
Language, xiii
Laser-based gravitational wave detectors, 99, 106
Law of Inertia (Newton), 78, 80, 91
Law of Motion (Newton), 174

Law of Universal Gravitation (Newton), xi, xiii, 26, 29, 74, 85, 86, 89, 95, 96, 174, 185, 186.
    See also General Relativity Theory
    flaws in, 73, 101, 102, 105
    postulate check for, 175-76
    premises of, 3, 26, 27, 28
    and weight of Earth, 177
Lead, 125, 127
Lesson plans. See also Student Handouts
    "Aristotle's Ideas About Gravity," 5-7
    "Building Blocks of the Universe," 119-29
    "Einstein's Dilemma," 114-16
    "Einstein's New Law of Gravity," 77-94
    "Einstein's Special Relativity," 58-71
    "Experiment of Effect of Gravity on Falling Objects Using Galilean Water Clock," 20
    "Galileo Asks Nature a Question," 11-17
    "Life Cycle of a Star, The" 137-48
    "Mysterious Encounter, A," 155-65
    "Principle of Relativity," 51-57
    "Problem of a Scientific Discrepancy, The," 101-8
    "Sample Inclined Plane Data Analysis Chart," 21
    "Sample Synectics Progression," 117-18
    "Statements to Be Used on Concept Attainment Cards," 31
    "What Is Space?," 39-42, 124
Light, 174
    bending of, by gravitational fields, 105
    and numbers, 53-54
    and photons, 59
    through prisms, 128
    reflected, 53
    speed of, 43, 60, 67, 69, 99, 106, 111, 179, 186, 187
    velocity of, in empty space, 37, 45, 46, 49, 50, 56, 61, 179
    visible, 34, 37, 38, 53, 56, 111
Light-year, 44
    definition of, 53, 56, 58
    measurement of, 34
Literature
    suggested follow-up units in, 174
Lorentz, H. A., 48
Lou Gehrig's disease, 153
Lyceum, The, 1, 8
Lyman, Frank, Jr., 24, 25

Magie, W. F., 49
Magnesium, 129, 133, 182
Magnetic fields, xi, 35, 74, 93
Magnetic poles
    and stresses, 36
Magnetic properties
    of space, 34
Magnetism, 109, 174
    and Special Theory of Relativity, 46
Magnets, 35, 174

Mass, xii, 77
   and acceleration, 73
   definition of, 24
   of Earth, 183
   Einstein's equation on energy and, 97
   of exploding stars, 187
   and gravity, 85, 175, 176, 186
   and speed, 67, 69, 179
   and stars, 131, 135
Massachusetts Institute of Technology, 99, 106
Materials
   "Aristotle's Ideas About Gravity," 5
   "Building Blocks of the Universe," 120
   "Einstein's Dilemma," 114
   "Einstein's New Law of Gravity," 78
   "Einstein's Special Relativity," 59
   "Galileo Asks Nature a Question," 11
   "Life Cycle of a Star, The," 138
   "Mysterious Encounter, The," 156
   "Newton Makes a Grand Hypothesis," 24
   "Principles of Relativity," 52-53
   "Problems of a Scientific Discrepancy, The," 101
   "What Is Space?," 39
Mathematical experiments, 47, 58, 61, 64, 66, 69
Mathematics, xiii, 109
   suggested follow-up units in, 174
Matter
   and curvature of space, 110
   definition of, 24
   discovery of, in universe, 169
Maxwell, James Clerk, xi, xiv, 35, 36, 43, 60, 62,
      74, 174
   Dynamical Theory of the Electromagnetic Field,
      A, 35
Mayans
   beliefs about world and universe by, 174
McKeon, Richard, 8, 33
Meaning of Relativity, The (Einstein), 184
Mechanical experiments, 52, 55, 57, 60, 68
M87 Galaxy, 152
Mercury, 98, 132
   and Einstein's General Relativity Theory, 104, 105
   orbit of, xii, xiii, 145
   rotation around Sun by, 96
   scientific discrepancy over orbit of, 101, 102,
      103, 181
Meteorites, 34, 154
Microwaves, 38, 111
Milky Way, xi, 100
Miniature black holes, 153, 154, 159
Minutes, 96, 101
Mirrors
   and photons, 54, 57
Misner, Professor Charles, 35, 45, 74, 151, 152,
      167, 169, 184
Models of Teaching (Joyce and Weil), 114
Molecules, 119
Molybdenum, 129, 189

Moon, xi, 34
   orbit around Earth by, 3, 26, 27, 28, 125, 175, 176
More, L. T., 49
Moses, xv
Motion. *See also* Uniform motion
   Galileo's experiments on, 2, 3, 9, 12, 13-17,
      18-19, 44-45, 55
   light and relativity of, 55, 60, 61, 62
Mt. Palomar telescope, 34
Mt. Parnassus, 166, 168
Moving clocks, xii
   versus stationary clocks, 179
Muons, 48, 63, 180

National Aeronautics and Space Administration
      (NASA), 33, 42, 157
National Laboratory, Japan, 179
Native Americans
   beliefs about world and universe by, 174
Natural systems
   and human obligation to preserve, 174
Negative electrical charge, 127
Neutrinos, 50, 111, 112, 113, 119, 120, 126, 134
   zero rest mass of, 50
Neutrons, 34, 111, 119, 125, 126
Neutron stars, 130, 135, 136 (fig.7.2), 140, 141,
      142, 148, 166, 171
   definition of, 138
New Law of Gravity (Einstein), xii, xv, 50, 73, 74,
      96, 97, 98, 149. *See also* General Relativity
      Theory
   and fate of universe, 154
   and gravitational waves, 99
   lesson plan on, 77-94
Newton, Hannah, 3, 27
Newton, Isaac, xi, xiv, 3, 23, 29, 37, 96, 109
   force equation of, 185
   ideas about gravity by, 26, 27, 34, 72, 102, 171,
      181
   Law of Gravity equation, 185
   Law of Inertia of, 78, 80, 91
   Law of Motion of, 174
   Law of Universal Gravitation of, xii, xiii, 3, 4, 26,
      27, 73, 74, 85, 86, 89, 95, 101, 102, 174,
      175-76, 177, 185, 186
   in "Play About Gravity," 77, 81, 85, 86, 87, 88,
      89, 90, 91, 92, 93, 94
   Principia, 4, 28
   on space, 33, 42
Newton's Assistant (John)
   in "Play About Gravity," 81, 87, 91
New York
   acceleration experiments in, 62, 69
Nickel, 129, 182
Nitrogen, 129, 133, 182
Non-hypotheses, 32
North Pole, 186

Nuclear chemistry, 126
Nuclear physics, 126
Nuclear power plants, 111, 180
Nucleus, 119, 125
    of atom, 56
Numbers
    and light, 53-54
    used by scientists, 51

Objectives
    "Aristotle's Ideas About Gravity," 5
    "Building Blocks of the Universe," 119
    "Einstein's Dilemma," 114
    "Einstein's New Law of Gravity," 77
    "Einstein's Special Relativity," 58-59
    "Galileo Asks Nature a Question," 11
    "Life Cycle of a Star, The," 137
    "Mysterious Encounter, A," 155
    "Newton Makes a Grand Hypothesis," 23
    "Principles of Relativity," 51
    "Problem of a Scientific Discrepancy, The," 101
    "What Is Space?," 39
Observation, xi, 1, 6, 7, 15
Oceans
    effect of gravity on tides in, 4, 28
Onnes, Kammerlingh, 43
Open universe, 166-67, 168, 169, 173
Oppenheimer, J. Robert, 37, 135, 149
Optical telescopes, 154
Oracle, the, 166, 168
Orion constellation, 132, 133
Ostwald, Wilhelm, 43
Oxygen, 125, 129, 133, 182
Ozone, 154

Pagels, Heinz R., 169
Parallel lines, 35, 109
Pencil
    breakdown of, 121 (fig.6.1)
Penrose, Roger, 47, 48, 167, 169
Penzias, Arno, 112
Penzias-Wilson photons, 113
Perihelion, 181
Periodic Table of Elements, 122, 187
Permittivity
    definition of, 178
Phenomenon
    definition of, 24
Phosphorus, 129, 133, 182
Photons, 54, 119, 126, 128, 131
    definition of, 120
    in electromagnetic fields, 59, 186
    emission by electrons of, 53, 56, 57
    Penzias-Wilson, 113
    speed of, 66, 68, 167, 111
    zero rest mass of, 50, 57, 112

Physical experiments, 58, 61, 62, 67, 69
Physicists
    numbers used by, 51
Physics, 43, 44, 45, 180
    nuclear, 126
    of radio and TV communication, 174
    theoretical, 153
Physics of Star Trek, The (Krauss), 174
Planets, 8, 27, 34, 93, 171. See also Earth
    advance of orbit of, 95 (fig.5.1)
    definition of, 23
    and gravity, 73, 74
    Jupiter, 23, 145
    Mercury, 96, 98, 132, 145
    motions of, 3, 28
    movement around Sun by, 75
    Pluto, 188
    rock, 134 (fig.7.1)
    Venus, 132, 146
Plastic tangram triangles, 52
"Play About Gravity, A," 78, 79, 81-94
Pluto
    gravity and Sun's relation to, 188
Plutonium, 111, 120, 125
Point of no return, 151, 156, 160
Polynesians
    beliefs about world and universe by, 174
Postulate, 109
    on curvature of space, 167
    definition of, 24
Potassium, 129, 182
Pregnancy
    and relativity of time, 66, 69
Premise
    definition of, 23
Princeton University, 105, 152, 153
Principia (Newton), 4, 28
Principle of Equivalence (Einstein), 50, 75, 90, 91,
        92, 110, 171
Prism, 53, 128
    light beams through, 56
"Problem of Space, Ether, and the Field in Physics"
        (Einstein), 35
Procedures
    "Aristotle's Ideas About Gravity," 6-7
    "Building Blocks of the Universe," 121-24
    "Einstein's Dilemma," 114-16
    "Einstein's New Law of Gravity," 78-79
    "Einstein's Special Relativity," 59-67
    "Galileo Asks Nature a Question," 12-17
    "Life Cycle of a Star, The," 138-40
    "Mysterious Encounter, A," 156-59
    "Newton Makes a Grand Hypothesis," 24-26
    "Principles of Relativity," 53-55
    "Problems of a Scientific Discrepancy, The,"
        102-4
    "What Is Space?," 40-41
Process knowledge, xiii

Projects
    for Follow-up Activities, 173
Props and costumes
    for "The Life Cycle of a Star Role-Play Script,"
        144
Protons, 34, 49, 111, 119, 125, 126, 152
Protostars, 131, 136 (fig.7.2), 140, 141, 142, 144-45
    definition of, 137
Proxima Centauri, 44
Pulsars, 135, 138
Puzzling scientific events, 156, 157
Pythagoras
    quotation by, 109

Quantum mechanics, 153, 162
Quantum theory, 169
Quartz crystal clock, 48, 64
Quasars, 34

Radar, 38
Radioactive clock, 48, 64
Radio Astronomy Observatory (West Virginia),
        98
Radios
    AM waves, 38, 128
    FM waves, 38
    "interference" on, 37
    physics of communication of, 174
    signals, 98, 105
    waves, 34, 59, 111, 130, 148
Radio telescopes, 98, 174, 187
Radium, 111, 120, 125
Radius
    of Earth, 177
Ramuz, C. F.
    quotation by, 43
Reading Activity
    for "Aristotle's Ideas About Gravity," 7
Red giant stars, 132, 134, 136 (fig.7.2), 140,
        141, 142, 145-46, 157, 182. *See also*
        Supernovas
    chemical elements manufactured by, 133
    definition of, 137
Reflected light, 53
Reines, F., 112
Relative, 54
    defined, 52
Relative motion, 44
Relativity, 1, 54-55, 150. *See also* General
        Relativity Theory; Special Relativity
        Theory
    and clocks, 48, 49, 50, 62-66
    Einstein's theory of, 45
    Galileo's principle of, 45, 46, 55, 59, 60, 61
    lesson plan on principles of, 51-55
Relativity field equations, 75, 93

Review Questions
    "Einstein's Special Relativity," 68
    "Life Cycle of a Star, The," 140
    "Mysterious Encounter, A," 159-60
    "Newton Makes a Grand Hypothesis," 26
Riemann, George F. B., xi, xiv, 35, 76, 109
Rock planets
    genealogy of star systems containing,
        134 (fig.7.1)
Rocks
    chemicals within, 187
Roemer, Oli, 43
Role-Play Script
    "Life Cycle of a Star, The," 138, 144-48
Russia
    acceleration experiments in, 62, 69

Salt
    breakdown of, 122 (fig.6.2)
"Sample Inclined Plane Data Analysis Chart,"
        16, 21
Savanna River Nuclear Energy Plant (Georgia),
        112
Schilpp, Paul A., 43
Schmidt, Maarten, 34
Schwarzschild, Karl, 135
Science, 104
    versus common sense, 2, 6, 7, 8, 48
    dimensions of, xiii
    mystery and wonder of, 173
    real advances in, 80, 90
    scales used in, 78
    suggested follow-up units in, 174
    unity of, 74
Science fiction stories, 174
Scientific inquiry, 173
Scientific values, 174
Scientists, 15, 102, 167
    experiments by, 1, 7, 8, 15
    moral obligations of, 174
    numbers used by, 51
    and open versus closed universe, 169
Seconds of arc, 96, 97, 101, 103
Selenium, 129, 182
Seyfert, Carl, 100
Seyfert Galaxies, 100
Shakespeare, William
    quotation by, 149
Shape
    of space, 35
Shipman, Harry L., 151
Silicon, 129, 133, 182
Silver, 134
Simultaneity, 59
    definition of, 58
    experiments on, 62-63, 69, 71
Simultaneous events, 187-88

Singer, Isaac Bashevis
   quotation by, 4, 29
Singularities, 135, 141, 147, 148, 149, 151, 155,
      161, 162, 168, 171. *See also* Black holes
   of collapsed universe, 169
   definition of, 138
Snyder, H., 135
Society
   science and, xiii
Sodium atoms, 122, 129, 182
Solar eclipse, 105
Solar system, 96. *See also* Earth; Planets
Sound, 174, 188
   relativity of volume of, 54, 55
   waves, 99, 174
South Pole, 186
Space, xi, 23, 29, 34, 39
   within atoms, 127
   curvature of, 42, 75-76, 93, 94, 97, 109, 110,
      151, 166
   definitions of, 33, 42
   discussion about, 40
   between distant galaxies, 106, 111
   and electrical permittivity, xiii, 178
   electromagnetic fields in, 36-37
   and gravity, 4
   model of, 41
   properties of, 34-35
   and time, 62, 69, 150, 168
   travel, 34, 174
   uniform motion throughout, xii
Spaceships, 34
Special Theory of Relativity (Einstein), xii, xiii,
      62-67, 74, 104, 173, 174, 186. *See also*
      General Relativity Theory
   conclusions from, 50
   experimental proof of, 45, 179-80
   graphic organizer on, 69
   postulates behind, 46
   published paper on, 61
   scientific community's reaction to, 49
Spectroscopes, 119, 123, 124
Speed
   limit in universe, xii, xiii
   and mass, 67, 69, 179
Speed of light, 67, 99, 106, 111
   and accelerator laboratories, 179
   and electromagnetic fields, 186
   and human biological system, 186
   and mass, 69
   and time, 69, 187
Spring (season)
   arrival of, 3
Spring clocks, 48, 64
Spring scales, 73, 78
Sramek, Richard, 98, 105
Stalin, Joseph, 97
Star cradles, 133

Starlight
   bending or deflection of, 97 (fig.5.2), 98, 105
Stars, 8, 140, 141, 142, 145. *See also* Black holes;
      Sun; Supernovas
   black dwarfs, 133, 136 (fig.7.2), 137, 140, 141,
      142, 146
   collapsed, 152
   companion, 160, 162
   critical masses in life cycle of, 135, 136 (fig.7.2)
   definition of, 23, 137
   double (or twin), 152
   exploding, 99, 106
   first-generation, 187
   genealogy of systems with rock planets, 134
      (fig.7.1)
   life cycle of, 113, 130, 138, 139, 140, 166, 187
   neutron, 130, 135, 136 (fig.7.2), 138, 140, 141,
      142, 148, 166, 171
   proto-star, 131, 136 (fig.7.2), 140, 141, 142,
      144-45
   red giant, 132, 133, 134, 136 (fig.7.2), 140, 141,
      142, 145-46, 152, 182
   Role-Play Script for Life Cycle of, 144-48
   and space, 34
   still-born, 136 (fig.7.2), 137, 140, 141
   time line for birth, life, and death of, 132 (fig.7.1)
   white dwarf, 130, 133, 135, 136 (fig.7.2), 137,
      140, 141, 142, 146, 166, 171
Static electricity, 36, 60
Stationary clocks
   versus moving clocks, xii, 179
Statistics/data analysis, 174
Still-born star, 136 (fig.7.2), 140, 141, 142, 145
   definition of, 137
Student Handouts
   "Aristotle's Ideas About Gravity," 7, 8-9, 10
   "Dissecting Atoms," 123, 125-28
   "Experimental Data," 12, 13, 15, 20
   "Galileo's Ideas About Gravity," 11, 15, 18-19
   "Graphic Organizer," 59, 61, 70, 101, 104,
      107-8
   "Life Cycle of a Star, The" 138, 139, 143
   "Mathematical Analysis of Experimental Data,"
      12, 15, 16, 22
   "Nature of Light, The," 52, 53, 56-57
   "Newton's Ideas About Gravity," 24, 26,
      27-29
   "Planning and Data Collection," 156, 159,
      160, 163-65
   "Reading on Light," 67
   "Rules for Writing Hypothesis," 24, 25, 30
   "Simultaneity Experiment Involving Light on a
      Train," 59, 71
   "Star Vocabulary," 138, 141
Student Worksheets
   "After the Play," 78, 80
   "Star Vocabulary," 138
Sulfur, 129, 130, 182

Sun, 8, 34, 74, 75, 95, 113, 131, 145, 151
  age of, 186
  and bending of light, xii, 105
  calculating weight of, 185
  Earth's orbit around, xi, 169
  eclipses of, 4, 28, 98
  and gravity, 96
  mass of, 76, 135, 149
  Mercury's orbit around, 181
  Pluto's relation to, 188
  speed of Earth revolving around, 186
  weight of, 94
Supernovas, 133, 136 (fig.7.2), 140, 141, 142, 147,
    148, 149, 157, 182
  Crab Nebula, 133, 135
  definition of, 137
  gold and silver synthesized within, 134
Suspended animation, 186
Swiss Federal Institute of Technology, 43
Swiss Patent Office, 43
Switzerland
  acceleration experiments in, 62, 69

Tangent line
  definition of, 23
Tangram triangles, 52
Tarfon, Rabbi
  quotation by, 169
Teacher (Mrs. Smith)
  in "Play About Gravity," 81, 82, 84, 85, 86, 87,
    89, 90, 94
Teacher Fact Sheets
  "Black Holes," 156, 157, 159, 161-62
  "Chemical Elements of the Human Body," 120,
    123, 129
  "What Is Space?," 40, 42
Teacher Keys
  "Graphic Organizer," 101, 104, 105-6
  "Life Cycle of a Star, The" 138, 139, 142
Teacher Samples
  "Graphic Organizer," 59, 69
Teaching Models
  "Advanced Organizer," 5, 101
  "BSCS Laboratory Work," 119
  "BSCS Style Invitation to Inquiry," 5
  "Classroom Meeting," 39
  "Concept Attainment," 23
  "Inductive Thinking," 51
  "Inquiry Training," 55
  "Role Play," 77
  "Small Group Investigations," 11
  "Synectics," 114
  "Teacher Enacted Role-Play," 137
Technetium, 122, 123
Telescopes, 99-100
  gamma-ray sensitive, 154
  Hubble, 73, 87, 115, 152

infra-red sensitive, 99-100
  Mt. Palomar, 34
  optical, 154
  radio, 98, 174, 187
  X-ray, 152
Television
  physics of communication of, 174
  waves, 38
Temperature
  of black holes, 159, 161
  of dead-star black holes, 153
  and electrons, 56, 57
  and photons, 57
Think-pair-share, 115
  components of, 24
Thorne, Kip S., 150, 169
  quotation by, 130
Thought experiments, 47, 58, 61, 63, 69
  of Einstein, 75
  on simultaneous events, 63
  on time and identical twins, 64-65
  on two views of same event, 47 (fig.3.1)
Three-dimensional space, 35, 42
Tides
  in lakes and oceans, 4, 28
Time, xi, xii, 174
  and black holes, 150, 160, 161
  and distance, 16, 17, 19-20, 59, 111, 175, 176
  and gravitational fields, 105
  and space, 62, 69, 150, 168
  and Special Theory of Relativity, 46, 48, 49, 50,
    62-66, 179
  and speed of light, 65, 187
Time travel, 8
Time-zero, 167
Tin, 129, 182
Tolstoy, Leo, 33
Traveling clocks
  and relativity, 48, 49, 50, 62-66, 69, 186
Tunguska, Yensei Valley (Siberia), 154
Twins, identical
  thought experiment on time and, 64-65, 69
Twin stars (or double stars), 152
Two New Sciences, The (Galileo), 18

Ultraviolet light, 38
Uniform motion, xii, 46, 50, 52, 59
  definition of, 58
  and Galileo, 55
  laboratories in, 74
  undetectability of, 44, 45
Universal speed limit, 62, 68, 69, 179
Universe, 8, 28. *See also* Galaxies; Planets; Stars
  closed, 167, 168, 171, 173, 184
  definition of, 23
  elements scattered throughout, 187
  equations for describing of, 109, 110, 114-15, 118

evolution of, xii
expansion of, 110, 113, 115, 118, 166,
     168, 169
facts about, 117
fate of, 154, 166, 171
and gravity, xi
"messengers" of, 111, 112
open, 166-67, 168, 169, 173, 184
University of Göttingen, 97
University of Maryland, 99, 106
UNK-I, Russia, 179
Uranium, 111, 120, 180

Vanadium, 129, 182
Venus, 132, 146
Verne, Jules, 174
Visible light, 34, 37, 38, 53, 56, 111
Vocabulary
   "Aristotle's Ideas About Gravity," 5
   "Building Blocks of the Universe," 119-20
   "Einstein's Dilemma," 114
   "Einstein's New Law of Gravity", 77-78
   "Einstein's Special Relativity," 58-59
   "Galileo Asks Nature a Question," 11
   "Life Cycle of a Star, The," 137-38
   "Mysterious Encounter, A," 155-56
   "Newton Makes a Grand Hypothesis," 23-24
   "Principles of Relativity," 51-52
   "Problems of a Scientific Discrepancy,
        The," 101
   "What Is Space?," 39
Vogt, Robbi, 99, 106

Vulcan, 96, 103, 104, 105

Was Einstein Right? (Will), 180
"Water clocks" (Galilean), 2, 12, 13, 14, 18, 19, 20
Wavelengths, 56
Weber, Professor Joseph, 99, 106
Weight, 5, 77. See also Mass
Weil, Marsha, 24, 114
Weinburg, Steven, 3, 28
Westfall, R. S., 33
Wheeler, John A., 135, 150, 151, 161
White dwarfs, 130, 133, 135, 136 (fig.7.2), 140,
     141, 142,
   146, 166, 171
   definition of, 137
White light, 37
Wightman, William P. D., 35, 74
   quotation by, 72
Will, Clifford M., 180
Williams, L. Pearce, 49
Wilson, Robert, 112
Writing
   suggested follow-up units in, 174

X-ray telescope, 152
X-rays, 34, 38, 111, 152, 160,

Yourgrau, W., 74, 167

About the Authors

Harry Gilbert is a retired rocket research scientist and teacher. He received his formal education at Case Western Reserve University (formerly Case Institute of Technology) and worked as a research chemist and engineer. Upon his retirement, he taught polymer engineering as an adjunct professor at West Virginia University. He also taught advanced chemistry and physics at Bishop Walsh Middle/High School in Cumberland, Maryland, where he was head of the science department for four years. His background and knowledge in physics and cosmology are derived from years of extensive reading and independent research on Einstein's life and works. Currently he is a freelance writer.

Diana Gilbert Smith has been teaching in public schools for nine years and is currently teaching fifth grade at Central Elementary School in Simsbury, Connecticut. She received her undergraduate degree in English and Drama from Kenyon College in Gambier, Ohio, with an emphasis in Shakespeare and Children's Theater. Diana received her M.Ed. in Curriculum and Instruction from the University of Maryland at College Park. She holds elementary and middle school teaching certificates in Maryland, Massachusetts, and Connecticut. She is a member of the Connecticut Science Teacher's Association and the National Science Teacher's Association. Diana has spent every summer since 1987 writing curriculum in drama, science, and social studies for students in grades K–8. Recently, she was a field test teacher for the SETI Life in the Universe series, also published by Teacher Ideas Press.

From # Teacher Ideas Press

OUT OF THIS WORLD Resources

BLAST OFF! Rocketry for Elementary and Middle School Students
Leona Brattland Nielsen

You'll launch excitement in the classroom with this complete teaching package on rocketry. It's packed with fascinating facts and motivational activities! **Grades 4–8**.
viii, 109p. 8½x11 paper ISBN 1-56308-438-4

INVENTING, INVENTIONS, AND INVENTORS
Jerry D. Flack

Flack's exciting, mind-stretching activities illuminate a rich, interdisciplinary field of study. Investigating inventions of the past and the present, funny inventions, and inventions we may see in the future provides a natural springboard to creative thinking. **Grades 7–9**. *(Adaptable for many grades.)*
xi, 148p. 8½x11 paper ISBN 0-87287-747-7

SIMPLE MACHINES MADE SIMPLE
Ralph E. St. Andre

Present scientific principles and simple mechanics through hands-on cooperative learning activities. **Grades 3–8**.
xix, 150p. 8½x11 paper ISBN 1-56308-104-0

MARVELS OF SCIENCE: 50 Fascinating 5-Minute Reads
Kendall Haven

Ideal for both read-alouds and reading assignments, these 50 short stories take just minutes to read but amply illustrate scientific principles and the evolution of science through history. **Grades 3** *and up.*
xxii, 238p. paper ISBN 1-56308-159-8

INTEGRATING AEROSPACE SCIENCE INTO THE CURRICULUM: K–12
Robert D. Ray and Joan Klingel Ray

Demystify space with substantive information and hands-on activities that integrate space science with other curricular areas. **Grades K–12**.
Gifted Treasury Series; Jerry D. Flack, Ed.
xxi, 191p. 8½x11 paper ISBN 0-87287-924-0

THE EVOLUTION OF A PLANETARY SYSTEM
SETI Institute

After exploring the evolution of our solar system, students apply the information they have gathered to simulate the possible evolution of a planetary system beyond our own. **Grades 5–6** *and up.*
Life in the Universe Series
Book: *xxviii, 220p. 8½x11 paper ISBN 1-56308-324-8*
Videotape: *Approximately 20 minutes ISBN 1-56308-410-4*
Classroom Kit: *Includes book, videotape, and full-color poster (24x36) ISBN 1-56308-411-2*

For a FREE catalog or to place an order, please contact:

Teacher Ideas Press
Dept. B47 · P.O. Box 6633 · Englewood, CO 80155-6633
1-800-237-6124, ext. 1 · Fax: 303-220-8843 · E-mail: lu-books@lu.com

 Check out the TIP Web site!
www.lu.com/tip